the magic of
Big Game

Also by Terry Wieland

Spanish Best: *The Fine Shotguns of Spain*

Spiral-Horn Dreams

the magic of
Big Game

by Terry Wieland

Countrysport Press
Selma, Alabama

This edition of *The Magic of Big Game* was printed by Jostens Book Manufacturing, State College, Pennsylvania. The book was designed by Saxon Design of Traverse City, Michigan. It is set in Centaur.

First Edition
10 9 8 7 6 5 4 3 2 1

Published by Countrysport Press
Craig Industrial Park, Building 116, Selma, AL 36701

Printed in the United States of America

ISBN 0-924357-77-0 Trade Edition

❋

For
JACK CARTER

and in memory of
TONY HENLEY

Everything a hunter should be

※

FOREWORD

That large mammals still so irresistibly attract us is one of what are generally referred to as "the big mysteries." Today, on the cusp of millennia, such a pull seems something that ought to have been lost to us so long ago that its continued existence strains belief. It's like discovering a bear track in a flower bed: Something doesn't belong here; and because we live in what Ortega y Gasset called a "rather stupid time," we assume that it must be the paw print that is out of place.

Terry Wieland, meanwhile, is someone who will wonder what a flower bed is doing surrounding a bear track. Then get down to measure the track to gauge the size of the bear.

A big-game hunter and author, Terry has written about the lurid passion for spiral-horned antelope and the not entirely sound ambition to encounter dangerous beasts. Needless to say, in reading Terry, even before meeting him, I identified kin.

Now Terry has written about the magic of big game, and the kinship is all the clearer. In these pages he recognizes, and celebrates, the strange attraction we still feel toward the megafauna; but in reality, as well as in Terry's writing, it's not quite as simple as that.

What Terry writes about is not some maudlin gravitation toward any and all big game ("...if you gravitate...to all you meet or know," a thoroughly exasperated D. H. Lawrence wrote of Whitman's poetic high crimes and misdemeanors, "why, something must have gone seriously wrong with you"), but of the unique pull exerted by the most magical ones.

All animals have power; nevertheless, though in our compulsorily egalitarian era it may not be correct to say, some animals have greater power than others. You have only to read Jack O'Connor on mountain sheep, Robert Ruark on Cape buffalo, or Jim Corbett on the (then) abundant tiger to realize that some animals simply possess a deeper mythos and live more vitally in that gray habitat of our minds than do others.

Terry understands this, and to his credit there are no lackluster animals anywhere in his book. Part of this is the animals themselves (it would be difficult to make the likes of bongo, elk, or polar bear boring!); but there is also the context in which they are found. There is far less magic in encountering a red stag in a deer park, for instance, than at the end of a long stalk through wind and rain on the Highlands heather; the power of a brown bear is raised exponentially when he is hunted with bow and arrow; and a world's-record whitetail reunited with the hunter who killed it, half-a-century after its vanishing from sight, is not a mere phenomenon, but one verging on the paranormal.

One question Terry's book does raise, and never completely answers, is what the exact nature of big game's magic is. There is, of course, a sugary, innocuous, Disneyesque magic known to everyone. Then there is another darker, riskier, and altogether more serious kind that only a very few ever experience. This is the magic of charms and enchantments, of being in thrall. It represents a force beyond us and often beyond our strength to resist.

Whatever the nature of big game's magic, it is ancient and not to be taken lightly. And whether it is the white variety, or that old black kind, it is a magic that definitely has Terry Wieland in its spell. For those who read this fine book, it is a spell they are likely to find themselves in, too, from the very first pages to the final, well-chosen word.

THOMAS MCINTYRE
Sheridan, Wyoming
November, 1998

TABLE OF CONTENTS

Foreword by Thomas McIntyre vii

Author's Preface xi

Acknowledgements xv

I THE CLASS OF '98 I

Introduction 2

Turn, Turn 4

The Big Five-Hundreds 34

The Mauser 98 57

Magic 78

A F R I C A

2 AND STILL CHAMPION

On the Trail of Mbogo 85

Vengeance 98

Corrida 114

A Sudden Silence 128

3 A PATCH OF RED 129

The Sué Bongo 131

The Biggest Bongo Ever 140

4 LEOPARD IN THE ROUGH 145

NORTH AMERICA

5   OUR FAVORITE GAME 161
    The Jordan Buck 164
    The Hanson Buck 169
    Bruce Ewen's Curious Buck 174

6   APACHE GOLD 181

7   BIG SKY, BIG HORNS 203

8   THE MOOSE OF FORTYMILE 215

9   DAY ONE, TEN A.M. 225

10 ONE WHALE OF A BEAR 235

11 BEARS ON ICE 249

EUROPE

12 THE HILL STAG 271

13 THE INNSBRUCK SANCTION 289

ASIA

14 TIGER, TIGER, FADING FAST 307

AUTHOR'S PREFACE

Sometimes an author will set out to write a book, and at the end of the process find that the book he has actually written is quite different than what was originally intended. This is one of those occasions.

I began with the idea of writing an anthology of original pieces —long magazine-type articles—telling the stories of how certain record-book big game animals had been taken in recent years. The impetus was provided by the Boone and Crockett Club's 22nd Big Game Awards, held in 1995. It so happened that this particular event included an extraordinary number, not only of high-ranking trophy animals of various species, but also a large number from individual species that, at one time, were thought to exist in such small numbers that the chances of them ever being hunted again, on any major scale, were remote at best.

The B&C gathering included, for example, bighorn sheep from the western states in surprisingly large numbers, a new all-time record whitetail, and representative elk, caribou and moose. Together, these suggested we were witnessing some dramatic changes in wildlife populations.

As the book progressed, I began to see some threads that ran throughout the different stories, and to wonder if perhaps there was not a theme there that was common to them all—a theme that had crept into the book like a Trojan Horse. Accordingly, I went looking for evidence to support it and, more often than not, found it elsewhere as well.

The theme I am referring to is the widespread resurgence of big game animals throughout North America that has occurred over the last century, since the dark days of 1898 when it appeared there would soon be no game animals left in any serious numbers anywhere on the continent. Once that theme was identified, many things snapped into focus, and I then expanded the book by including several pieces that dealt with related subjects such as changes in firearms since 1898, the evolution of the hunter himself not just in America but throughout the world, and the overall state of game and big game hunting as it exists today.

The result, I hope, is not just a collection of unrelated articles about isolated events, but a more cohesive picture of the state of big game hunting in 1998, a year which just happens to be the 100th anniversary of several pivotal events in the world of guns and hunting.

It would not be overstating to say that the outlook for hunting 100 years ago was bleak virtually everywhere in the world. Game populations in North America were at the lowest ebb, as a result of rampant over-hunting, and sometimes deliberate extermination; in southern Africa, the game animals had been all but shot out of the original Dutch colonies, and settlers were just beginning to move into the great game country of East Africa. It was generally accepted everywhere that civilization was good, that settlement of a country meant putting it under the plough, and that in order to do this, the game animals would have to go.

Even Theodore Roosevelt, a gentleman who can, with justification, claim to be the father of game conservation in modern America, believed in the benefits of so-called progress and civilization. He might mourn the passing of the great game herds, and he might do everything possible to preserve token herds of animals to show future generations what once had been, but to halt the ploughs and beat the plough shares back into broadhead arrows? Never.

Fortunately, animal numbers reached a kind of low tide around 1900 to 1920, and then slowly, through a combination of factors and influences, began to come back. That they came back from unbelievably low numbers to what they are today—who would believe that around 1921, there were only 13,000 pronghorn antelope in the entire United States?—is partly due to conservation efforts and partly to force of circumstance. The resurgence in caribou numbers in the far North since the low point of the mid-1960s, for example, can be attributed to little more than natural cycles. Perhaps, though, realizing that such natural cycles can, do, and will occur is itself a valuable lesson for mankind, which displays more managerial arrogance toward the natural world with every passing day.

To an extent, every story in this book is the story of a comeback. Some, like the whitetail in America, are irrefutable and seemingly permanent; others, like the polar bear, are more fragile, and still others, like the tiger, may be completely ephemeral. But in almost every case, recreational hunters—I hate to use the word "sport" in connection with hunting, given its corrupted modern meaning, in spite of the fact that it originated with hunting in the dim distant past—recreational hunters are largely responsible for what game animals we do still have. "Recreation" is a particularly apt word, I feel, because hunters continually recreate themselves when they hunt, and through their conservation efforts they have helped to recreate at least a semblance of the game herds of the past.

Recreational hunters have fought the efforts of farmers, ranchers, loggers, real estate developers, anti-malaria swamp-drainers, ski hill operators, anti-tsetse fly activists, oil exploration outfits, pipeline companies, and the U.S. Army Corps of Engineers. We have not always won, but in recent years at least, we have always tried. Sort of like hunting, when you think about it.

ACKNOWLEDGEMENTS

Writing a book (or to be precise, publishing a book you have written) is the greatest of all pleasures in life, bar none. One reason for this is that almost any work of non-fiction is as much a job of compilation as anything, and in the course of compiling and writing you form many new friendships, as well as renewing friendships from the past.

Of my new acquaintances, I am particularly grateful to Jack Reneau of the Boone and Crockett Club, who went far out of his way to assist with information, photographs and background material.

I also wish to thank everyone who hunted the animals and shared their experiences with me, including Bill Clark (Africa), John Crouse (Alaska), Bruce Ewen (Saskatchewan), Jack Frost (Alaska), Don Hotter (Northwest Territories), and Don McVittie (Baffin Island).

Then there are the guides, the professional hunters and the outfitters—Davie Fraser and Mike McCrave in Scotland, Walter Sailer in Austria, Duff Gifford and Gordon Cormack in Tanzania, and Jerome Knap in Canada's far north. And the game biologists—Joe Jojola from the Fort Apache Reservation, and Kevin Lackey of the Rocky Mountain Elk Foundation.

Jim Morey was my companion on two of the hunting expeditions—to Scotland and Austria—and a fine companion he was, although his singing would cause you to jump off an Alp if you were not already paralyzed by fright.

I am also grateful to illustrator Bruce Langton, to Bob Hunter, publisher and provider of much encouragement, and to Bill Buckley, my editor. Bill's Ivy League insistence on accuracy and good grammar was sometimes infuriating but always helpful. And finally, my special thanks to an old friend, Robin Hurt, who was, as always, generous with his time, experience and advice.

1

❋

THE CLASS OF '98

*The world's pioneers have almost invariably belonged to one of two
classes. It has been the love of sport, or the lust of gold, which has led
men first to break in upon those solitudes in which nature and her
wild children have lived alone since the world's beginning. Hunters or
gold prospectors still find the mountain passes...living as hard as
wolves, and content to think themselves rich in the possession of a few
gnarled horns and grizzled hides.*

Clive Phillipps-Wolley
Big Game Shooting
The Badminton Library, 1894

❋

1

INTRODUCTION

Some years stand out in history. For hunters, 1898 was such a year. There were no world wars started, no continents discovered; if you could point to a single pivotal event in North America, it would be the Klondike Gold Rush, which for the first time brought Alaska to the attention of the nation as something more than Seward's Folly— a vast, worthless expanse of ice and snow. Gold changed everyone's perception. Gold will do that.

In Africa, gold was also the focus for miners who were swarming over the Witwatersrand in the Transvaal, setting the stage for the Second Anglo-Boer War. That conflict, the greatest armed robbery in history, really began in 1898, although the first shots were not fired until the next year. In East Africa—Kenya and the Uganda Protectorate, as they were then known—construction of the Uganda Railway was well underway, and settlers were trickling in from England to take up land in the highlands north of Nairobi. The very first professional hunters were shooting elephant, black rhino, and lions to clear the land for white settlement, or to make way for black tribes on native reserves.

Altogether, 1898 was an eventful but not really remarkable year. Unless, of course, you were a hunter—and even then, it would not have seemed out of the ordinary at the time. It is only with the benefit of considerable hindsight that today we can measure the impact of its disparate events. The Klondike Gold Rush, for example, led to the settlement of Alaska and the opening up of its tremendous reserves of big game. The British march up the continent of Africa continued, from the Cape through the Transvaal, and the conquest of the Rhodesias; the settlement that began in Kenya eventually led to the acquisition (after 1918) of Tanganyika—then, as now, the greatest single storehouse of game animals in the world.

In England, gunmakers responded to the demands of the

early African professional hunters for harder-hitting rifles by introducing the first of the Nitro Express cartridges (the .450 NE by John
Rigby, in 1898), and in Germany Paul Mauser produced the rifle that
was destined to dominate big game hunting over the next 100 years—
the Mauser 98. The 98 began life as a military weapon, but it was as
the world's finest all-around hunting rifle that it really made, and con-
tinues to make, its mark in the world.

Eighteen ninety-eight was also the year in which we can pinpoint a shift in attitude towards the game animals themselves. By that
year, overall wildlife numbers in North America were the lowest they
have ever been: The bison were gone from the Great Plains, along
with most of the elk and all but a handful of pronghorn antelope.
In just a few years, a combination of market hunting, politics, and
land-clearing had all but wiped out the vast game herds that inhabited the continent for thousands of years. Many thought the animals
were gone forever, but they were wrong. Certainly the bison could
never return in the numbers they once enjoyed, but both elk and
pronghorn have made amazing comebacks, as have the white-tailed
deer. In the end, only the passenger pigeon and a few localized subspecies actually disappeared forever.

As it turned out, 1898 was not the end of the game animals, as many concluded at the time. Instead, it was the beginning
of a serious battle to save them. And, as with the exploration of
unknown lands, the people in the forefront of that battle were hunters. In North America, it was Theodore Roosevelt and his friends; in
Africa, it was Frederick Courteney Selous, Sir Samuel White Baker,
F.R.N. Findlay, and a whole generation of English shooting men who
had gone out to Africa enthralled by the tales of the early hunters,
only to find that the fabulous game herds witnessed by Roualeyn
Gordon Cumming and William Cornwallis Harris were long gone—
like the passenger pigeon and the bison of North America.

It would be a grim debate indeed to determine which was
the most egregious slaughter of game and rape of a country—the
despoiling of the American West, or the conquest of South Africa.
Just when you read an account of unbridled slaughter of the bison
and think to yourself that nothing could surpass that, you read of a

game drive in South Africa in which, for the amusement of a visiting dignitary, some 6,000 game animals were killed in a single day, with some of the game (in this case, a stampeding herd of panicked zebras) trampling several of the native beaters to death. Debating which was worse overall is like comparing Nazi Germany with Stalinist Russia. The debate itself demeans the events and is completely meaningless to those who died.

Finally, 1898 was the year in which Kruger National Park actually came into being. An 8,000-square-mile preserve in the eastern Transvaal, along the border with Portuguese East Africa (now Mozambique), Kruger was established in an attempt to provide some sanctuary for the hard-pressed big game animals of South Africa. Today, Kruger is perhaps the greatest game preserve in the world, ranking with the Selous in Tanzania and Yellowstone Park in America.

In spite of the obvious successes in the last 100 years, only a fool would suggest that the battle is won; it is not yet even over, and it never will be. But the events of the last century, which would have seemed like a pipedream in 1898, at least prove that it is possible not to *lose* the battle. Perhaps that is the best we can hope for.

❈

TURN, TURN
An American Tale

When the white man came, North America was, according to all reports and reliable estimates, one vast cauldron of game. There were 20 million white-tailed deer, and they were found all over the continent. Up to 60 million bison roamed the plains, sharing their territory with another 30 to 40 million pronghorn antelope. The elk was found from the Atlantic to the Pacific, passenger pigeons rose in clouds that stretched from horizon to horizon, and when the ducks flew their numbers darkened the sun.

By the year 1900, all this had changed. The passenger pigeon was gone, wiped out, and wildfowl numbers were perilously low. There were, perhaps, 300,000 whitetails in the entire country, and none at all in some states. Elk were down to 90,000, pronghorns reduced to a few scattered pockets totalling fewer than 13,000, and only 300 bison survived. Three hundred, when just a few years before there had been 60 million!

The story of how all this came to pass is the story of hunting in America. But it's not the whole story. How waterfowl were revived, how pronghorns rebounded, how the bison was saved, and how whitetails are as plentiful now as ever before in history is also the story of hunting in America. It is a story with no beginning and no end.

❋

The United States of America has been in existence for almost 225 years, and its history of hunting and wildlife can be divided into three distinct periods: 1776 to 1850, 1850 to 1925, and 1925 to the present. Each period is roughly three-quarters of a century, and the end of each saw the end of an era; the beginning of each saw the curtain rise on a new act. Take 1850—the heyday of the market hunter east of the Mississippi and the mountain man in the far West. Thomas Meacham was a professional hunter in St. Lawrence County, New York. He hunted deer for venison and skins, he hunted wolves on contract, he shot bears for their hides. Unlike many of his brethren, Meacham was a literate and painstaking man who kept precise records of his activities. When he died in 1850 after a lifetime of hunting, his journals showed that he had killed more than 200 each of bears and wolves, as well as 77 cougars—and 2,550 white-tailed deer. Meacham may have been exceptional, but he was not unique. A hunter from Herkimer, New York, reportedly killed 76 deer in one season.

Thomas Meacham died just about the same time that Henry William Herbert came on the scene. Herbert was an English aristocrat who arrived in America in 1831, began writing hunting and fishing stories a few years later, and in 1849 published a book called *Frank Forester's Field Sports*. This was followed in 1853 by *American Game in its Seasons* and *The Complete Manual for Young Sportsmen* in 1856. Three years later he died, and the name Henry William Herbert passed into obscurity. As Frank Forester, however, Herbert left a lasting legacy— the first real attempt to introduce the concept of ethics and fair play in hunting in a country which viewed game as limitless, and game laws as an imposition of tyranny. Under the circumstances, both attitudes were perfectly understandable.

In Europe, hunting had long since ceased to be a pursuit of food for survival and had become largely an activity of the aristocrats and the privileged few. Kings and nobles hunted with falcons or pursued foxes on horseback; royal forests and deer parks were home to birds and animals which were protected from the peasants by strict game laws carrying fierce penalties for poaching. The peasants might wish to hunt, for recreation as well as for food, but there were severe restrictions, and in some countries it was forbidden altogether. When these peasants struck out across the sea for parts unknown and stepped ashore into a world of endless forests and teeming game, they had arrived in heaven. Until the forests were cleared and crops planted, food came in the form of anything that could be taken with a gun. There were no game laws, no bag limits, no seasons, no restrictions, and any attempt to impose such was resisted or ignored. Every man was a hunter, and hunting was a God-given right. Having come so far to escape the strictures of the Crown, they were not about to allow any local government to impose game laws when birds and animals were not only necessary for food but, as any fool could see, unlimited and unending.

Gradually, towns grew up and people became urbanized, but America retained its taste for game. Cattle and chickens they might have, but these could never compete with a tenderloin of whitetail or a juicy breast of canvasback. Demand for game meat was fierce and constant, and market hunters were only too happy to fill that demand. Thomas Meacham was one of thousands who made their living by the gun and whose avowed purpose in life was to kill as many as possible, with as little expenditure of ammunition as possible. It was simple economics, and no one can really blame them. They were hunting for a living, not for recreation.

Even those who hunted for themselves, however, were slow to embrace the concept of sport hunting with a code of conduct. Such things were already accepted in Europe, but in a sort of inverse snobbery were sneered at in the colonies as affectation. "Flying shooting," the taking of birds on the wing, had been known in Spain since about 1640, and had gradually spread across Europe until the term "sitting duck" had become a jeering epithet; not in the Americas, though, where sportsmen endeavored to shoot their birds on the ground or in the water until well into the 1800s. Shooting at a bird on the wing was a gesture born of desperation, not a manifestation of sportsmanship.

In 1909, Ernest Thompson Seton made one of the earliest attempts to estimate how many whitetails were in America before the white man, and arrived at a figure of 40 million. Leonard Lee Rue, a modern authority on deer, reckons that figure is high; he estimates the actual number might have been about half that. Regardless, all down the eastern seaboard it did not take the new settlers long to reduce whitetail numbers to a fraction, and wipe them out altogether in some places.

Deer hides were a major item of trade with Europe. In a period of just 18 years, from 1755 to 1773, 600,000 deerskins were shipped to England from the port of Savannah, Georgia. How many more were killed for domestic use is anyone's guess. The magnitude of the deer "harvest" is illustrated by the fact that the *Mayflower* landed at Plymouth in 1620, and Rhode Island's first permanent settlement was established in 1636. Just ten years later, in 1646, in an attempt to preserve what few deer it had left, Rhode Island passed a law establishing the first closed season, and over the next few years the other colonies followed suit. The laws were not universally accepted; deer were food and a hungry man makes his own rules. Still, it was the beginning—sort of—of a new era for the wildlife, and it came not a moment too soon.

If there were 20 million whitetails in America, how many

ducks might there have been? A zillion seems like a fair and reasonable estimate, but while the deer abounded no one could be bothered hunting ducks on any scale. As deer numbers declined, however, the colonists turned to waterfowl. In 1783, America's first actual hunting book was published. *The Sportsman's Companion*, written by a British officer serving in the colonies, was a guide to birdshooting, including the use of dogs for pointing and retrieving and even cautions against overshooting. Like many first books on any subject, it was not widely known and its advice even less widely followed. The War of Independence was an inauspicious time for a British officer to be telling the American citizen what do to or how to do it.

※

By 1850, the American West was, if not opened up to settlement, at least well-known from the travels and adventures of the mountain men. Jim Bridger, Kit Carson, Uncle Dick Wootton, and the rest had led the way, and word had trickled back about the vast plains, the gigantic herds of buffalo, the elk, and the grizzly bear. The plains Indians had domesticated the horse, become proficient riders, and had adapted their methods of hunting accordingly, especially for the bison, the main animal on which their livelihood depended. Like most aboriginal hunters, the chase was both vocation and sport. The practice of riding in the midst of a stampeding buffalo herd, and shooting the animals with bow and arrow while trying to keep your mount when the merest slip meant death beneath the pounding hooves, was exhilaration beyond description. That was a sporting endeavor by anyone's standards, and hunters began to arrive from as far away as Europe and Russia to give it a try.

In 1854, an Irish baronet by the name of Sir St. George Gore arrived in St. Louis to begin one of the epic hunting trips of all time. This was an age of excess all over the world, but Sir St. George set a standard that allows him a place of questionable honor even among such infamous hunting excessives as Roualeyn Gordon Cumming and John Hanning Speke. Gore's odyssey through the West lasted three years. During that time, with Jim Bridger as a guide, he travelled the plains with an entourage that included 28 vehicles and 112 horses. For his own use he had a carriage and a Kentucky thoroughbred, and was accompanied by four dozen hunting dogs. He took with him 40 servants, 18 oxen, and three milk cows. The estimated cost of his safari into the Wild West: a half-million dollars. But what a hunting trip it was! In three years, Sir St. George's personal bag included 105 bears, 1,600 deer and elk, and 2,000 of the huge, woolly plains bison. It was a fitting beginning to a half-century of one of the two most terrible periods of wildlife exploitation in the history of man: The despoiling of the American West.

Other notables who crossed the Mississippi for the same purpose included writer Washington Irving and the painter, George Catlin. In 1871, General Philip Sheridan and "Buffalo Bill" Cody organized the famous "Millionaires' Hunt" for a group that included James Gordon Bennett, owner of the New York *Herald Tribune*, and Anson Stager, founder of Western Union. The group's bag did not approach Gore's: They took only ten each of elk and antelope, and 100 buffalo—but then, they only hunted for ten days. A year later, General Sheridan went west once more, this time in the company of General George A. Custer to escort Grand Duke Alexis of Russia. His Grace was here to buy guns for the Tsar's army, and he was anxious to test them in the best possible manner—riding hell-for-leather among the charging bison and shooting them with his new Smith & Wesson .44s. This was the sport of kings as enjoyed by the kings of commerce.

By that time, of course, buffalo hunting in the West had become a big business to the point where the buffalo hunters were almost *out* of business. The bison, which once had roamed over the entire continent from the Atlantic seaboard to the Rockies, and from Mexico to the Northwest Territories, had been steadily driven back until, by 1820, there were none left east of the Mississippi. In 1830, the plains buffalo were about all that remained, but they still numbered around 50 million. The growth in demand for buffalo robes, for use in sleighs and carriages, sent hundreds of men west in search of their fortunes. They enlisted the plains Indians to hunt for them, and in the years leading up to the Civil War an estimated three-million bison a year were being killed for the trade. The Civil War itself forced a lull in the bloodshed, but the flood of dispossessed Southerners, demobbed soldiers, and all-around freebooters who headed west after 1865 spelled a sure end for the plains buffalo.

There was the market for hides, and there was a market for the meat to feed the crews building the transcontinental railroads that were pushing west. At the height of the slaughter it is estimated there were 20,000 men in the field hunting buffalo. The full-time professionals resented the intrusion of amateurs who wasted both meat and hides by killing far more animals than they could skin, butcher, and transport, but there was little they could do about it. The surplus of hides drove the market price down, making the trade barely economic even for the efficient professionals. Frank Mayer was a professional buffalo hunter on the plains for nine years. His self-imposed quota when he was hunting was 50 bulls a day. When the animals were down, Mayer left the carcasses to his skinners while he cleaned his rifles and loaded fresh ammunition for the next day. The skins he sold for two or three dollars apiece. At the end of his career, Mayer totalled up his expenses for wagons, stock, equipment, and his helpers' wages and subtracted it from the money he made from selling the hides. His bottom line: A net income of $3,000 a year. There may have been fortunes to be made in buffalo hunting, but if so it was not the hunters themselves who made them.

As is usually the case, the big money changed hands higher up. One company in St. Louis, Missouri, shipped 250,000 hides east in a single year; another, in Dodge City, Kansas, shipped 200,000 hides the first year the railroad hit town. At an auction in Fort Worth, Texas, 200,000 hides were sold in just one day. The railroads provided both a market for the meat and a means of shipping meat and hides to the East; they were also a major instrument of destruction of the bison. The Union Pacific reached Cheyenne, Wyoming, in 1867. Its line divided the Great Plains in two, and the bison into a northern and a southern herd. The southern herd was the first to go. In 1871, the Santa Fe railroad reached the heart of its summer grazing grounds, and over the next four years buffalo hunters killed millions. By 1875, the southern herd was all but exterminated. At the same time, oversupply had killed the market; fully-lined robes were selling in the East for as little as nine dollars, and hides were selling at source for 65 or 70 cents apiece. Still, the hunters kept at it. Politics entered the fray, with the northern buffalo becoming a pawn in the Indian wars that swept the plains in the 1870s, culminated in Custer's defeat at the Little Bighorn in 1876, and finally ended with the Battle of Wounded Knee in December, 1890.

In early 1872, the bison in the northern herd were estimated at seven million. By the end of that year, four million of them had been killed, and another million died in 1873. The Cheyenne and Sioux watched this slaughter, and the encroachment of white settlers, with growing trepidation and, ultimately, despair. The death of Custer and his men at Little Bighorn was but a sideshow in a much larger tragedy. By 1877, the year after the battle, there were barely a half-million bison left, and that dwindled to 75,000 by 1885, and a scant 200—two hundred!—by 1889. At which point, the government decided the bison needed official protection, and the hunt was ended. With the bison died the whole way of life of the plains Indians, who were then confined to reservations. The bison's former range was occupied by settlers, and the high plains were turned under. Buffalo grass was replaced by wheat and barley. A new era began in the history of the American West.

※

Elsewhere, in the settled parts of the United States, hunting had passed seamlessly from being a necessity of life to being a way of life. From Vermont's Eastern Kingdom to the Georgia pines, boys graduated to manhood by being accepted into the company of hunting men. Unfortunately, the necessary adjunct to a hunting society— game to hunt—was in decline almost everywhere.

The North American elk is a typical example. Today, we think of the elk as an animal of the mountainous West, but when the first settlers came it was indigenous to just about every state. Being a large animal with excellent meat and good hide, the great antlered beast became a hunter's prize, and there began the elk's long retreat.

※

The elk disappeared from Vermont and New Jersey around 1800, and from the Carolinas about the same time; they were last sighted in New York in 1847, and in Michigan in the 1870s. They hung on in the mountains of Pennsylvania until 1867, when the last elk in the Alleghenies was reportedly killed by an Indian, Jim Jacobs. They were gone from Ohio by the 1840s, from Missouri by the 1890s.

Forest and Stream, 1876:

> *...owing to a savage and indiscriminating warfare that has been inaugurated against them within the past few years, their numbers are decreasing more rapidly than ever before... An elk skin is worth from $2.50 to $4.00, and to secure that pitiful sum this beautiful life is taken and 300 to 500 pounds of the most delicate meat is left on the ground.*

The last native elk in Wisconsin was killed in 1875, in Iowa in 1885, in Minnesota in 1896.

Although the extirpation of the plains buffalo is well documented, the fate of the elk is less well known. They were highly prized by both Indian and white man for their hides, their meat, their antlers, and their canine teeth. These "tusks" were used by Indians to decorate clothing, and by white men as watch fobs. Members of the Benevolent and Protective Order of Elks paid high prices for the tusks, which were the organization's unofficial badge of membership. The advent, in swift succession, of the caplock, then the cartridge, then the repeating rifle gave professional hunters the means to capitalize on the demand for elk hides and teeth, and within about three decades they had been effectively swept from the plains.

In the early 1880s, Theodore Roosevelt, then in his twenties, moved west to become a rancher on the Little Missouri River in the Dakota Territory. Even by that time, as Roosevelt later wrote, the depredations of the market and hide hunters had turned the Dakotas from a paradise to a wildlife wasteland:

> *In 1881, (bison) were still almost as numerous as ever. In 1883, all were killed but a few stragglers, and the last of these stragglers that*

I heard of was seen...in 1885. Elk were plentiful in 1880, though never anything like as abundant as buffalo. Only straggling parties have been seen since 1883, and the last one I shot near my ranch was in 1886.

Roosevelt went on to document the demise of every other big game species: mule deer, pronghorn, mountain sheep, bear. Sadly, he concluded, "Nowadays (1905), settlers along the Little Missouri can kill an occasional deer or antelope; but it can hardly be called a game country."

⁂

If any one man can be thanked for the great turnaround in game populations over the last 100 years, it is Theodore Roosevelt. He returned to the East in 1886 to go into politics, but what he had seen in the West stayed with him, and he was determined to do something to save what remained of the game. He was not the only voice for conservation by any means, nor even the first voice; but he was a man of courage, determination, and energy, and in 1901, he became President of the United States.

By 1900, game of every kind was in dreadful shape virtually everywhere in the country. Centuries of profligate hunting had taken their toll. Today we blame market hunters for the loss, but they were not totally at fault. With the exception of the buffalo and one or two other species, the game taken by farmers and ranchers and sport hunters, and those who just wanted to eat, far exceeded what the market hunters killed. And of course, then as now, the greatest culprit was loss of habitat. As the land was cleared, the forests logged, and the plains tilled, the animals retreated or died.

In 1894, there were only 300 plains bison left alive. East of the Mississippi the white-tailed deer had been decimated or eradicated. Incredibly, by the early 1900s, whitetails were gone from Ohio, Indiana, Illinois, Iowa, and southern Michigan—all magnificent whitetail states today. In 1910, the total whitetail population in the Midwest was estimated at fewer than 2,000.

⁂

In the East, by the end of the colonial period, every state had emulated Rhode Island and introduced some sort of protection for deer. The results varied. By 1900, New Jersey had fewer than 200 deer, while in Massachusetts, New Hampshire, and Vermont they were so scarce that even seeing a track made the local papers. In the West, however, game laws came slowly. This was not surprising, since many people had moved west to *escape* restrictions, not impose them, but as each territory achieved statehood, game laws naturally followed. Minnesota, for example, became a state in 1858 and immediately introduced a closed season for deer and elk; in 1871, it prohibited the export of game meat for sale in other states, imposed a bag limit on deer (five) in 1895, and introduced its first big game hunting license in 1899. Other states were taking similar action, but their effect on market hunters was neither immediate nor significant. Through the 1880s and 1890s, game laws were an inconvenience at best, a nuisance at worst, and market hunters continued to kill deer, elk, the remnants of the plains buffalo, pronghorns, and bighorn sheep to sell to railroads, logging camps, and mines. In the East, market hunting for ducks—especially the succulent canvasback—provided a staple item for the menu of every fashionable hotel. America's taste for game meat had not abated one whit, and the population, a mere 1.5 million at independence, numbered 45 million by 1876, with hungry immigrants still pouring in by the tens of thousands.

Obviously, the only way the carnage could be slowed was by federal action. In 1900, Congress passed the Lacey Act, restricting interstate commerce in game meat, and the era of the market hunter passed into history. The Lacey Act was a catalyst. In the next few years one measure after another was taken to save what was left of America's game populations. In 1901, Theodore Roosevelt became president; four years later he created the United States Forest Service, and by 1908 almost 150-million acres of land had been set aside. Yellowstone became the nation's (and the world's) first national park in 1872, and millions more acres of parkland were set aside during Roosevelt's administration.

In the late 1800s, Roosevelt and some friends banded together to form the Boone & Crockett Club, to promote the concept of fair chase among hunters. It was North America's first major hunters' organization.

The country's first wildlife refuge, on Alaska's Afognak Island, had been established in 1892; Roosevelt seized on the concept with a vengeance, and Florida's Pelican Island Refuge was established by executive order in 1903. He followed this with 50 more refuges, in 17 different states, by the end of his first term; another 36 were set up during his second term in office. His "bull moose" tactics infuriated some, but there is no arguing with the result, and the conservation movement continued to grow. By 1963, the U.S. had 289 national wildlife refuges totalling 28,500,000 acres. Roosevelt's immense contribution to conservation was honored in 1947, when the government established Theodore Roosevelt National Park, 110 square miles of badlands along his beloved Little Missouri River in North Dakota.

From 1900 to 1935 was a period of struggle for both game and legislators. Almost every species was at an all-time low. Pronghorns, once almost as numerous as bison on the prairies, now numbered a measly 13,000; elk totalled perhaps 90,000 across the country, holed up in remote mountain strongholds. Wildfowl numbers had tumbled, and in 1916 the United States and Canada signed an international treaty to protect migratory birds. Congress ratified the treaty in 1918, and bag limits were introduced immediately. The national refuge system continued to expand. In 1924, Congress authorized $1.5 million for the purchase of bottomlands along the upper Mississippi. This became the Upper Mississippi River Wildlife and Fish Refuge, a vital section of the Mississippi Flyway that today provides both protection for wildfowl and fine hunting opportunities for duck hunters.

✳

But what of hunters? What of recreational hunting? Legislators legislate for one reason: public pressure. And the public, including a great many sport hunters, were the continuing pressure that forced the adoption of so many protective measures. As well—as with

Roosevelt and the Boone & Crockett Club—individuals and groups were busy in a thousand different ways. Although no big game species had been lost completely in the orgy of commercial exploitation of the late 1800s, some bird species had been—most notably the passenger pigeon. The wild turkey had been driven from much of its previous range, and some individual species like the northeastern pinnated grouse, or heath hen, had been eradicated. The prairie chicken had been reduced to a pitiful remnant and was continuing to lose ground.

For some of these birds, help could be provided, but not for others. The wild turkey recovered and then some, and the prairie chicken is making a painfully slow comeback. They have been augmented by the introduction of foreign species such as the ringnecked pheasant, the Hungarian partridge, and the chukar. Today, these are three of the greatest game birds in the West—all introduced by hunters. Similarly, exotic big game species arrived and began to take hold. Texas ranchers were particularly enthusiastic about it, and today on Texas ranches you can hunt the big nilgai antelope, the axis deer, and dozens of other species. Some of them, like the black buck, are no longer huntable anywhere else in the world. Then there are the accidental species that are now notable game animals, such as the Texas wild hog. In the 1930s, when the Depression struck, many families could not feed their stock and turned them loose to fend for themselves—which they did, admirably. Then Russian boars were introduced to cross with the feral hogs and give them greater hardiness. The result? One fine game animal—exciting hunting and good eating.

Many of these successes were individual efforts. But there were group efforts as well. In spite of federal measures on behalf of waterfowl, ducks continued to struggle through the 1920s. It was a long road back and when the Depression struck in 1929, followed by the great drought of the 1930s, duck populations went into another serious decline. In 1929, a group of businessmen and sportsmen formed a foundation called "More Game Birds In America, Inc." The foundation financed research into the status of waterfowl and other game birds, which found that loss of habitat was rampant on the prairies. This led, in 1937, to the formation of Ducks Unlimited—the first, the most powerful, and arguably the most effective single conservation organization ever formed. And the founders were duck hunters.

That year saw another milestone: Passage of a bill that has done more for wildlife than any other single piece of legislation. The Pittman-Robertson Act, formally known as the Federal Aid to Wildlife Restoration Act, was signed into law on September 2, 1937. It levied an 11 per cent excise tax on sporting arms and ammunition, the monies gathered to be distributed to the states to finance wildlife-management programs. It was supported by everyone—conservation groups, state wildlife agencies, the Bureau of Biological Survey (later the U.S. Fish and Wildlife Service), and the manufacturers and hunters themselves. DuPont, Remington, and the Federal Cartridge Company were especially enthusiastic.

The sporting arms and ammunition companies had already taken steps on their own. In 1911, alarmed at the state of wildlife populations, they got together to found the Wildlife Management Institute, an organization devoted to the scientific management of game based in Washington, D.C. Ever since it has been a leader in studying and publishing game-management information. When Pittman-Robertson was passed, the Wildlife Management Institute became actively involved in working with its various programs.

One of the key provisions of the Pittman-Robertson Act was that, to qualify for a share of the funds, states had to guarantee that hunting-license fees would not be diverted to non-hunting programs. Within a year, 43 out of 48 states had done so, and eventually the other five followed suit. This provision laid the basis for wildlife management at the state level as it is today. As for Pittman-Robertson, the money began to flow into Washington and out to the state agencies. As of today, hunters, through the excise tax on their purchases, have provided close to *one billion dollars* to finance state wildlife programs.

The formation of Ducks Unlimited in 1937 was both an actual and a symbolic change in direction for American hunters. Since then, other formal groups have sprung up devoted to protecting and propagating the species of their particular interest: the Rocky Mountain Elk Foundation, the Foundation for North American Wild Sheep, the Ruffed Grouse Society, Pheasants Forever, the Wild Turkey Foundation. In 1969, big game hunters, led by C.J. McElroy, founded Safari Club International, an organization devoted to conservation of wildlife and also protection of the hunter. Today, membership in one or several of these organizations goes with owning a hunting license. Membership is not required but is, in many circles, expected.

Both for hunters and for the hunted, these groups arrived none too soon. Since 1950, the growth of anti-hunting sentiment in America has been rapid. Many people, especially those who live in cities and have no personal hunting background, do not understand recreational hunting either as an activity for the individual or as an essential tool of wildlife management. And truth to tell, in all too many cases hunters have not helped their own cause. In 1898, the bison was the endangered species. In 1998, it is the hunter himself who is endangered. This is ironic, considering what has happened to wildlife over the past 100 years.

The bison, reduced to 300 animals in 1894, now numbers well into the tens of thousands. There are managed herds in parks such as Yellowstone and Canada's Woods Buffalo National Park in the Northwest Territories, and there are huntable populations on private ranches throughout the West. The pronghorn antelope has bounced back. Where once it complemented the grazing of the buffalo on the plains, it now complements herds of cattle, living side by side with them in every western state. The pronghorn has become one of America's greatest game animals and numbers well into the millions. Elk, while gone forever from much of their original range, are thriving throughout the West and small herds are still being reintroduced. They were eradicated in New Mexico by 1895; today, reintroduced, they are a major game animal. So too in Arizona, where the native Merriam's elk was replaced by Rocky Mountain elk. Colorado, one of the greatest elk states, had only 500 to 1,000 animals in 1910; reintroduction and careful management has increased the population to more than 100,000 today.

But the greatest story—perhaps the greatest wildlife story of all time—is the white-tailed deer. Reduced to about 300,000 at the turn of the century, there are now an estimated 20 million whitetails, they are found in every state, and are unquestionably America's favorite game animal. Game laws played a part, but mostly the deer rebounded because of its natural resilience and adaptability. There is no conservation group for the whitetail, and it doesn't need one, thank you. Give it a little edge habitat and some acorns, and the whitetail would cheerfully inhabit Central Park. All they ask is an even break.

❄

African Looking-Glass

The history of game animals in Africa is considerably shorter and in many ways much simpler than in North America. Except for South Africa, which has been inhabited by whites almost as long as the Americas, the colonized history of the major game countries of central and East Africa (Tanzania, Kenya, Zambia, Zimbabwe, and Botswana) is barely a century old. In that time white settlers moved in to establish farms and till the fields, and professional hunters were there ahead of them to shoot for ivory, skins, and meat, and later to shoot animals on control.

Although millions of animals were killed, and hundreds of thousands are still killed each year, Africa as a whole was never subjected to the wholesale slaughter that virtually swept the American West clean of game in less than half a century. With some notable local exceptions, such as the gold-mining district of the Rand in the Transvaal, there was not the widespread mining, logging, and railway-building to establish a demand for a steady supply of game meat. There were no fashionable hotels building a reputation on their game-meat cuisine to keep the market gunners in business, and certainly there was no political pressure for the extirpation of a particular game animal, such as that which occurred over the plains bison during the

❄

wars with the Sioux and the Cheyenne.

Where they held sway—which happened to be most of the game-rich areas—the British very quickly established game preserves, closed seasons, and a licensing system that controlled all but the most determined poachers. And truth to tell, even where poaching was at its worst, it seemed to have surprisingly little impact on game populations until very recently. Even in the native reserves of Kenya, where professional hunters were hired to go in and clear out rhino, elephant, and lion by the hundreds, and sometimes by the thousands, it did not appear to make more than a dent in the animal population. No matter how many lions were killed, there never seemed to be a shortage.

The exception, of course, was South Africa, and there the parallels with North America are most pronounced. The Cape Colony, and later the Orange Free State and parts of the Transvaal, had their counterpart to the plains bison in the immense herds of springbok, the dainty little antelope that traversed the veldt in hosts that numbered in the millions. For the Afrikaner settlers (descendants of the original Cape Dutch), with their near-mystic worship of flocks, crops, and farms, wild animals were but an obstacle to be overcome or eliminated in their biblical quest for the land of milk and honey. To the average Afrikaner, a Zulu and a springbok occupied just about the same position on the ladder of life, and were equally likely to be flung off it at the earliest opportunity. Unlike the English, the Afrikaners of the time had little use for game, except as a source of cheap meat and leather. One by one, the great game animals were shot out in what is now South Africa. Elephants, rhinoceros, hippopotamus, lions, giraffes, and Cape buffalo were eradicated from the Dutch settlements. By 1898, in what is now Cape Province, the Orange Free State, Natal, and part of the Transvaal, the great herds that William Cornwallis Harris hunted in the 1830s were but a memory.

When Jan van Riebeeck landed in Table Bay in 1652, he found all the major African game animals in abundance. Where

Church Square later stood, in what is now Cape Town, there was a swamp infested with hippopotamus and Table Mountain reportedly was swarming with hartebeeste, eland, and steinbok. All the predators were numerous and remained so: In June, 1694, lions killed nine cattle within sight of the settlement.

As well as the common species, the Dutch also found animals that were unique to the locale. Generally speaking, a leopard is a leopard whether it is found in the Cape or Kenya, as is a lion; a few antelope species are found without variation throughout the continent, but not many. Most are distinct subspecies that are found in localized areas, and in those areas only. This makes the subspecies especially vulnerable, and woe betide the edible antelope who found his succulent self living cheek by jowl with the Cape Dutch, for he was not long for this world.

The most famous example is the *blaaubok* (blue buck), a relative of the sable and the roan that was found in only one small corner of the Cape colony, near Swellendam. It was extinct by the year 1800, and only scattered eyewitness accounts, as well as five known mounted specimens, now remain to remind us it once existed. These specimens, listed in Rowland Ward, show an animal with sweeping, scimitar-like horns, mounted on a predominantly grey-blue body. While most accounts describe them as having horns longer than a roan, the longest listed (at Leyden Museum) is slightly more than 24 inches; if it had been a roan, it would not even make the book. The other specimens, all described as being taken in the 18th century, are in Paris, Uppsala, Stockholm, and Vienna.

Another animal that came perilously close to the same fate was the bontebok, a damalisc whose relatives include the blesbok, the tsessebe of Botswana, and the topi of East Africa. It was shot out to the point that, by 1931, according to one account, there were only 17 left in the world. And the black wildebeest (a.k.a. the white-tailed gnu) was similarly reduced until only a handful remained.

From 1652 to 1800, Dutch settlement slowly spread east toward the Great Fish River, but expansion to the north was limited by the Great Karoo, the semidesert of the interior that was a major obstacle for a hundred years. The Karoo was famous for one aspect of wildlife, the springbok. This dainty little animal, which is now one of South Africa's national symbols (South African Airways is known as "The Flying Springbok" and all the national sports teams seem to be called the Springboks), dominated the South African interior much the way the bison did the plains of South Dakota. Travellers and hunters encountered the springbok in herds numbering into the millions, and their migrations were a serious factor of life for the original inhabitants (bushmen and Hottentots) and later for white farmers, who likened the springbok hordes to a plague of locusts.

It is difficult, from our vantage point in the late 20th century, to appreciate the psychological effect that the sight of a massive wildlife congregation can excite in a person. To see bison in a herd, shoulder to shoulder, stretching to the horizon and beyond, until the entire prairie is "one gigantic buffalo robe," as one chronicler described it; to ride for days in a straight line, yet have the animals always before you; to stand at the fence you have built to contain your sheep and watch as an irresistible flood of animals moves, inexorably, down upon you, innocently but relentlessly intent on overrunning that fence and stripping your pasture bare, perhaps even gathering up your precious sheep and carrying them off like a biblical river in flood—those are emotions that we can only wonder at and, in a sense, envy. It is an emotion comprised all at once of helplessness and rising panic; of a racing heart and an urge to turn and run, and an equal urge to laugh and throw your hat in the air, to sit down and watch and be enveloped by this tide of life, all at the same time. Occasionally modern man gets a glimpse of that emotion when he finds himself in the midst of what passes for a great herd today, and can only imagine what it must have been like on the plains of South Dakota, or the high veldt of the Orange Free State when the Afrikaners of the Great Trek crossed the Karoo in 1835.

William Cornwallis Harris, the British army officer who ventured into the interior of southern Africa on the first organized hunting expedition in 1836, and later wrote of his adventures in *The Wild Sports of Southern Africa*, encountered those great game herds. His description inspired Roualeyn Gordon Cumming, who also came and hunted, and later wrote about it, and in turn inspired others such as

Frederick Courteney Selous, whose own writings have inspired countless thousands since then to go to Africa to hunt and to see. Each in
his turn described what the wildlife was like then, and each could
only wonder what it had been like for his predecessors, when the game,
by all their reports, had been so much more plentiful. Harris described
how he could sit on the tailgate of his wagon with three loaded rifles,
and with his eyes closed point each in a different direction, one after
the other, pull the trigger, and bring down an animal, so thick were
they around the wagon. Gordon Cumming wrote of riding at full
gallop, killing animals all around him with gun, knife, and spear.

　　While many of South Africa's animals were familiar to those
men, at least by reputation, such as the lion, elephant, and rhino, many
of the lesser plains game were completely new. South Africa had a
wide variety of antelope, with different horns and colorations, and
many of the early hunter-explorers became engrossed by what they
saw from a naturalist's point of view as much as from a hunter's.
Harris, for example, is credited with discovering the sable antelope,
which was known for a few years as a "Harris buck." William
Cotton Oswell, the benefactor who funded David Livingstone's trans-
Kalahari trek to Lake Ngami in 1849, and accompanied him on the
journey, probably discovered both the red lechwe and the sitatunga
(at least the southern race; John Hanning Speke discovered the northern some years later during his expedition with James Grant in search
of the Nile).

　　Wondrous as the individual animals were, and stupendous
as they were when encountered in herds of millions, it did not stop
the pragmatic Boers from attacking them with a ferocity reminiscent
of a war. When the *voortrekkers* departed the Cape in 1835 to escape
the British, they were setting off into an interior which few had seen,
and almost all feared. Aside from natural hazards like the waterless
Karoo, and the bleak high veldt of what is now the Orange Free State,
there were warlike Zulus and Matabele as well as the usual animal
predators. The Boers treated all the animals they encountered as a
gift from God, to be dispatched as they saw fit and put to any use
possible. In the early years, for example, the eastern part of the Free
State, on the escarpment above the Drakensberg passes that lead down

into Natal, was known as *riemland* for the excellent *riems* (leather straps and thongs) that could be made from the hides of giraffes that were killed there. Many a Boer kept body and soul together by killing the giraffes and making *riems* for reins, whips, and harnesses, and trading them for the necessities of life. As a result, the giraffe population of the Free State was but a memory within a few years. Lions that preyed on Boer stock, leopards and cheetahs that stalked their sheep, hyenas and wild dogs that skulked along behind the lines of Cape wagons heading north and east, were all enemies to be eradicated if possible. And eradicated many were. In the case of the springbok, the conflict assumed many aspects of a war; certainly, there were parallels here with the plight of the North American bison and the passenger pigeon, and at least one writer of the time compared the springbok hosts with those ill-fated creatures half a world away.

Early writers, Harris and Cumming among them, wrote wonderingly of the springbok they encountered. By 1906, however, barely a half-century later, writers were looking for eyewitnesses who could tell them what it had been like in that golden era, for by that time the main springbok hordes were gone. They had been all but wiped out, either by hunters after hides and meat or by farmers determined to protect their land from their depredations. Frederick Roderick Noble Findlay was an Englishman who hunted in southern Africa during the 1890s and returned home to write a book about his experiences called *Big Game Shooting and Travel in South-East Africa*. The book in its original form is exceedingly rare, and even reprints are hard to come by. It is not renowned for its writing style, which is ponderous at best, but the book is certainly notable for its prescience, and Findlay for his gilt-edged connections. Findlay, like a few others of his time, realized with great alarm that the indigenous animals of Africa were facing decimation, if not extinction, and he devoted the last chapters of his book to calls for legislation and individual action to save them.

Findlay's aunt was Olive Schreiner, a noted South African author who wrote *The Story of an African Farm*. This novel, published in 1881, is one of the most famous works of literature to come out of South Africa, and reprints and special editions abound. Olive

Schreiner was equally concerned about wildlife in southern Africa, and lent her prestige to the cause of wildlife conservation. She wrote part of one chapter of Findlay's book calling for the establishment of game preserves and national parks. Another uncle, C.S. Cronwright-Schreiner, wrote an article on the springbok migration that appeared in the May 1899 issue of the English magazine *Zoologist*. Findlay reproduced the article as part of a chapter, and Cronwright-Schreiner's account leaves you shaking your head.

At the time, a distinction was made between the *hou-bokke* (literally "kept-buck"—those that stayed permanently in one area) and the *trek-bokke*—those that gathered in hordes and migrated, blanketing the veldt like a field of wheat. Cronwright-Schreiner:

> *Congregating in millions, they moved off in search of better veldt, destroying everything in their march over the arid flats. The 'trek-bokke' can only be compared, in regard to number, with the bison of North America or the pigeons of the Canadas. To say they migrate in millions is to employ an ordinary figure of speech, used vaguely to convey the idea of great numbers; but in the case of these bucks it is the literal truth.*

When springbok were on the move, they were as unstoppable as the tides. They would invade small towns, crowding down the streets, and men and boys could go among them and kill them as long as they had strength to swing a club. Cronwright-Schreiner again:

> *Native herdsmen have been trampled to death by the bucks and droves of Africander sheep carried away, never to be recovered, in the surging crowd. So dense is the mass at times, and so overpowering the pressure from the millions behind, that if a sloot (gully) is come to so wide and deep that the bucks cannot leap over or go through it, the front ranks are forced in until it is levelled up by their bodies, when the mass marches over and continues its irresistible way.*

The main springbok activity centered on the northern Cape colony in the vicinity of Namaqualand. Opinions varied as to the reasons for their periodic migrations, but most observers agreed that drought was a major factor. In 1892, a government official in Namaqualand, W.S. Scully, actually broke out government stores of rifles to arm the resident Boers to repel the invasion of springbok, much as if they had been rampaging Zulu *impis* or the descending hordes of Attila the Hun. They were threatening to overrun the cultivated parts of Namaqualand, and "it was only with some difficulty that the invasion was repelled," Findlay reported.

In 1896, a relative told Cronwright-Schreiner that the *trek-bokke* were on the move near Karee Kloof in the northwestern Cape. Certain that such mass migrations would soon be a thing of the past, he was determined to witness it for himself. Leaving Kimberley by train, he travelled along the Orange River, then continued by wagon until he reached the edges of the migration. What he found was more like a monstrous carnival than anything else. The springbok were on the move in millions, and with them, like flotsam on a river in flood, were various other antelope unable to resist or escape the tide of animals. Along the edges, hundreds of lions, leopards, hyenas, and wild dogs preyed on the bucks as they moved, while hunters slaughtered them in thousands and tens of thousands. The owners of one small general store alone were buying hides at a rate of 3,000 a week. It was estimated that in the Prieska district alone, several hundred thousand springbok had already been killed out of that migration. Cronwright-Schreiner and his companions skirted the herd; never were they out of the sound of gunfire, and they constantly passed wagons loaded with carcasses. It took them days to outstrip the hunters and reach an undisturbed portion of the herd:

> At length our wish to see large numbers of (undisturbed) bucks was gratified. On driving over a low nek (pass) of land a vast, undisturbed, glittering plain lay before us. Throughout its whole extent the exquisite antelopes grazed peacefully in the warm afternoon winter sunshine. It was as beautiful as it was wondrous. Undisturbed by the hunters, they were not huddled together in separate lots or running in close array, but were distributed in one unbroken mass over the whole expanse, giving quite a whitish tint to the veldt, almost as though there had been a very light fall of snow.

Cronwright-Schreiner and his two companions, all of them farmers, sat down to watch and to attempt a reasoned calculation of the numbers they were viewing. Eventually they reached an estimate of 500,000 in sight from that one spot, at one moment in time; it was but a small part of a larger herd that extended a 23-hour march in one direction, and several more hours in the other, which they calculated to be a piece of country 138 miles long by 15 miles wide. While the land was not covered equally densely throughout, still there must have been millions of animals in the herd, all on the move at one time.

This migration, in 1896, was the last of the large-scale treks of the springbok. Their numbers were chopped away, then whittled away, until all that remained were small individual herds. Although little is written about it, presumably the Second Anglo-Boer War of 1899-1902 contributed mightily to the reduction in springbok numbers. Aside from the massive troop movements that took place, the British employed a scorched-earth policy in which they burned farms and crops, confined the Afrikaners to concentration camps, and criss-crossed the veldt with double lines of impenetrable fences. No doubt this decimated any wildlife that remained. Most Boer accounts of the last long months of bitter resistance dwell on the pitiful condition of their troops as well as the people at large, and the starvation that was rampant throughout their lands. If there was game in any quantity for the wandering Boer commandos to shoot for food, no historian has seen fit to mention it.

❊

By that time, more than the springbok were gone. The fantastic herds that had roamed the high veldt of the Orange Free State disappeared so quickly it left observers wondering if perhaps they had not dreamt it all. When the *voortrekkers* first entered the territory, herds of gnus and quaggas were so huge that a Frenchman, A. Delagorgue, reported in 1847 that "where the soil was light and dry, their feet had so broken up the ground that it almost resembled land under tillage." As Findlay later reported, however, "the commercial value of skins was no sooner discovered by the Boers and hunters generally, than a bloody and reckless war of extermination was commenced on those same plains, and the countless thousands of game vanished like a dissolving mirage before the approach of man."

Another writer, H.A. Bryden, in *Gun and Camera in South Africa*, told of one particular hunt that took place in 1860 in the eastern districts of the Free State. The Duke of Saxe-Coburg-Gotha paid a visit to the fledgling republic and was greeted with an organized hunt that surely must rank with the most incredible spectacles of all time. A thousand natives were recruited to drive the game, and at the height of the drive there were 25,000 head of game within sight of the Duke's hunting party. Thousands of animals were killed (the highest estimate is 6,000), including blue and black wildebeeste, zebras, quaggas, ostriches, blesbok, hartebeeste, and springbok. One herd of zebras panicked and charged some of the beaters, killing several and injuring many others.

"Now these plains stand bare and desolate," Findlay wrote. No wonder.

The last hippopotamus was killed in the Orange Free State in the 1890s near the small town of Memel, in a marsh called Seekoeivlei. Elephants were down to a few, as were the white rhinoceros. The bontebok, reduced to a few hundred, existed only on a couple of farms near Swellendam. Every other species was a shadow of its former self.

Aside from the blaaubok, the other notable animal to be hunted to extinction was the quagga (*equus quagga*), an odd relative of the zebra that sported zebra-like stripes on its forward quarters, but resembled a horse everywhere else. The last known specimen died in London's Zoological Gardens sometime after 1875; its skin was mounted and put on display at the Museum of Natural History. The fate of the quagga is recounted by E. Ray Lankaster in his 1905 book, *Extinct Animals*. Lankaster was the director of the natural history departments of the British Museum, and his book is a compilation of lectures, complete with reproductions of the slides he used to illustrate them, which he delivered to a gathering of students in London in late 1903. According to Lankaster, the quagga was quite common in South Africa as recently as 1860, but "this animal has now entirely ceased to exist, owing to the fact that the country over which it ranged has been taken up and cultivated by white men. There are no more living quaggas anywhere. This animal has become extinguished in our own lifetime."

Lankaster was not alone in his concern for the rapidly vanishing wildlife of southern Africa—or Africa as a whole, for that matter. The scramble for Africa, as it will be known forever to history, was well underway by that time, with the European powers gobbling up vast tracts of land. Colonists were moving in steadily, and the animals were retreating in the face of settlement and cultivation. Belgium had the Congo, Germany had Tanganyika and South-West Africa, Portugal had Angola and Mozambique, France held much of central and west Africa, and Great Britain had, more or less, everything else. If the missionary societies were anxious for the souls of the black tribes of Africa, various animal-loving organizations were no less concerned for its uncounted (albeit dwindling) millions of wild animals.

In 1900, the International Convention for the Preservation of Wild Animals, Birds, and Fish in Africa convened in London. Representatives of Great Britain, France, Germany, Italy, Spain, Belgium, and Portugal met to define territorial boundaries and impose measures to preserve the animals that were left. The delegates agreed to a set of principles, a list of guidelines and regulations, and a series of schedules listing the animals and birds which were to be affected. Its signatories agreed to impose certain measures, such as bag limits and licensing requirements, and overall the agreement would not look too terribly out of place as a piece of game legislation today. Broadly speaking, it covered all territory between the Sahara and the Zambezi River, from the Indian Ocean to the Atlantic.

On May 19, 1900, the convention was signed. One of the signatories, on behalf of Victoria Regina, Queen of the United Kingdom of Great Britain and Ireland and Empress of India, was E. Ray Lankaster, director of the natural history departments of the British Museum. Clearly there was a small coterie of concerned individuals in England and Europe, just as there was in the United States. This convention became the basis for many of the game regulations that were subsequently imposed in East Africa and the Rhodesias, and while it was far from perfect, it was a huge advance over the unfettered slaughter that had already taken place south of the Limpopo.

It now remained, if possible, to salvage something from the wreckage in South Africa. To be fair, the history of South Africa was not one long blood-fest with no attempt to mitigate the slaughter. Ordinances had been passed in various parts of the patchwork of colonies and *voortrekker* republics that was South Africa, from the time of the Great Trek in 1835 until the beginning of the Anglo-Boer War in 1899. The Ohrigstad Republic, for example, prohibited the "extermination of game" in 1846; in 1858, the South African Republic (later the Transvaal) prohibited "unnecessary shooting" of game, and elephant hunting was severely curtailed. In 1870, the Volksraad of the Transvaal Republic passed legislation approving the appointment of game rangers and introducing various restrictions on hunting and trapping, as well as closed seasons on some animals. These regulations were extended in 1891 and 1893, and in 1894, a game preserve was established at Pongola, a luxuriantly tropical area in the eastern Transvaal on the border of Swaziland. Exactly how much effect these decrees and proclamations had on hunters in the field is open to question; certainly they had little on individual Boer farmers concerned with springbok devastating their crops or hyenas savaging their sheep. In fact, well into the 20th century—for that matter, until the era of Robert Ruark in Kenya—Afrikaners had a reputation for shooting anything that moved and for filling their licenses not once in a season but many times.

In 1898, Paul Kruger, President of the Transvaal, proclaimed Kruger National Park, an 8,000 square mile expanse on the border of Mozambique. Work had begun on the park several years earlier, but it was not until 1898—over serious opposition, one might add— that it became a reality. Considering the immense pressure of other concerns—the British were about to launch their war to seize the Rand goldfields—the plight of the wildlife must have been severe to warrant Oom Paul's attention in that fateful year. Today, Kruger is the foremost game park in Africa, full to overflowing with everything from elephant on down.

As well, efforts were made to save individual species in their native areas. The bontebok, by Findlay's time, numbered no more than 200. A few farmers, concerned about the decline in their numbers, banded together beginning in 1864 to give the remaining handful of animals a sanctuary on their land; and without the intervention of these men named Van der Byl, Van Breda, and Uys, the bontebok in all likelihood would have followed the blaaubok and quagga into extinction. As it was, they hung on until 1931, when a mere 17 survivors were used as the basis for a herd in Bontebok National Park near Bredasdorp. Eventually, these were relocated to another park near Swellendam, where they gradually bounced back; by 1970, there were 211 bontebok, and today there are thousands scattered on parks and game ranches throughout South Africa.

In 1965, when James Mellon wrote *African Hunter*, the outlook for hunting in South Africa was bleak from a game point of view. The great herds were gone, and the untamed veldt had been replaced by carefully cultivated farms. Although there were individual bunches of springbok, blesbok, and wildebeest here and there, South Africa was not game country. Almost all land was privately held, and the Afrikaners, with few exceptions, were farmers first and foremost.

In 1906, F.R.N. Findlay laid out a grim accounting, species by species:

> *The true or mountain zebra is now almost exclusively confined to a few of the higher mountain ranges of the Cape Colony. The vast herds of eland have vanished. The large herds of buffalo are seen no more. The immense herds of hartebeests and sassaby are sights of the past. The sable antelope is rare. The stately gemsbok, the regal koodoo, the Lichtenstein hartebeest, and the majestic waterbuck are fast disappearing from South Africa, and even the blue wildebeest and the zebra are but, as it were, a shadow of the countless herds which once beautified the landscape. The wonderful giraffe (is reduced to a few). The hippopotamus, once so numerous, has suffered equally with its terrestrial friends; it is disappearing like the others...*

The other South African antelopes, such as the inyala, reedbuck, impala, mountain reedbuck, vaal rhebok, springbok, bushbuck, oribi, steinbok, duiker, klip-springer, and other of the smaller antelopes have all suffered severely and form today but an infinitesimal part of what they once were.

It took the better part of 80 years to arrest the decline and eventually reverse it, but today the situation is entirely different, and the change is due almost completely to hunters, hunting, and the revenue that hunting brings. In the 35 years since *African Hunter* was published, hunting in South Africa has become a big business. Game ranching is a major money-maker for holders of large tracts of land, and even smaller farmers (those with 5,000 acres and less) have resident herds of blesbok, springbok, blue and black wildebeeste, and zebras. There are mountain reedbuck and all kinds of small antelope living on the rocky slopes of the *kopjes* that dot the land. Perhaps the most notable change has been in the attitude of individual Afrikaner farmers. When Mellon visited South Africa in the early 1960s, he found Boers who were preoccupied with farming and with sheep and cattle; a few (a very few) were interested in game animals and allowed them living space and pasturage. The dearth of other kinds of wildlife was also noticeable. For example, vultures were almost unknown in South Africa, and other birds of prey, as well as terrestrial scavengers like hyenas, were rare. Tradition had it that vultures killed newborn lambs, and so they were shot on sight. It is notable that the International Convention of 1900 lists, in Schedule I, Series A of species "protected because of their usefulness," the vulture and the secretary bird (a large terrestrial eagle). Even today the vulture has not completely recovered in South Africa; the sight of half a dozen of the huge, dihedral-winged birds, floating in lazy circles, is enough to draw comment. Yet there are still farmers who insist they should not be tolerated.

Still, today the vulture, the secretary bird, the brown hyena, and the black eagle are all valued, protected where possible, and in many cases cherished by the farmers on whose land they live. The farm where I lived briefly in 1994 had a secretary bird in residence, and my life would have been forfeit had I accidentally shot it; the same with a pair of black eagles that lived in the cliffs above a farm near Harrismith where I used to shoot rock pigeons. It seems today that every second farmer you meet in South Africa has his own safari company, complete with crests on shirts and baseball caps. Holding one of the quickie South African PH licenses, he will "guide" you to hunt on his property for (guaranteed) world-class blesbok, or impala, or blue wildebeeste. So sophisticated have these farmers become that there is a two-tiered pricing system: one for Afrikaners coming from Pretoria to shoot for biltong, another for Americans coming from Peoria armed with U.S. dollars.

Perhaps the most notable recovery has been that of the white rhinoceros, the second-largest land mammal in the world, which was shot to near-extinction in South Africa by 1900. They exist in only one other place on earth, a small enclave on the Uganda-Congo border (not the most secure of dwelling places), but in South Africa today, for a hefty trophy fee ($25,000 and up) a hunter determined to take one of these great prehistoric beasts can do so on various game ranches, or even to reduce numbers in preserves. South Africa has become, once again, a notable storehouse of game, and while the herds do not roam the veldt freely as they did in the days of the *trek-bokke*, the fact that they are valued and protected on private land at least partly makes up for it.

The lessons that were learned in South Africa in the 1800s were incorporated into the Convention signed in London in 1900 and applied in the rest of the continent, from Rhodesia to Kenya. It did not stop poaching on a grand scale, by natives for meat, by ivory hunters both white and black, or by those who take the black rhino's horn for sale in the Middle East. But it did produce a basic set of rules to apply, and to a great extent they were applied effectively. Several generations of professional hunters have grown up in British East Africa and the Rhodesias learning their trade in the game departments, managing preserves and parks, and shooting on control. To the extent that big game hunting still flourishes in Africa, it does so to a large degree because of that Convention, because of the efforts of hunters like Oswell, Selous, and Findlay, animal-lovers like

Schreiner and Lankaster, and in the century that followed, the men who ran the game departments from the Cape to Khartoum.

❊

THE BIG FIVE-HUNDREDS
The .500 Nitro Express

If the shooting world were rational and logical, the .500 Nitro Express would have long ago been acclaimed the greatest of the big-bore rifle cartridges, and everything else (including the vaunted .470) would have fallen by the wayside.

The shooting world, however, can be anything but logical, and strange coincidences combine to sink even the best cartridge—at least for a time. Such has been the lot, for most of the last century, of the .500 Nitro Express. For much of its long life people have been predicting its imminent demise because of lack of demand, and for just as long, the .500 has been hanging on grimly—adored by a few but ignored by most. But now, suddenly, at the age of 100 years plus (and considerably longer if you count its blackpowder forebears) the .500 Nitro Express is healthier than ever and appears set to outlast most of its rivals.

The .500 is unique in one way: Nowhere that I can find does any authority have a single negative thing to say about it. From John Taylor to Craig Boddington, from J.A. Hunter to Arthur Alphin, everyone with first-hand experience agrees the .500 is in a class by itself. It is acknowledged to be a noticeable cut above the .470 class in knock-down power. Taylor calls it "a real killer" on elephant and rhino, and Boddington says it is "a horse of a different color" when you start comparing the big nitro express cartridges in power and performance.

Yet for decades it was an unloved child. Why? Perhaps because, as far as we know, the .500 was *nobody's* child. Like Topsy, it "just growed." Its origins are lost in the mists of time. Excellent cartridge though it was, as gunmakers introduced their own proprietary cartridges and beat the drums for their *wunderkind*, the .500 had no one to extol its virtues except a few people like J.A. Hunter and John Taylor—both professional hunters of impeccable credentials, but lonely voices all the same.

❋

In the transition from smooth-bore muzzleloaders to rifled, breech-loading cartridge guns, it was only natural that gunmakers would settle on the .50 caliber as a standard. An even half-inch is so sensible that it would be surprising if the .50 had *not* become the standard. North America had the muzzleloading .50 Hawken and its ilk in the 1840s, which were followed by the .50-caliber Sharps and other buffalo cartridges of various lengths and configurations. In Britain, where big game hunting meant travel to India or Africa, the .50 caliber was adopted early in the game, and several cartridges were developed for it.

Tracing the origins of a particular caliber can be both fun and frustrating. Take the .577 as an example. How on earth did someone settle on .577 as a bullet diameter? Why not .550 or .600? The answer lies in the transition that was taking place at the time.

The first British military cartridge rifle was the Snider (or Snider-Enfield) .577, adopted in 1866. It was a conversion of the existing Enfield muzzleloading rifle, which was a 24-bore. In the English system of measurement, 24-bore is quite logical (two dozen lead balls to the pound) and was popular both as a shotgun and a muzzleloading rifle. Such a ball is .577-inches in diameter, so the bullet for the new cartridge also had to be .577 caliber. For many years old-style brass 24-gauge shells were available, and they can be cut off to make .577 Snider cartridges. Hence the .577, which later gave birth to the .577 Nitro Express and a handful of others.

Sometime before 1880, there came along a blackpowder cartridge called the .500 Express. It was a straight-taper, rimmed case, three inches long by half an inch at the mouth—a simple, elegant, sensible design. I have seen photographs of a .500 Express break-open hammer gun made by James Woodward, sometime around 1875.

❋

It is obviously a "best" gun, which suggests the .500 was well established even by then.

According to legend, James Purdey & Sons coined the term "Express" to describe the speed and flat trajectory of the new breechloading, small-caliber rifles (relative to muzzleloaders, at least) that they were building for their clients, equating them with the express trains that were, at that time, the last word in land transport. If Purdey did, indeed, originate the term, then it could well be that Purdey's originated the .500 Express cartridge as well. Certainly, the firm was among the very first to chamber rifles for it, and continued to do so for many years. In 1880, the Marquess of Ripon was appointed Viceroy of India, and immediately placed an order with Purdey's for a battery of big game rifles—a 4-bore and four .500 Express doubles. Whether the new Viceroy was following accepted practice or setting a new standard, this battery quickly became the *beau ideal* for sportsmen going out to India.

The .500 Express blackpowder cartridge came in two versions—one three inches long, the other 3¼-inches. Ballistically, the two were very similar. The shorter case held 136 grains of blackpowder and fired a 340-grain, copper-tubed, lead-core bullet at 1,925 fps (2,800 ft-lbs) or a 380-grain, solid-lead bullet at 1,850 fps, for a muzzle energy of 2,890 ft-lbs. The longer case took 142 grains of powder and was loaded with a 440-grain, copper-tubed bullet at 1,775 fps (3,080 ft-lbs) or 480-grain, solid-lead bullet at 1,700 fps (3,080 ft-lbs). While there was not a great deal of difference ballistically between the two, there was a tremendous difference in the performance of the lighter bullets in both. The copper-tubed bullets had a small copper cylinder imbedded in the nose which, on impact, would drive back into the lead and cause it to mushroom. These bullets "set up," as the British say, very quickly—too quickly, in the case of dangerous game. For this reason, the heavier, solid-lead bullets were much preferred.

Even so, the .500 Express blackpowder was not, by the standards of the day, a suitable rifle for really big game such as elephant and rhino. In India, it was a tiger rifle; in Africa, it was a good medium-bore for lion and large antelope. Even as late as 1894, the

Badminton Library's *Big Game Shooting* (a hunter's bible of the time) recommended, for a shooter going out to India, a double 8-bore for elephant and rhino, a .500 Express double for tiger, and a .400 Express for the smaller stuff. If you were going to Africa, they recommended you augment this with a single-barrel 4-bore and replace the .400 with a .450. The mainstay of the African battery was the .500 Express, however, and they suggested taking a full complement of ammunition for it—solid, soft-nose, and copper-tubed bullets. It was the rifle you would carry most often and use to bag the most game.

John "Pondoro" Taylor—ivory hunter, poacher, and author of *Big Game and Big Game Rifles* and *African Rifles and Cartridges*—was a great admirer of the .500 in both blackpowder and the later smokeless version. Although he was anything but anxious to face a Cape buffalo with the old blackpowder round, he wrote that he had used it extensively for man-eating lions and found it a "powerful weapon against soft-skinned game when properly handled." His rifle, by the way, was a hammerless double. His praise was reserved for the solid-lead bullet, however, not the copper-tubed version, which he said broke up too quickly. He also had trouble with the paper patch. Occasionally a piece would break off and get in behind the extractors and keep the rifle from closing, but this was a problem with any cartridge using paper-patched bullets.

From its inception in the 1870s until the advent of cordite in the 1890s, the .500 Express was one of the standard calibers, along with the .577 and .450. The only one of the three that was considered suitable for elephant in its blackpowder incarnation was the .577, and even that was marginal.

During that period some beautiful guns were built in .500 Express, both doubles and single-shots. The aforementioned Woodward is a gorgeous piece. How many "best" .500s were made is impossible to pin down, but since Purdey's had been making them for such prominent shooters as the Marquess of Ripon since at least 1880, we know there are definitely some out there, with the greatest names engraved on the barrels, and still eminently shootable one way or the other.

In 1887, the British Army discarded the .450 Martini-Henry

in favor of the .303 British, first in blackpowder form and then, in 1892, loaded with the then-new cordite smokeless gunpowder. Cordite is a double-based powder made of nitrocellulose, nitroglycerine and mineral jelly, extruded in strands like string (hence the name) and cut into lengths for loading. Performance-wise, compared with American smokeless powders, cordite is lower pressure but hotter burning, heading off some potential problems but creating others. Once the British Army adopted it, however, it was only a matter of time before civilian gunmakers wholeheartedly did so as well, and the 1890s saw a complete transformation of the rifle world. A few of the best of the blackpowder rounds were reborn as smokeless cartridges, but most fell by the wayside.

Among those that survived were the two greatest: the .577 (now the .577 Nitro Express) and the .500 Nitro Express (in both three-inch and 3¼-inch configuration). The smokeless .500 was an instant success, and in 1893, Purdey's built a hammerless sidelock double in three-inch .500 NE for the Maharaj Rana of Dholpur (and a lovely piece it is).

Very quickly there were four .500s extant—two blackpowder and two smokeless. So highly regarded was the blackpowder round, however, that Kynoch introduced a fifth, transitional cartridge, the ".500 Nitro For Blackpowder Express"—a low-pressure, low-velocity cordite load expressly for use in the old blackpowder rifles. It offered slightly improved performance, firing a 400-grain lead bullet at 1,900 fps, for a muzzle energy of 3,530 ft-lbs, and remained available well into the 20th century. Its ballistics, however, were nothing compared to the new full-house, smokeless .500 Nitro Express, which fired a 570-grain bullet at 2,150 fps—5,850 ft-lbs of first-rate elephant gun. With the advent of cordite, the day of the old 8-bore and 4-bore rifles was finally dead. As the old century turned to new, the .577 reigned as the king of nitro-express cartridges (750-grain bullet, 2,050 fps, 7,010 ft-lbs) with the .500 NE as a very worthy crown prince. The two cartridges looked set to dominate big game hunting for the foreseeable future, but then a series of events intervened. When they were over, the big loser was the .500.

The first blow came in 1902 when W.J. Jeffery decided to

trump the .577 by introducing a still more powerful cartridge, the .600 Nitro Express. That toppled the .577 from its position as most powerful cartridge. Then, in 1907, the British Government banned the use of .450-caliber rifles in India and the Sudan. There were political troubles in both regions, and the government wanted to prevent .450-caliber sporting bullets from being used in the thousands of contraband Martini-Henry rifles that were still floating around.

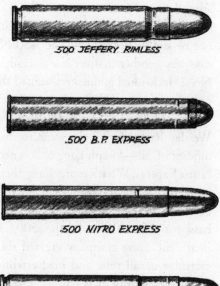

.500 JEFFERY RIMLESS

.500 B.P. EXPRESS

.500 NITRO EXPRESS

There had been a host of .450-caliber blackpowder cartridges, but adapting them to smokeless powder presented problems because most of them had very thin brass and could not withstand the higher pressures of cordite. An exception was the .450 Nitro Express, introduced in 1898 by John Rigby & Co. from an existing

.505 GIBBS

blackpowder case. The .450 Nitro Express proved so popular that Holland & Holland took the blackpowder .500/.450—a .500 3¼-inch case necked down—adapted it to smokeless powder, and called it the .500/.450 Magnum Nitro Express. It had no pressure problems either, but in 1903, Eley Brothers, the cartridge manufacturers, decided to settle the issue once and for all. They created the .450 No. 2 Nitro Express, using a newly designed, long, thick-walled, necked case that would resist the higher pressures of cordite with no problems.

The .450 wars were in full swing when the government lowered the boom and a large chunk of the market for them dried

THE MAGIC OF BIG GAME

up. Since these had been very popular cartridges, the London gunmakers scrambled to develop legal replacements that would more or less duplicate the ballistics of the .450s (480-grain bullet, 2,150 fps), which had proven so deadly on game yet so kind to the shoulder of the man holding the rifle. It being easier to adapt an existing case than design a whole new one, the various companies looked around for cases to neck up or down.

The .450 NE 3¼-inch was a straight-tapered case, so it could not be simply necked up. The .450 No. 2's long, heavy, bottleneck case was another matter; it was easily necked up to make the .475 No. 2. Individual gunmakers wanted their own rounds, however, and one after another they settled on the .500 NE as a starting point.

Holland & Holland necked it down to create the .500/.465; Westley Richards did the same to make the .476, and—most significant of all—Joseph Lang & Son necked it down to make the .470 Nitro Express. What's more, Lang then released its brainchild to the trade, for anyone to chamber in any rifle, sidelock or boxlock, "best" or trade gun. Using the .500 Nitro Express 3¼-inch case as the basis for the .470 (as did the .500/.465; the .476 used the three-inch), the Lang company created the most popular nitro-express cartridge of all time and inadvertently relegated its parent case to eventual obscurity. It is tempting to present this in a Shakespearean or even Biblical context, but there were sound ballistic and logistical reasons for the popularity of the .470.

Taken together, the creation of the .600 NE combined with the entire .470-class of cartridges made the .500 NE neither fish nor fowl. Henceforth, the .577 NE and the .600 NE were the powerhouses, the sledgehammers with knockdown power when a wounded elephant was on top of you in thick brush. The .577 NE, particularly, was the tool of the professional ivory hunter—the James Sutherlands of the world, and the John Taylors.

The .470-class cartridges were all ballistically very similar (480-grain bullet, 2,150 fps) and were available in rifles that weighed between 10 and 11 pounds. The early .500 NE rifles weighed better than 12 pounds, so they were caught in between—less handy than the .470s, but without the sheer power of the really big boys. Logically, someone could have argued that they were more powerful than the .470s without the horrendous weight and recoil of the .577 and .600, but few did. Why? The age-old laws of commerce: Holland & Holland wanted to sell .500/.465s, since they had put money into developing it; similarly, Westley Richards and the .476, and everyone else with the .470, the .475 No. 2, and the newly developed .475 Nitro Express, a straight-tapered case that resembled a scaled-up .450 NE. The .500 Nitro Express went from glamor boy of the smokeless cartridge world to unwanted child, available henceforth only on special order.

❋

This is not to say the .500 NE had nothing unique to offer ballistically, because it did.

Like its predecessor, the .500 NE came in two different cartridge lengths, three-inch and 3¼-inch, but they were loaded with identical bullets and offered virtually identical ballistics. The longer case allowed slightly lower pressures (with a corresponding drop-off in muzzle velocity of about 25 fps) but otherwise there was no difference. The shorter case could be fired in the longer chamber, but not the reverse. These two advantages did not seem to carry much weight, however, and the three-inch case quickly gained an ascendancy. George Caswell of Champlin Arms, who has dealt in double rifles for more than 30 years and has probably handled more of them than anyone else on earth, says three-inch .500 NE rifles probably outnumber those chambered for the longer case by ten to one.

"That's just a guess—a gut feeling—because I've never kept count. But the 3¼-inch is decidedly more rare," Caswell says. "But then, .500 NEs of either kind are scarcer than their popularity would warrant."

Altogether, Caswell estimates that no more than 500 .500 NE double rifles were made up until the 1980s.

"Take Purdey as an example. Up to the 1980s, Purdey built a total of about 350 double rifles; of those, only 16 were .500 NEs. By comparison, they made six .600 NEs. How many of the .500s were the long case, I have no idea. One? Two?"

Of these estimated 500 rifles, by far the majority are boxlocks (most double rifles are boxlocks, period), although we know some exquisite sidelock "bests" do exist.

A small coterie of African professional hunters appreciated the advantages of the .500 NE. One such was J.A. Hunter, who arrived in British East Africa in 1905. For the next 50 years, J.A. (as he was known) hunted professionally, either taking out clients, hunting for ivory, or shooting on control. It is said he shot more big game animals than any other modern professional. Working at a time when elephants were more plentiful than Cape buffalo (the rinderpest epidemic of 1896 had decimated the buffalo from Ethiopia to the Cape), J.A. Hunter killed 1,400 elephant, 1,000 rhinoceros, 350 Cape buffalo, and uncounted hundreds of lions and leopards.

In 1938, he published *White Hunter*, an account of his exploits in Africa. In the book he listed his three favorite cartridges, in order, as the .475 No. 2, the .450 No. 2, and the .470 Nitro Express. Sometime after that book was written, however, J.A. Hunter came into possession of a Holland & Holland .500 NE, and he never looked back. When he published volume two of his memoirs in 1952, he wrote:

> I have mainly relied on a .500 d/b hammerless ejector fitted with 24-inch barrels and weighing 10 pounds, five ounces, made by Holland & Holland. In my opinion, Holland & Holland are the best in rifle makers, just as I would give honors to James Purdey & Sons for the best in smooth bores. My .500 has never let me down. It is quite adequate for all big game, including elephant. I have never seen it fail to stop a charge...and as a result, I have never felt the need of burdening myself by carrying one of the heavier guns which, excellent though they may be, are cumbersome things and do give the shooter a certain amount of punishment.

One objection to the .500 was that its recoil made it necessary to make it up in a heavier rifle—12 pounds or more. John Taylor, for one, disputed this. The .500, he said, could nicely be made up in a rifle weighing 10½ pounds that was easy to carry and light to handle, but which did not kick unduly. The fact that Hunter's rifle weighed only 10 pounds, five ounces supports this view.

On paper, the .500 certainly packs more wallop to the rear than a .470, but how much of that is actually felt by the shooter depends to a great extent on stock design. I once test-fired some new Holland doubles in London. We had a .700 H&H, a .500/.465, and a .500 NE. I fired the .700 first (big, *big*, recoil), then picked up the .500. By comparison, it felt like a 12-gauge shotgun. Then I tried the .500/.465, which is reputed to have a lighter recoil than others in its class, never mind the .500. That thing whacked me, unpleasantly so; figuring it was all relative—that the shock of firing the .700 was wearing off—I fired two more from the .500. It still felt like a pussycat, and another two from the .500/.465 still felt like a pair of left hooks from Floyd Patterson. The two rifles weighed about the same, but the .500 NE fit me better and was more comfortable to shoot. I would love to have fired it all day long.

At the other end, however, the .500's punch is unquestioned. John Taylor's system of "knockout values," which he says reflects actual field performance (exactly what the mathematical formula was, no one knows), awards the .600 NE a knockout value of 150.4; the .577 gets 126.7. The .470 is measured at 71.3, and nothing else in its class gets more than 74.2. The .500 NE, on the other hand, is awarded a knockout value of 87.8, comparable to the .505 Gibbs.

On a practical level, Taylor reckoned a knockout value of 50 was needed to put an elephant down. A value of 60 to 80 would knock him out for five or six minutes even if the shot missed the brain, while the .577 would knock him down for 20 minutes, and the .600 for half an hour. Presumably, the .500 would put one down for ten minutes or so. If you are hunting for ivory, shooting elephant in any numbers, the difference could be vital.

Taylor's assessment of the .500 Nitro Express was that it was decidedly more powerful than the .470-class cartridges, "a magnificent weapon for elephant, rhino and buffalo…but the bullet is really too massive for lion." Unfortunately, he added, writing in 1948, Kynoch was indicating even then that they planned to discontinue the .500 Nitro Express because demand for the cartridge was so small.

If only 500 double rifles had been built for it, that was certainly understandable. At any rate, Taylor cautioned against ordering one unless you could be certain ammunition would be available. Otherwise, he said, "It's a really powerful cartridge and a great killer."

⁂

In 1962, Eley-Kynoch finally did give notice that it was discontinuing virtually all the great old nitro-express cartridges. It would produce a few years' supply, but after 1963, no more.

Some gunmakers, such as Holland & Holland, immediately stockpiled as much ammunition as they could find in calibers they manufactured, including the .577 NE, the .600 NE, the .500/.465, and the .500 NE. The orange and red Kynoch boxes were stored in a special room in their premises at Bruton Street in London. That forestalled problems for H&H and its clients but not for everyone else, and for the next 25 years the .500 NE became harder and harder to find. Professional hunters who still used the .500 NE, such as Robin Hurt, Geoff Broom, Gordon Cundill, and a few others, hoarded what few rounds they had left, pulling the big guns out only when their clients had one of the Big Five wounded in the bush. Demand for new .500s dropped off to almost nothing because of the uncertain ammunition situation. And so it stood until the 1980s. But the big .500 was not dead, just sleeping.

In the early 1980s, Jim Bell of Brass Extrusion Laboratories, Ltd. (B.E.L.L.) began producing what was called BELL Basic Brass—cases for the old nitro-express cartridges. Since the .500 NE 3¼-inch was the basis for some of the most popular cartridges, it was natural to produce it first and foremost. Suddenly, double-rifle owners had a supply of brass again and could start loading and shooting in bulk. It was, quite literally, the beginning of a second life for the .500 Nitro Express.

⁂

We are now into the present, and the future, of this wonderful old cartridge, and there are several factors to look at: buying an old rifle, loading for and shooting one, and buying a new one. First, buying an old rifle.

By George Caswell's estimate, there are maybe 500 .500 Nitro Express rifles around from the golden age, with a few more being made all the time, as we shall see. There are some "absolutely super" Purdey and H&H sidelocks around, says Caswell, but by far the majority of .500 Nitro Express rifles are boxlocks. Another major name in double rifles is John Rigby, but it seems the company never made a .500 in the old days—at least not to Caswell's knowledge. "I have never seen a Rigby .500," he said. "I don't think they ever made one." This would be logical, since Rigby introduced the .450 Nitro Express in 1898 to compete with the .500. When the .470 was introduced in 1907, that became a Rigby standard. Significantly, however, when John Rigby & Co. was acquired by American investors in 1998 they added the .500 NE to the list of available calibers, which also includes the .470 NE and .577 NE.

Other than Purdey and H&H, Caswell says, the .500 was a favorite of Boswell, John Wilkes, and the Army & Navy Stores, but he has also seen .500s made by Westley Richards, the fourth big name in English double rifles. "Let me put it this way," he said. "Many people made them, but they didn't make many."

Caswell also sees a surprising number of the old .500 Express blackpowder rifles, some with damascus barrels, but even some top lever, hammerless rifles with fluid-steel barrels. Champlin Firearms will custom load ammunition and regulate individual rifles, both smokeless and blackpowder; for the latter, the ammunition is loaded with the original-type paper-patched bullets. As a cartridge, the .500 Nitro Express seems remarkably tractable—accurate and tolerant of variations in ammunition.

"We have had to re-regulate very few .500 NE rifles," Caswell told me. "We seem to be able to find loads they will shoot accurately pretty easily."

Although 3¼-inch-chambered rifles are considerably more rare than three-inch chambers, they command no premium on the used-rifle market. For that matter, the .500 NE commands no premium over other cartridges, but nor is it valued lower. Caswell says there might be a tiny difference to a serious collector, but nothing substantial.

Since the advent of BELL brass in the 1980s, a number of manufacturers have begun offering .500 NE ammunition and cases, including Westley Richards and the newly constituted Kynoch in Britain, and Harald Wolff Mastergunworks in Europe. In the United States, the major name in nitro-express cartridges is Art Alphin's A-Square Co., Inc. A-Square has been the angel of life for dozens of old nitro-express cartridges. Its current loading in .500 NE uses the three-inch case, and is available loaded with solids, softs, and the super-soft "Lion Load." There is some question about the wisdom of firing solids like the A-Square Monolithic in double rifles. Art Alphin insists they are fine, based on extensive testing with his pressure barrels. A-Square ammunition is available in its "Triad" form—all three bullet types matched ballistically to shoot to the same point of impact. I know they do this in a bolt rifle; if they will also do it in a double rifle which was originally regulated for something different, then Art Alphin qualifies as a ballistic genius. Probably, they will do it in some and not in others. Every double rifle is an individual, as George Caswell points out.

The other question is cartridge length. Should you fire three-inch cases in a 3¼-inch chamber? The answer is, why not? The short cases fit just fine. The danger lies in the effect it will have on the chamber. It is argued that the hot gases will slightly erode the last quarter-inch of chamber and then, if you fire the full-length cases, the brass will expand into the pitting (microscopic though it may be) and cause extraction problems. Art Alphin thinks that is a moot point.

"I would guess it would take at least 500 rounds before any problem would show up. We have done some testing with a .458 Lott pressure barrel, shooting .458 Winchester ammunition, which is exactly analogous to the .500 NE. So far we have fired about 260 rounds with no discernible corrosion at all. So I am certain you could fire at least 300 rounds of .500 NE, and probably more since the pressures are considerably lower."

A more likely cause of problems would be powder particles and other debris building up against the shoulder of the chamber. This could cause case sticking or, more likely, difficulty in chambering a 3¼-inch case. A thorough cleaning immediately after firing, however, should prevent that. Exactly how major a problem this might be is debatable anyway: There are very, very few 3¼-inch-chambered .500 NEs out there to begin with. Alphin has been making the .500 NE since the early 1980s. During that time, he says, he has received only "two or three" requests for 3¼-inch-cased ammunition. Around 1993, he did a run of the longer cases, which he sold as a lot to Huntington Die Specialties.

Art Alphin is a big admirer of .500-caliber cartridges of all kinds, having developed more than a few himself. He says the .500 Nitro Express is "a good one, with a lot more killing power than the .470." In fact, he says, if someone is ordering a new double rifle and is looking for killing power, not resale value, and does *not* order a .500 NE instead of a .470, then "he needs professional assistance, my friend. It's not only more powerful, it's more practical. There are all kinds of .510 diameter bullets available, including gas-check lead bullets for light loads. The .500 Nitro Express just makes more sense, for a shooter, than the .470."

Now who would ever have expected to hear that? As for the ammunition, Alphin says, the .500 is a consistent seller that he plans to make "in perpetuity." The ammunition supply problem that John Taylor worried about in 1948 seems to be, at long last, solved.

And speaking of ordering a new .500 NE double, you can get one from H&H, if you are feeling wealthy, or from Rigby in either sidelock or boxlock form, or for a little less money a Rogue River Rifleworks boxlock based on the Merkel design. There are also several continental makers. Craig Boddington used a Heym on an elephant hunt in Mozambique some years back and praised it highly. The .500 NE three-inch is a standard offering from Beretta, and it is available on request from makers like Auguste Francotte. The new Krieghoff Classic double rifle, introduced in 1995 and now available off-the-shelf, could then be had in .500 N.E. for less than $10,000, which is a bargain in double rifle terms.

❀

Finally, who uses one? What purpose is there today for a cartridge that John Taylor deemed excellent for elephant and rhino, but too *much* gun for lion and a little overpowered even for Cape buffalo? George Caswell says the .500's biggest fans today, the people who search out the rifles and shoot them, tend to be "good shooters who are cartridge knowledgeable."

As a working cartridge, though, perhaps its real future lies with the African professional hunter who still has to deal with big game under the worst circumstances. Robin Hurt has a William Evans .500 Nitro Express that he reserves for use in only the most dire situations. And recently Russ Broom Safaris (Pvt) Ltd. of Zimbabwe adopted the .500 caliber as its standard back-up rifle: .500 A-Square for the bolt actions, and .500 Nitro Express for the double rifles.

So here it is—a hundred years old and counting, and looking at a bright future. Maybe the shooting world's not so irrational after all. We just require a little time.

❀

The .505 Gibbs

Very few cartridges have been privileged to be immortalized in literature, but the .505 Gibbs is one of those few. On April 19, 1936, Ernest Hemingway completed *The Short Happy Life of Francis Macomber*, a short story about a safari in Africa, a love triangle, and a tragic, enigmatic ending. The hero of the story, if there is one, is the professional hunter, Robert Wilson—a stocky man with "machine-gunner's" cold blue eyes, sandy hair, a ruddy complexion, and a "short, ugly, shockingly big-bored .505 Gibbs."

By story's end, Wilson's .505 Gibbs had become practically a character in itself, mentioned each time with awe, but not always with accuracy. Hemingway, who prided himself on knowing how things really were, committed one of the great ballistic gaffes when he referred to the .505 as having a "muzzle velocity of two tons." But no matter. With the publication of *Macomber*, the .505 Gibbs became the synonym for a certain type of stopping rifle: graceless but deadly, a professional's weapon.

Exactly how Hemingway came to choose the cartridge is really anyone's guess, although the choice served a hidden purpose beyond establishing the character of its fictional owner, Robert Wilson. Wilson was closely modelled on Hemingway's white hunter on his first safari, Philip Percival. Percival himself carried a .450 No. 2 double rifle and never used a .505 Gibbs. Another famous professional hunter of the time, Baron Bror von Blixen-Finecke, did use a .505 Gibbs, however, and since "Blix" was as famous for his *affairs d'amours* as he was for his big-game hunting, he probably served as a model in that respect. Von Blixen was a friend of Hemingway, and appears in his fiction in a couple of places, most notably as 'the Baron' in *Islands in the Stream*. At any rate, by arming Wilson with the .505, Hemingway was deliberately distancing him from his real-life counterpart, Percival.

It is not really surprising that he chose the .505, however, because at that time, in the mid-1930s, it was a well-known (if not widely used) cartridge in the United States. When Hemingway was preparing for his safari, he haunted the old Abercrombie & Fitch store in New York. A&F was a major importer of guns and rifles and even had a shooting range in the basement. Probably, in the course of buying rifles for his safari, Hemingway saw the .505 that he eventually described in his story; certainly his descriptions of that .505 have a ring of awestruck truth about them. And truth to tell, the .505 Gibbs is one awe-inspiring cartridge.

※

When we think of the big British elephant guns, we usually mean "nitro express"—long, rimmed, cordite-stuffed cartridges for the great double rifles. Comparatively, the British designed relatively few big cartridges for repeating rifles. Those they did come up with, however, were very, very good. They included the .416 Rigby, the .425 Westley Richards, the .404 Jeffery, and of course, the .375 Holland & Holland.

Of the British gunmakers, some (such as Purdey, Boss, and Joseph Lang) were known primarily for their shotguns, although they also made rifles. Others were rifle makers first, shotgun makers second. Around the turn of the century, gunmaking in Britain had its own rigidly defined class system. At the top of the heap were the London gunmakers. Companies in Birmingham could insist they were as good, and many probably were, but Birmingham did not have the cachet London enjoyed.

Oddly enough, while the greatest names in shotguns were London names (Purdey, Boss, Holland & Holland), most of the companies that specialized in rifles originated elsewhere. John Rigby began in Dublin and Westley Richards in Birmingham, while George Gibbs started out in Bristol.

The company began life, in 1835, as J. & G. Gibbs and, in 1842, George became the sole owner. From the beginning, Gibbs was a rifle maker. In 1841, he made a 4-bore, two-groove rifle for the great explorer Samuel White Baker. The rifle fired a three-ounce lead ball, propelled by 16 drams of black powder. This was the forerunner of Baker's famous "Baby," a 4-bore, three-groove rifle made for him several years later by Harris Holland and carried on his epic journey down the Nile. Baker spoke highly of the earlier Gibbs rifle, however, insisting it could put down "anything that walked." Baker's description of the rifle in *The Rifle and the Hound in Ceylon* (published in 1854) was the first—but not the last—time a great writer extolled the virtues of a Gibbs rifle. A few years later, Frederick Courteney Selous did likewise; this time, the rifle was a Gibbs-made Farquharson chambered for the .450 Express, and Selous hunted elephant with it for more than 30 years.

George Gibbs was seriously into riflemaking, working hard to innovate and perfect his products. In 1865, the firm was awarded the sole rights to the new Metford rifling system, designed by William Metford and introduced the same year. Metford's rifling employed seven grooves, and both the lands and grooves were shallow and slightly rounded. The original design was .461 caliber and quickly proved itself to be both highly accurate and easy to keep clean—an important factor with blackpowder rifles. Gibbs held the rights to Metford's design for 14 years. In 1870, Gibbs began putting Metford barrels on Farquharson actions, a combination that dominated rifle matches in the United Kingdom for the next 30 years.

By 1900, blackpowder was giving way to smokeless (cordite, in the U.K.), and the Mauser bolt-action rifle had been perfected. British gunmakers began building repeating rifles on Mauser actions, and most of the big names designed at least one proprietary big-bore rimless cartridge of their own. Not surprisingly, the most common approach was to develop a rimless cartridge that would duplicate the ballistics of an existing nitro-express rimmed design. In 1909, Westley Richards introduced the .425; in 1910, Jeffery followed with the .404 (a rimless .450/.400, ballistically), and a year later Rigby unveiled its .416. All were fine cartridges in essentially the same class in terms of power, propelling a 400-grain bullet at a velocity of about 2,200 fps.

George Gibbs (the founder died in 1884, but the company retained the name) took a slightly different tack. The company decided to duplicate the power of the .500 Nitro Express. Sometime around 1910 (the date is vague) it came out with the cartridge it called the .505 Rimless Magnum—better known to all the world as the .505 Gibbs.

By any standard, the .505 was a beast. It fired a 525-grain bullet at a muzzle velocity of 2,300 fps and energy of 6,190 ft/lbs. The case alone was more than three inches long (3.15"), .635-inches in diameter at the base, and the loaded cartridge approached four inches in length! Beside the .505 Gibbs, even the formidable .460 Weatherby looks diminutive. Naturally, such a bulky round would not fit into just any action, and getting it to feed properly was a challenge. Nevertheless, Gibbs's offering in the big-bore magazine-rifle stakes attracted an immediate following and, while it never achieved the popularity of cartridges like the .416 Rigby (to say nothing of the .375 H&H), it was definitely here to stay.

The .505 was not without rivals, although there was only one that really mattered, and that was the .500 Jeffery. According to all the ballistics tables, the .500 Jeffery shades the .505 in terms of sheer power, although it is a slightly smaller case, and for years every mention of the .505 Gibbs referred to it as the second-most powerful cartridge in its class.

The .500 Jeffery is obscure in its origins and rare today in terms of both rifles and ammunition. It is identical to the only true big-bore cartridge offered in Germany, the 12.5x70mm Schuler. Everything about this animal is vague. Who introduced it, Jeffery or Schuler? No one knows for certain, but my guess is Schuler. When was it introduced? Again, no one knows, but it is assumed to be in the 1920s, long after most of the other big-bore cartridges were well established. The confusion is compounded, in the case of the German cartridge, by the fact that it is most commonly referred to in America as the 12.7x70mm Schuler, but is listed in German catalogs as the 12.5x70mm Schuler. If you run across a Schuler rifle with 12.5x70 stamped on the barrel, what you have is a .500 Jeffery.

The published ballistics for the .500 Jeffery are a 535-grain bullet at 2,400 fps and 6,800 ft./lbs of muzzle energy. If this is real, as opposed to estimated, guesstimated, or pure wishful thinking, that is some cartridge, folks. Personally, I consider it highly doubtful.

The .505 Gibbs was a proprietary cartridge; ammunition was loaded by Kynoch and sold exclusively by George Gibbs. Ammunition for the .500 Jeffery, however, was never loaded in England; it was available only from the Continent, apparently, and loaded rounds today are an exceedingly rare collector's item. Even if you could find a .500 Jeffery rifle (and Jeffery reportedly made only 23 of them), you would never fire the original ammunition in it. The bottom line of all this is that getting ammunition to test is next to impossible, so determining definitively which was ballistically superior, the .505 or the .500 Jeffery, is about as likely as proving that Joe Louis could have flattened Muhammed Ali. Regardless, both cartridges were highly respected in Africa. John Taylor wrote that having tested one .505 Gibbs rifle, he would recommend it highly to anyone who preferred a magazine rifle for dangerous game. He added that, by way of a test, he shot a Cape buffalo bull at 196 long strides and hit him square on the shoulder. The buffalo "dropped instantaneously" and was dead in less than a minute. "It's a magnificent weapon, if you like a magazine, and has adequate power for all emergencies," Taylor concluded.

Strangely enough, Taylor had considerably more experience with the .500 Jeffery, having shot three of them, and was even more effusive in his praise. Considering how scarce .500 Jefferys have always been, it is very odd that three of only 23 ever made should pass through Taylor's hands. Regardless, he loved it.

"This is the most powerful sporting magazine rifle that has ever been placed on the market," he wrote. "It's a glorious weapon..." He added that he preferred it to the .505 but could not really say why; he suspected it was because Jeffery put a generously dimensioned fore-end on his rifles, and that made them easier to handle and shoot.

Obviously, whether or not the published ballistics were genuine, the .500 Jeffery certainly performed in the field. Taylor was never reluctant to condemn shoddy rifles or ammunition produced on the Continent, and given the fact that .500 Jeffery ammunition was available only from Germany, it must have done the job or he would have said so in no uncertain terms.

As to which cartridge is really better, well, the .505 is a longer, fatter case with greater capacity (and attendant problems of magazines and feeding). The .500 Jeffery is shorter and more compact, but that means you are working with considerably higher pressures to obtain the same results. If the original figures are correct, the chamber pressures in the .500 must have been tremendous; in the heat of Africa, with a bolt action, dealing with dangerous game, that is not good news. Perhaps if Taylor had shot a .500 Jeffery for an entire season or two, he might have had a few words to say on that subject.

Another odd thing about the .500 Jeffery is that it has a rebated rim—that is, the rim has a smaller diameter than the base. This is not necessarily a bad thing; the .425 Westley Richards also has a rebated rim. Theoretically this can lead to feeding problems, but it does not appear to have been an issue. Of course, with so few .500s ever made and used, it is hard to say whether it was given a thorough test.

The neck of the .505 Gibbs is considerably longer, allowing for double crimping grooves, which gives the case a death grip on the bullet. This is very helpful with heavy-recoiling cartridges. The .500 Jeffery, with its noticeably shorter neck, does not grip as firmly, so in theory at least the .505 is superior in that regard. This, however, is quibbling. Taylor's friend Fletcher Jamieson, a Rhodesian, owned a .500 Jeffery with which he shot more than 300 elephant, among other things, and experienced no difficulties. And that is actual practice, not idle theory.

⁂

Unlike most of the big British elephant guns, the .505 Gibbs crossed the Atlantic and developed something of a following in America, probably because it was a rimless cartridge and could be chambered in a bolt-action rifle, and because then, as now, there is always a handful of people who get a kick out of shooting the biggest thing around.

At that time, the bolt rifle was just beginning to make inroads in the civilian market. The only commercial bolt rifle available was the Remington Model 30, itself a sporterized version of the Enfield P-17. The Winchester Model 54 was introduced in 1925. Mauser 98 actions were available from Germany, both in military guise and as the Oberndorff Mauser actions the major British firms used for their magnum rifles.

Major Townsend Whelen was then officer commanding the Frankford Arsenal, and he introduced Seymour Griffin, a fledgling New York stockmaker, to James V. Howe, a young Frankford gunsmith with a talent for metalworking. In 1923, Griffin and Howe went into partnership to form what is now America's oldest custom gunmaking firm. In the same year, in Cleveland, Hoffman Arms began operating. Both companies specialized in making custom hunting rifles based on Springfield military actions. James Howe stayed with the company for only six months before leaving to work for Hoffman Arms. He had developed an interest in the .505 Gibbs, however, and began developing loads for it. These he sent to the Frankford Arsenal ballistics laboratory to be chronographed and pressure-tested, and the results are very interesting. Working with a 525-grain bullet (origin unknown), Howe obtained velocities ranging from 2,250 to 2,455 fps with HiVel #2. Breech pressures ranged from a mere 28,850 psi to a high of 45,375 psi—not by any stretch of the imagination a severe test of a magnum Mauser action.

Handloaders and gunsmiths were not alone in their interest in the .505 Gibbs. The big ammunition companies were also working with it, although they never loaded commercial ammunition. DuPont provided data for the cartridge with IMR #15 ½ powder— a light load at 2,000 fps, and an elephant-bouncer at 2,520 fps. The latter gave muzzle energy of 7,402 ft./lbs, which is enough to get anyone's attention.

From the beginning, American shooters were almost as preoccupied with the recoil of the .505 Gibbs as they were with its power down range.

"The cartridge is tremendously powerful with an excessive amount of recoil," wrote Philip B. Sharpe in 1937. "Major John W. Hessian, of Winchester, told me several years ago that he once had a wonderful session of approximately 40 consecutive rounds with this cartridge, and that he was unable to enjoy life for the following two weeks."

Tales of dislocated shoulders and broken collarbones were attached to the .505, whose recoil became the stuff of legend. To the American shooting public, which had no remotely comparable domestic cartridge, it must have seemed incredibly severe; the British, however, attached no particular awe to it, and John Taylor pronounced it a veritable tabby cat: "I had expected considerable recoil, but was most agreeably surprised to find how little there was. (It) is very pleasant to shoot, and very accurate."

Perhaps both are correct. The British made their magazine rifles heavy, running upwards of 11 pounds in some cases; if the Griffin & Howe rifles were the more normal American standard of nine pounds or under, the recoil would be much more noticeable.

Given the availability of the Enfield P-17 action, which is

big and strong and ideal for conversion to a cartridge like the .505, it is surprising that more of them were not made. Probably, difficulty in obtaining ammunition was the great stumbling block. There is no case that can be converted to .505 Gibbs; if you could not get factory ammunition, the only recourse was to turn cases from solid brass rod, and that is a lot of time and expense unless you happen to be a machinist.

Today, there is no problem obtaining either loaded .505 Gibbs ammunition or new brass cases. The A-Square Company makes both, and loads its .505 ammunition in both softs and solids to original Kynoch specifications. As well, the new Kynoch in England is offering ammunition in both .505 Gibbs and .500 Jeffery.

A-Square also loads two proprietary .50-caliber rimless cartridges of their own design, the .500 A-Square and the slightly shorter .495 A-Square. Both are based on the .460 Weatherby belted case. Art Alphin developed both cartridges back in his wildcatting days and now loads them with heavier bullets, and to greater energy levels, than the original .505 Gibbs. The .495 shoots a 570-grain bullet at 2,350 fps and 6,989 ft./lbs, while the .500 fires a 600-grain bullet at 2,470 fps and 8,127 ft./lbs. A handloader can improve the .505 Gibbs's performance significantly if he has a mind (and a need) to, and I once asked Art Alphin why he chose to go with the .460 Weatherby belted case instead of the Gibbs.

"Very simple," he told me. "Back in 1975, when I developed the .500 A-Square, .505 Gibbs cases were extremely scarce and hard to come by. At that time I was strictly a wildcatter—I wasn't making my own cases yet—and I went with what was freely available. But yes, if the .505 Gibbs had been available, I might not have ever developed the .500 A-Square." Today, thanks to Alphin, the .505 Gibbs is more freely available in the United States than it has ever been.

As a cartridge, the .505 Gibbs probably carries more reputation on the basis of limited use in the field than any other big-bore in existence. But even so, its deadly reputation is amply deserved. It is a cartridge that should receive, if anything, more attention and respect than it does. If brass had been readily available through the years, the .505 Gibbs would have spawned an extended family of wildcats based on its cavernous case necked up, down, and sideways.

In 1996, Safari Club International honored the .505 Gibbs when it auctioned the fifth in its "Dangerous Game" series of rifles built on Oberndorf magnum Mauser actions. The "Elephant Rifle," made by John Bolliger's Mountain Riflery, was a .505 Gibbs, and it came complete with 100 specially produced and headstamped .505 Gibbs cartridges, custom-made by A-Square. When you think of it, there is no other cartridge that would suit the ultimate bolt-action elephant rifle quite so well. It would certainly get Ernest Hemingway's vote.

THE MAUSER 98

The evolution of the modern bolt-action rifle resembles in many ways the development of the classic English game gun. The mechanism for the game gun, which is virtually identical whether it is used to produce a Purdey sidelock 12-gauge or a Rigby .500 Nitro Express double rifle, appears to us, today, to be simple and logical. You look at it and wonder why on earth anyone would try to do it differently. That is the essence of genius: to produce a mechanism that will perform a series of sometimes complex activities, yet do them with simplicity and logic.

In the case of the English game gun, the final form, which reached its apex around 1900, was the result of 50 years of intense competition and innovation among several-dozen independent gunmakers. Each specific feature can be traced to the workshop of a specific maker and sometimes even to the brain of a particular craftsman. The break-action concept itself was French (Casimir Lefaucheux) but introduced to Britain by Joseph Lang; the double underlug that locks the barrel in place was a Purdey development; the top lever that moves the bolts that lock the lugs (the Scott spindle) was from William Middleditch Scott, of W. & C. Scott fame; the boxlock action came from William Anson and John Deeley, both of whom worked for Westley Richards, and the two most common release mechanisms for fore-ends originated in the same fertile minds—the Anson plunger and the Deeley latch. Other examples include the Greener crossbolt, the Jones underlever, and Southgate ejectors. As patents expired, the best approaches became universal, and the also-rans were relegated to the scrap heap or became arcane signatures of one or two gunmakers—Stephen Grant's allegiance to the side lever, for example.

The end result, however, was a device that even non-shooting independent engineers agree may be the closest thing to mechanical perfection ever devised by man. The fact that the English game gun is still being manufactured in essentially the same form a century later is fairly conclusive.

※

It is also 100 years since the Mauser 98 was introduced, and the parallels between its development and the English game gun are uncanny, with one notable exception: the Mauser was refined and perfected by one man, over the course of a little more than a decade. Paul Mauser started with a single brilliant concept, and carried it through to perfection step by step. In the end, what he produced was the finest repeating hunting rifle ever developed. It is not exaggerating to say that the Mauser 98 revolutionized hunting at its level, just as the nitro-express cartridges did for the hunting of dangerous game.

Until the Mauser came on the scene, hunters looking for long-range rifles for medium-sized game—a stalking rifle for hunting red stag in Scotland, for example, where ranges might run to 200 yards, or for wildebeest on the Serengeti plain—were limited to single-shot rifles such as the Farquharson or various break-action designs. In the United States the lever action, as made by several companies, was superseding the single-shots, but the lever had several inherent limitations. The major one was power—or rather the lack of it. Most were limited to cartridges like the .44-40, or with smokeless powder, the .30-30. The most powerful cartridge ever chambered in a lever action was Winchester's .405 in its 1895 rifle, but the .405 was considered marginal even for soft-skinned dangerous game such as lion.

In Europe, the single-shot was as much a pedigreed gun of the hunting gentleman as the double—handmade, often elaborately engraved with game scenes, and sporting carved walnut stocks. While single-shots could be very accurate, and could be made just as powerful as any nitro-express double, they had one built-in drawback: They fired only one shot.

By 1890, with hunters flocking to the newly colonized parts of Africa such as Kenya, Tanganyika, and the Rhodesias, there was a serious need for a rifle that was powerful, accurate, reliable, durable, and—not least of all— affordable for the average hunter. Not everyone was the second son of a lord with a family account at Holland & Holland.

When Paul Mauser was working on his various designs for Mauser bolt-action rifles, the needs of colonists did not enter into the equation. He was designing a military rifle with which he hoped to win military contracts and make his fortune. It is a time-honored tradition, however, that military designs spawn sporting rifles, because many of the demands of hunters in remote parts of the world are the same as those of infantrymen in a water-filled trench. Each needs a rifle that is reliable, easy to dismantle, easy to clean, not prone to breakage, that can be repaired when necessary with a minimum of hand labor, and which will fire every time you pull the trigger regardless of mud, rain, snow, or dust storms.

Paul Mauser did not originate the concept of the bolt action. Most historians trace the bolt back to the Dreyse needle gun of the 1840s, and subsequent to that a dozen designers took the basic approach and developed it in their own way. In Austria, Baron von Mannlicher developed the Mannlicher-Schoenauer rifles and carbines, which would be Mauser's main competition around the world for half a century. James Paris Lee, an American, worked on different designs that evolved into the Lee-Metford, and later the Lee-Enfield, which was the British service rifle until after 1945. In Norway, the Krag-Jörgensen was developed and became briefly the American service rifle. France, whose quirky independence knows no bounds, had the Lebel. Each of these saw service—sometimes very arduous service—and each has a commendable record as a military rifle; each, in fact, has merits as a sporting rifle, and many an elephant has fallen to a Lee-Enfield firing the .303 British cartridge. But not surprisingly, each had its failings.

There is an old axiom that in 1917, the Americans were armed with a target rifle (the Springfield), the Germans with a hunting rifle (the Mauser 98) and the British with a battle rifle (the Lee-Enfield). There is enough truth in it to keep people quoting it to support their preferences for each of the above. In the case of the Lee-Enfield, the positive traits that make it a battle rifle are its very slick, fast, rear-locking bolt, and its detachable ten-round magazine, which was years ahead of its time.

In 1890, designers seeking to develop a bolt action as we know it today had to make some immediate decisions on specific features: would it have front locking lugs, rear lugs, or lugs positioned somewhere in the middle of the bolt? Would it have a box magazine, a tubular magazine, or a rotary magazine? Would it cock on opening or on closing? Would it have a single-shot feature which would allow soldiers to keep the magazine fully charged and in reserve, while loading and firing the rifle one shot at a time in the traditional way?

Peter Paul Mauser was 21 years of age when, in 1859, he was conscripted into the army as an artilleryman. Soon after, he was assigned to work as an armorer at the Royal Armory at Wuerttemberg, where he became familiar with breech-loading weapons of the day. After leaving the army he embarked on a career as a gunmaker, and his immediate goal was to design a rifle that improved on the Dreyse needle gun, which since 1840 had been the principal service rifle of the Prussian Army. The Prussians had used the Dreyse to good effect in the intervening 30 years, including their devastating victory in the Franco-Prussian War of 1870-71, and become a significant power in Europe because of it.

While technically the Dreyse was a bolt action, it was a very rudimentary one at best. In reality, it was a transitional design between the muzzleloading percussion rifle and the breech-loader. It was a single-shot percussion rifle that employed a paper cartridge loaded into the chamber from the rear. The "needle," which operated much like a modern striker, penetrated the cartridge and detonated a primer attached to the base of the bullet. Mauser immediately recognized that the Dreyse could be improved upon in several ways.

He began with an idea to modify the Dreyse by making the firing pin self-cocking as the bolt was cycled. This rifle evolved into one that used metal cartridges instead of paper, and the first of the Mauser rifles was born. For the next 20 years Mauser built up his business, designing new rifles—each an improvement on the last—and selling them to the armies of Europe and eventually South America and Asia. Up until 1888, most of the rifles produced by Mauser were single-shot blackpowder weapons.

In 1888, with France's adoption of the Lebel, the whole picture for military rifles in Europe changed. The Lebel featured a box magazine and fired an 8mm smokeless cartridge. Shortly afterward, Germany adopted the 1888 Commission rifle, an arm which employed certain Mauser features as well as a box magazine of the type invented by the Austrian, Ferdinand Ritter von Mannlicher, Paul Mauser's great rival. Several inventors claim to have originated the box magazine; it is often credited to James Paris Lee, but a trio of English gunmakers actually patented an earlier one, in 1867. It follows that the basic idea would be seized upon and perfected, which it was. The concept of the detachable box (and hence one which would allow infantrymen to carry fully loaded spares) saw its first large-scale use in the Lee-Enfield series. Mannlicher designs, on the other hand, were usually part of the trigger guard/floorplate assembly and loaded from the top with stripper clips.

The 8mm Commission cartridge (actually 7.9mm, although it is never designated as such) was also an important development because it was rimless. This feature is credited to the Swiss inventor,

Colonel Rubin, of Schmidt-Rubin rifle fame. It was a breakthrough because it eliminated a serious problem with rimmed cartridges in box magazines: the possibility of the rim of the top cartridge getting behind the one below and causing a jam. If this seems like a minor concern, keep in mind that the British Lee-Enfield used a rimmed cartridge, the .303 British, and its rim forced them to undertake all kinds of safeguards to ensure against this problem. Stripper clips for the .303 are more complicated than for the Mauser cartridges, and loading the magazine is slower and requires more care to guard against this happening. The Bren gun, which was the British platoon-level automatic rifle until after 1945, also used the .303, and the rim had to be taken into account in various parts of its design, including the magazines. Altogether, eliminating the rim simplified life for rifle designers and foot soldiers alike. The rimless 8mm cartridge adopted for the German 1888 Commission rifle was the forerunner of all the famous Mauser cartridges that followed.

The third important feature of the Commission rifle was its dual opposing locking lugs. Again, this concept was not new, the first patents along this line having been taken out by an Englishman named Terry in the early 1850s; the concept was also used in the American Green percussion rifle. The first designs placed the lugs at or near the rear of the receiver. Mauser put them instead at the head of the bolt, locking into the receiver ring where it joined the barrel. The receiver ring is the strongest single part of an action—in fact, it can be made just about as thick and hefty as the gunmaker requires—and relieves the rest of the receiver of any requirement for great strength. This was a significant advance because it allowed the designer greater leeway in designing the magazine well, the trigger mechanism, and related features such as the ejector, without the necessity of ensuring sufficient strength to withstand the pressures of firing. Even the bolt itself, behind the locking lugs, could be slimmer and lighter as a result.

By 1892, the basic Mauser design had evolved into an efficient system that employed a bolt with two opposing locking lugs that cocked on closing, had a three-position safety on the bolt shroud, and a box magazine holding five cartridges. When the United States Army held trials in 1892 to select a rifle to replace the trapdoor

Springfield .45-70, Mauser entered five different models. They performed reasonably well in some ways but not so well in others; in the end, they were beaten out by the Norwegian Krag-Jörgensen, largely because it performed better in single-shot mode and with rimmed cartridges—two features which even then were obsolescent.

Mauser fared better in the Spanish government rifle trials of 1892, and the result was the Spanish Mauser Model 93—after the Model 98, the best-known and most widely used of the Mauser designs. It was chambered for the 7x57 cartridge, one of the great cartridges of all time. One of its most advanced features was a five-round box magazine that held the cartridges in a staggered column. This allowed the floorplate to be flush with the stock, which both protected it and made for easy carrying; the magazine follower had a ridge on one side, and the spring was "W"-shaped. This magazine design is found today on the vast majority of bolt-action rifles, both military and civilian.

The American government made its choice, and the Spaniards made theirs. In 1898, they went head to head in the Spanish-American War, and while the U.S. won overall, the Mauser 93 won the battle of the rifles. Its superiority to the Krag-Jörgensen was apparent to all. Tens of thousands of rifles were captured by the Americans, who carried out extensive testing of both rifle and cartridge and incorporated many of its features into a new rifle of their own design. Barely a decade after it was adopted, the Krag was shouldered aside by the new Springfield, a modified Mauser design, firing the rimless .30-03 cartridge, forerunner of the .30-06. The .30-06 is slightly longer and larger caliber than the 7x57, otherwise they could be twins, and the rifle owed so much to Mauser that the U. S. government ended up paying royalties to the German company for years for patent infringement.

The Spanish-American War, however, was but a scuffle in comparison with a major conflict the British were preparing to fight on the other side of the world, one that would pit the Mauser against another great rival, the Lee-Enfield.

The war in South Africa that began in 1899 is known by various names. British histories call it the Second Anglo-Boer War (the first was in 1881, won by the Boers at the Battle of Majuba); the Afrikaners call it the *Tweede Vryheidsoorlog*, or Second War of Independence. At the time, the British held the Cape Colony and Natal, while the Transvaal and the Orange Free State to the north were independent states governed and largely populated by Afrikaners, the white descendants of the original Dutch colonists who landed at the Cape in 1652. The discovery of the vast gold deposits of the Witwatersrand near Johannesburg was the cause of friction between the Boers (Dutch for "farmer") and the British. The Transvaal and the Orange Free State armed themselves with Mauser rifles, and in 1899 invaded Natal in an attempt to defeat the small British force there and win the war before reinforcements could arrive. The British, as is their wont when they go to war in the fall, expected to win by Christmas; instead, the conflict dragged out over three years and cost a staggering £ *200 million*. It was Britain's longest and most costly war since Napoleon. There were more than 100,000 casualties on the British side, including 22,000 dead; of the original Afrikaner population of less than 90,000, almost one-third died in the war—many of whom were women and children who perished of disease, starvation, and neglect in that great British innovation, the concentration camp.

Why did such a lopsided contest go on so long and at such great cost? What allowed the Afrikaners to resist the might of the British Empire so stubbornly and effectively for three long years? A large part of the credit must go to the Mauser rifle. In the early stages of the war, the Mauser, in the hands of the bush-wise Boers, was the great equalizer although, truth to tell, the real reasons for this have been exaggerated and distorted by a century of historians and history teachers intent on showing that the Boers somehow had an unfair (!) advantage.

The dominant myth about the Mauser, which showed up first in newspaper reports of the time, concerned its accuracy and long range, and its effectiveness in the hands of Boer "sharpshooters." In reality, the Mauser had no great range advantage over the Lee-Enfield and no firepower advantage at all; as for accuracy, beyond 500 yards any target shooter will tell you the Mauser may be more accurate than a Lee-Enfield, but it is not such a factor that it would defeat entire armies. Newspapermen in 1899 were generally as ignorant about ballistics as reporters in 1999, and just as prone to jump to conclusions and trumpet inaccuracies to the sky. Such inaccuracies, repeated often enough and loud enough, eventually become accepted wisdom. In the case of the Mauser, a major cause of these erroneous conclusions was its rear sight.

The actual model that saw the most use in South Africa was the 95, a slightly altered 93 that was sold to several countries, the Orange Free State among them. Free State rifles were made by DWM (*Deutsche Waffen-und Munitionfabriken*) and can be identified by the O.V.S. stamped on the receiver, standing for *Oranje Vrystaat*. There were minor differences between the O.V.S. 95 and the Spanish 93, among them the use of a cartridge with a slightly shorter neck (the 7x53 Mauser). Another difference was the rear sight.

The Mauser 93's open rear sight was a finely machined little mechanism graduated from 400 meters to 1400 meters. On the Model 95, it was 400 to 2000 meters. The thought of shooting at something 2000 meters away—two kilometers!—is ludicrous even when considered in terms of modern marksmanship, but it made eminent sense when you look at the military practices of the day. Infantry tactics of the 19th century, in the era before the machine gun, used massed rifle fire to lay down a beaten zone. Riflemen would set their sights at a particular range and fire in unison on command. Markers on the battle field, put in place when the defensive position was established, would allow officers to estimate range quite accurately. A hundred rifles fired in this way could lay down a curtain of bullets that would devastate infantry or cavalry advancing in close order at a deliberate walk, as was the custom of 19th century European armies. It would also destroy large-scale charges by primitive warriors, as the British themselves proved at the Battle of Omdurman, among others. As well, by having soldiers set their sights at different ranges, and firing in unison at an attacker in the distance, they could lay down an extremely effective beaten zone. The British Lee-Enfield itself had a sight graduated to 2000 yards.

There are two interesting sidelights to this conflict involving the Lee-Enfield on the British side, as well. The Boer War was the first large-scale conflict in which technical aspects of armament became the subject of newspaper articles and political debates—with the same accuracy and results we see with journalists and politicians today, one might add. In the first instance the British had only recently switched from the Lee-Metford to the Lee-Enfield. Both were chambered for the .303 British, which began life as a blackpowder cartridge. The Metford was so-called because it employed the shallow Metford rifling, which was fine with blackpowder but not with the higher pressures and velocities of smokeless- powder cartridges. Naturally, a Metford and an Enfield would not shoot to the same point of impact with a given sight setting. Supposedly, as a result of the War Office not taking this into account, thousands of reservists were sent out to Africa with rifles which fired 18 inches wide at 500 yards. Even by modern standards, that is not a devastating fault in a rifle that is intended for normal infantry use, and it is easy to correct, but the fact was trumpeted as evidence of War Office bungling. All the relevant facts of the matter will probably never be known.

More serious was the use of "dum-dum" bullets, a term that has come to mean a military bullet that has been altered to expand on impact—an inhumane weapon that causes horrifying wounds. In fact, Dum-Dum was the British military arsenal in India where ammunition was produced. The armorers there did originate the "dum-dum" bullet, which was a standard solid with the nose cut off and the jacket serrated with a file. The British Army used these cheerfully until they were outlawed by the Hague Convention. By that time, however, the term "dum-dum" had entered the language. When ammunition crates were captured by the Boers and they saw the name "Dum-Dum" stencilled on the side, there was international outrage. All it really meant, however, was that the ammunition came from that particular arsenal—proving yet again that a little knowledge is a dangerous thing. Ironically, the Boers themselves used dum-dum bullets of their own later in the war, and the British took to shooting any prisoner found with such ammunition in his possession.

Subsequent accounts and explanations of what happened in South Africa have referred to the Boers' expert marksmanship, and there are breathless accounts of them shooting at 500 yards, 1000 yards, and more. The graduated rear sight is introduced as evidence of this. A popular fantasy has grown up of Boers calmly estimating distances up to a mile and more, jacking up their rear sights, and picking off unsuspecting British soldiers. This is, of course, ridiculous. The reality, however, was more than bad enough.

The Boer War was the first large-scale conflict of the 20th century and set the stage in many ways for the First World War, which followed in 1914. By 1899, the British had abandoned red tunics and bright brass buttons in favor of khaki serge. Khaki, incidentally, (pronounced *kar-kee*) is a Persian word meaning "dust," and the cloth derived its name from its color. Appropriately enough, this change came about largely because of the Battle of Majuba in 1881, when the Boer defenders used shiny British helmet badges and belt buckles as aiming points. One of the dead was the British commander, Maj. Gen. Sir George Colley. Infantry uniforms and rifles had changed, but it took the bloody lessons of the Boer War to force a revolution in infantry tactics. In effect, the basic techniques of modern warfare in the age of the machine gun were invented during the Natal Campaign by General Sir Redvers Buller in response to the devastating effects of massed rifle fire from Boers in dug-in positions. It was the forerunner of the trench warfare of 1914-18.

Ever since 1900, Buller has been denigrated, defamed, and blamed for every blunder and misfortune that befell the British in that war, especially in the early stages. Generations of schoolchildren throughout the old British Empire have been taught that Buller's incompetence caused the early reverses, and that the day was saved by the arrival of Field-Marshall Lord Roberts. In fact, this was anything but the truth, as Thomas Pakenham explains very convincingly in his modern history, *The Boer War*. Buller was a victim of a bitter rivalry within the British War Office between two factions, one headed by Roberts (the "Indians"—soldiers who had spent most of their service in India) and the "Africans," headed by Lord Wolseley. Without getting into the details of the dispute, suffice to say that Buller was in the Wolseley camp, while Leo Amery, the brilliant young correspondent of *The Times*, and Rudyard Kipling, poet laureate of the war, were admirers of Roberts. Amery was largely responsible for the massive, seven-volume *Times History of the War in South Africa*, which presents the gospel according to Roberts and has been one of the most influential works on a conflict that was Britain's greatest military embarrassment between 1815 and 1914. Needless to say, since Roberts hated Buller and the public was demanding a scapegoat anyway, poor Sir Redvers comes out on the short end. While Pakenham makes a valiant effort to rehabilitate Buller's reputation (Buller was an excellent soldier, a fine if not brilliant general, and a very brave man who won the Victoria Cross during the Zulu Wars), it is unlikely that anything can now save his name. Sir Redvers Buller was a victim of circumstance, of incompetent subordinates, of malicious rivals, of partisan newspaper correspondents, of weaseling politicians, of Boer opponents who refused to fight a war by the accepted rules—and, let it be said, of the Mauser rifle.

If any evidence is needed that Buller was a great soldier, in the face of all the above he eventually won the Natal Campaign and handily defeated the forces that opposed him—the military ones, at least.

❋

In 1898, Sir Redvers Buller was commander of the British Army Corps at Aldershot, the major training base; he was designated Commander-in-Chief in South Africa when it became apparent that war was in the offing. Buller knew the Boers and the country very well (he was suspected of having Boer sympathies, another mark against him) and warned the garrison commander to dig in south of the Tugela River in the event the Boers invaded; there, they could hold out comfortably and wait for reinforcements. Instead, the commander, Sir George White, allowed himself to be trapped and besieged in the town of Ladysmith. The relief of Ladysmith became the major strategic requirement when Buller arrived, to his intense disgust since he had specifically warned against it, and he was forced to try to fight his way through the nightmare of fast-flowing rivers, gorges, and natural defensive positions that the Boers now occupied.

The Boers, who were farmers, hunters and frontiersmen, good shots, expert horsemen and natural guerrilla fighters, could not fight the British in set-piece battles on the European model. What they did, under General Louis Botha's direction, was dig into strong defensive positions and prepare to lay down a blanket of fire against the advancing British infantry and cavalry. The early results were devastating. Infantry units attacking in the old manner, at a measured walk in close order, found themselves decimated by a withering storm of rifle fire. Observers were appalled, newspaper correspondents among them, and the first myths of the Mauser rifle were born. More than a weapon, the Mauser became a symbol. Postcards from South Africa during the war bore the slogan "God and the Mauser—United in the Fight for Freedom and Justice."

The Battle of Colenso, in which Buller's army corps tried to force its way across the Tugela River on the road to Ladysmith, was their first serious confrontation with massed rifle fire from defensive positions. The British artillery, attempting to get their guns into position, encountered rifle fire from a mile away. It was not accurately placed individual shots, it was massed fire. In any such situation more than a few bullets will hit their mark, which is exactly what happened. Thomas Pakenham recognized the reality, and described it this way:

> A mile was extreme range for effective rifle fire (but) the two 15-pounder batteries found themselves in the center of something to which military textbooks had yet to give a name: in this zone of fire, the air crackled like fat in a frying-pan. There was no question of the Boers being brilliant marksmen. Indeed, one of the things that struck some survivors most forcibly was how poor was Boer marksmanship, supposed to be one of their great points of superiority to the British. It was the sheer volume of rifle fire—the emptying of a thousand Mauser magazines—that had the force of machine-guns and gave the British the impression that they were facing twenty thousand Boers.

In hindsight, it is easy to condemn the soldiers and their commanders for not adapting more quickly to the changed conditions of war the Mauser brought about—and in fact, of course, the Boers could as easily have been armed with Krags, Lee-Enfields, or Lebels, and inflicted exactly the same punishment on the British Army. But they were armed with Mausers, and so it got the credit. It takes time, however, to change the habits of a lifetime, and professional armies as organizations are not noted for their flexibility and adaptability. First, an intelligent commander is needed to analyze the problem and determine how it can be counteracted. Then he has to convince his subordinates of what is needed (simply giving orders is not sufficient) and train them accordingly. Finally, the troops themselves must be taught the new method of fighting. Doing all these things amid the life-and-death stresses of battle is a vastly more difficult proposition than retraining at a quiet military base in peacetime.

The answer, which Buller finally hit upon in the course of several battles, was the technique now known to armies around the world as "fire and movement," and it is still the most basic, most reliable infantry tactic known. Rather than advancing at a measured pace, the infantry attacks in short rushes, exposing themselves only when their comrades are providing covering fire to keep the enemy from firing back. A simple approach? Absolutely. But developing the method and training infantrymen to carry it out effectively under fire could not be done overnight. Fire and movement, and the use of creeping artillery barrages ahead of advancing infantry, were the innovations that allowed Buller and the British Army of Natal to finally lift the siege of Ladysmith and eventually defeat Botha and the Boer army in the east.

By the time the Boer War ended in 1902, modern warfare had been transformed. Every aspect of it, from uniforms, to transport, to hospital facilities, to treatment of civilian populations, to the equipment of the individual soldier, was radically different than it had been. Now the spade was almost as important as the rifle, for the trench was recognized as the most effective defense against massed rifle fire. The process would be hurried along in 1914 by the advent of the machine gun, but the basic changes began in South Africa. As Thomas Pakenham puts it,

The reason for those humiliating reverses was not the marksmanship of the Boers, nor their better guns or rifles, nor the crass stupidity of the British generals—all myths which the British people found it convenient to believe. It was that the smokeless, long-range, high-velocity, small-bore magazine bullet from rifle or machine-gun—plus the trench—had decisively tilted the balance against attack and in favor of defence.

The Mauser rifle was not solely responsible for this transformation by any means, but the attention given it during the Boer War made it the popular symbol of the technological advances that changed warfare once and for all, from a gentleman's pastime to a horrifying bloodbath. Like the Americans after 1898, the British after 1902 undertook a thorough study of the rifle that had come so close to defeating them and designed a comparable rifle of their own. The result was the Pattern '13 Enfield, developed at the Royal Small Arms Factory at Enfield Lock. The P-13 was chambered for a newly developed 7mm cartridge, the .276, which was similar to the Canadian .280 Ross (many Canadians served with the British in South Africa and suffered the effects of the Mauser). Because of the looming prospect of war in Europe, the British did not want to get caught in the midst of a weapon/cartridge changeover, and the P-13 evolved into the P-14, chambered for the old .303 British. It in turn became the P-17, chambered for the .30-06. In this way, both the Springfield and the Enfield "P"-series rifles were children of the Mauser, developed in the United States and Britain as a direct result of battlefield experience against the Mauser Model 93.

Even before the Boer War began, Paul Mauser had made serious improvements upon the 93. The next milestone was the Swedish model, introduced in 1894 and modified in 1896; the designer then drew upon it to put together his crowning achievement, the Mauser Model of 1898.

The Mauser 98 could be used in engineering schools to demonstrate the virtues of continual refinement and simplification of a mechanism. As model followed model, and the lessons of field use came in, Mauser methodically eliminated problems and improved the functioning characteristics, generally simplifying the mechanism at the same time. This process reached its apex with the 98, and although there were dozens of variations on it over the next half-century, the essential design remained unaltered. The greatest virtue was its simplicity, because simplicity is the first essential element of reliability. The 98's bolt consists of just eight parts in total, not one of which is a screw, nut, bolt, or pin, and it can be readily disassembled without tools.

Each feature of the action has a purpose. Nothing is included that does not have a function, and many perform more than one. The floorplate is opened by pressing a pin in a recess, using the nose of a military spitzer-bullet cartridge—something no soldier was likely to be without, and if he was, why would he want to open the floorplate? Similarly, the 98 has no manual cocking piece attached to the striker, a feature that requires more complex and expensive machining operations. It also adds weight and slows the lock-time. Instead, the 98 has a vertical groove in the rear of the cocking piece, into which fits the rim of an 8x57 cartridge; using that as a hook, the striker can easily be re-cocked. Incidentally, excessive lock-time was a recognized failing of the Swedish Mauser and is corrected in the 98.

On the left-hand side of the action as you view it from the rear is a half-moon cutout on the side of the receiver. The primary function of this notch is to accommodate the thumb as it presses cartridges into the magazine from a stripper clip, but it also allows gas to escape from the left lug raceway should a cartridge rupture.

The bolt has another safety feature missing on the Swedish model: a third locking lug (or safety lug) on the bottom of the bolt just forward of the bolt handle. It fits into a recess in the floor of the receiver, but engages only if the forward lugs fail; as well, it helps to block any escaping gas. The bolt shroud has a circular flange for the same purpose.

The safety mechanism of the 98 is a masterpiece. It has three positions: The first allows the rifle to be fired, the second locks the striker but allows the bolt to be cycled, while the third locks the striker and the bolt in place. In the middle position the bolt can be removed, and the bolt itself easily dismantled. This safety's only drawbacks in its military configuration are that it precludes the use of a riflescope, or requires that the scope be mounted uncomfortably high, and it is also not easily operated simply with the thumb of the right hand. Otherwise, it is the best safety ever developed. It locks the striker in place, rather than merely blocking the trigger. This seems a minor point until you have a rifle accidentally discharge with the safety on; then you look at things differently.

The final major improvement incorporated in the 98 is that it cocks the striker on opening the bolt rather than on closing it. This is done by a camming action. In fact, it is partly cocked on opening, and cocked the rest of the way when the bolt is closed, but it makes a noticeable difference in the ease of cycling the bolt.

The feeding system of the 98—what is now referred to as controlled-round feeding with a claw extractor—is the most dependable ever developed, under all conditions. Again simplicity is the key. At no time is the cartridge left to its own devices: it is held in place, guided into the chamber under control, and withdrawn and ejected, again under control. Even if you cycle the bolt with the rifle vertical, or upside down, or on its side, the magazine feeds easily and the rifle will load, fire, and reload, shot after shot. Gravity plays no part in its function, nor can it disrupt it. Another virtue of this system is that a properly tuned rifle can be reloaded in almost complete silence, with no rattle. In dealing with elephant in close cover, a wounded Cape buffalo, or a nearby enemy soldier, this is a priceless advantage.

By the time Paul Mauser had finalized his new design, the German Army was looking for an updated replacement for the Commission 1888 rifle and naturally chose the 98. This gave them the finest and most up-to-date infantry weapon in the world.

As we have seen, the British were in the process of copying the Mauser in everything but name to replace the Lee-Enfield, and the Americans were well on their way to doing the same thing with the Springfield. In Austria-Hungary, also, the superiority of the Mauser was recognized, and they made plans to replace their Mannlichers with a variation on the 98; this work was suspended in 1914, because they did not want to get caught in a changeover, exactly the situation in which the British found themselves with the P-14. Had the war been delayed by a year or two, all the major combatants except France and Russia would have been fighting with essentially the same infantry weapon.

⚜

The Mauser's performance in South Africa did not escape the notice of big game hunters, and when the Boer War ended there were thousands of Mausers still in private hands or in military stock-piles, along with prodigious amounts of ammunition. Naturally, many began using these for hunting, either for food or trophies. One prominent Englishman who immediately took to the Mauser was Frederick Roderick Noble Findlay, who hunted in South Africa in the early 1900s and published a book about his adventures, *Big Game Shooting and Travel in South-East Africa*. Findlay was notable in that he hunted almost everything with a Mauser rifle, from the Cape buffalo on down. One of his Mausers was a standard military 7mm of the type used by the Boers—most likely a Model 95. The other was an 8mm sporting model.

The Mauser company at Oberndorf did not begin any large-scale manufacture of sporting rifles until after the 98 was introduced, at which point firearms for hunters became a significant part of their business. The 98 action was manufactured in three different lengths, short, standard, and magnum, and they were the basis for several different models of sporting rifle. These were exported to the United States and Great Britain as well as sold to hunters on the European continent. Other German gunmakers added the Mauser to their list of products, some used actions produced at Oberndorf, while others made their own actions under license. In Leipzig, Wilhelm Brenneke made rifles and designed cartridges, among them, in 1912, the 7x64 (virtually identical to the .280 Remington). Other well-known names who produced Mauser sporters were J.P. Sauer & Sohn, Heinrich Krieghoff, and Gebruder Merkel. In the United States, the New York sporting goods firm of Von Lengerke & Detmold became sole agent for *Waffenfabrik Mauser*, and their first advertisement for Mauser rifles appeared in 1900 in the magazine *Shooting & Fishing*. Shortly after, Abercrombie & Fitch began importing Sauer rifles.

In Great Britain, John Rigby & Co., the oldest and tradition-ally the most innovative of the London gunmakers, recognized the potential of the Mauser as a sporting rifle and signed an agreement to become the London agent for the German company. This arrange-ment gave Rigby a head start of several years over rivals like Holland & Holland, although soon every English riflemaker was building rifles on Mauser actions.

Which maker's name was on his 8mm Findlay does not bother to mention. He was more concerned with justifying his use of a magazine rifle in hunting, and explaining that it was not at all unsporting. He even devoted a chapter of his book to the technical and sporting aspects of his two Mausers. The 7mm military rifle he considered clumsy and rather ungainly to look at, but he described its mechanism as "delightfully simple." He also comments on the speed at which a score of shots can be fired, but immediately has-tens to add that he himself had not experimented in that direction. His concern was that the Mauser had acquired a reputation with the public as a weapon of devastating speed of fire and long-range accu-racy, and that many would consider it unsporting of him to use such a weapon for sport hunting—much as we might regard a man today who hunts with a submachine gun.

Findlay was a serious student of rifles and ballistics as well as a good hunter, and he goes into some detail comparing the trajec-tories of the Mausers to the Lee-Metford and the old Martini-Henry, as well as to the large-bore express rifles of the time. He also looks at terminal ballistics—bullet performance on game—a subject which was virtually ignored in that era. To most sportsmen, a bullet was a bullet was a bullet. Not Findlay. "The penetration and expansion of a bullet depends greatly on the range from which it is fired, its ve-locity on striking, and, naturally, on the nature of the substance with which it comes into contact," he wrote, and went on to examine bullet performance and penetration on an nyala and a rhinoceros. This attention was unusual: for most gentlemen-hunters of the time, such technical arcana was frightfully *infra dig.*

Although he usually had a Gibbs .450 Nitro Express in reserve, most of his hunting was done with the Mausers. On one occasion, he wrote, at ranges of 30 to 80 yards with his 8mm Mauser, he killed three Cape buffalo out of a herd that thundered past.

> *The lightness, accuracy, high velocity, and flat trajectory of its bullets, the absence of recoil and smoke, the inconsiderable report, the rapidity with which it can be reloaded, the number of its cartridges which can be carried with ease, and the deadly effect of its bullets on large and small game, provided discretion is used in the choice of the bullet calculated to prove the most effective, mark the large-bore Mauser (8mm) as a splendid rifle for the sportsman. I do not for a moment wish to contend that it is a better rifle than, for instance, a .450 or .461 express by Gibbs of Bristol,—each has its special advantages,—but it is decidedly a good rifle.*

The only problem with the Mauser as a sporting rifle, as Findlay saw it, was when it was used by a "despicable gunner who shoots for the mere pleasure of killing and with the object of topping his friend's so-called 'record bag,' and he will have no great difficulty in slaying a dozen Burchell zebras, and wounding many more in a single day…" In the hands of a "careful and considerate sportsman," however, Findlay said the Mauser was "an almost ideal weapon."

These sentiments were echoed by others, and gunmakers everywhere took to the Mauser as a starting point for building sporting rifles. In London, the availability of the Mauser 98 made possible an entire class of new dangerous-game cartridges. In 1907, Rigby took the 7x57 and renamed it the .275 Rigby, which it remains in Britain to this day, and two of the most famous big game hunters of the 20th century, Jim Corbett and Walter Dalrymple Maitland Bell—"Karamoja Bell"—used it to great effect, one on man-eating tigers in India, the other on elephants in Africa. Neither use was intended by either Mauser or Rigby, but there is no arguing with the results.

The transition from blackpowder to smokeless was just as important to big game hunters as it was to the military. Smokeless powder gave higher pressures, and hence higher velocities; this was not an unmixed blessing, however, especially when used in break-action double rifles, and the nitro-express cartridges (the first of which, the .450, was introduced by Rigby in 1898) all had long, roomy cases to keep pressures down. The Mauser 98 could withstand much higher pressures, and the camming action of the bolt minimized the possibility of a case becoming stuck in the chamber. Recognizing this, London gunmakers flocked to design large-bore rimless cartridges for magazine rifles. Probably the first was Holland & Holland's .375/.400 Belted Nitro Express, which appeared in 1905, and within a few years new big-bore cartridges for Mauser rifles were sprouting like dandelions in May: the .425 Westley Richards came along in 1909, the .404 Jeffery and .505 Gibbs in 1910, the .416 Rigby in 1911, and the most famous of all, the .375 H&H, in 1912.

On the continent, the Mauser spread like wildfire. In 1889, in Liege, Belgium, *Fabrique National d'Armes de Guerre* (FN) was founded specifically to build Mauser rifles for the Belgian government. FN later became one of the largest and best-known makers of Mauser sporting rifles in the world. In Sweden, it was Husqvarna, in Denmark Schultz & Larsen, in Czechoslovakia, Brno.

In his book *Mauser Bolt Rifles*, Ludwig Olson attempts to estimate the total number of Mauser 98 rifles manufactured in the 100 years since its introduction. Taking all the military production into account, he believes the number is more than *100 million rifles* altogether. And that is not counting civilian production, nor does it include the obvious Mauser descendants like the American Springfield and the British Enfield. Each of those, in turn, spawned civilian designs for hunting. The Enfield led directly to the early Remington bolt action, the Model 30; Winchester's revered Model 70 is directly derived from the Mauser 98, as is the modern Dakota 76.

Civilian production of Mauser 98 actions, either in mass- or custom-production, has continued in an unbroken line to this day. The last mass-producer of actual, unaltered 98s, Zastava in Yugoslavia, suspended production when that country disintegrated in the early

1990s. Today, there are still a few extremely high-quality Mauser 98 actions being built, notably by Hartmann & Weiss in Germany; these are very expensive, simply because the Mauser action, while simple to operate, is costly to manufacture. The built-in simplicity requires a multiplicity of expensive machining operations. In fact, over the years, most of the changes that have been made when a Mauser-derived action has been introduced have been an attempt to reduce production cost by eliminating some of these machining operations.

Through it all, the Mauser 98 sails on, the darling of professional hunters who admire its ruggedness and dependability, a favorite of custom riflemakers who turn hundred-year-old surplus military actions into works of art that sell for tens of thousands of dollars, and the delight of farm boys who buy a surplus rifle for a few bucks and happily hunt deer and woodchucks with it. The Mauser 98 is, quite simply, the greatest rifle, of any type, ever designed.

MAGIC

It was a day like you find late in the fall, when the leaves are off the trees and the snow comes gently in wet flakes—when the sky is gray and motionless and you learn how good canned soup can be, steaming on a woodstove, and the snow you stamp off your boots lies unmelting on the cabin floor.

Claire was an old man even then, a man who had hunted deer up there for longer than I had been alive. He started with his father just after the first war, saw his father's last hunts, taught his son what it was all about, and then sort of adopted me when his sons went off and married. I was not an orphan, except in the sense of being a kid in thrall to hunting but trapped in a family of indoorsmen, and I took to Claire and his old '94 like a tack to a tire.

It was the last day of the season, a Saturday when everyone was out for one last time. The deer were starting to yard up, and even seeing one was a long shot at best. With a new rifle and a pair of new dubbined boots and my first deer license, out in the woods with real ammunition, it did not matter to me how long the odds were; I still expected a big buck to appear the way bucks did in *Outdoor Life*, heavy-horned and silhouetted against the snowy timber. Wet and cold but supremely unmiserable, even the long trip back across the lake to the cabin, with the waves slapping and ice building up on my precious Marlin, felt good to me. And the smell of that soup on the stove as I lugged more firewood into the cabin—I can still feel it all today.

We were on the last of the coffee when Claire took his pipe out of his mouth and started to talk, looking into the fire. It felt awfully good, that fire, and if Claire wanted to talk for a while rather than get right back out there, it was okay with me. It was a long way across the lake with only a chilly stand to look forward to. Afternoon optimism is tough.

"We might see a deer later, and we might not," he said. "There aren't as many as there used to be. Haven't been for quite a few years. I'd like to see you get your first one, but other than that, I don't much care if I shoot another one. I just like to be up here hunting them."

Many fall days have slipped away since that one. Many big wet flakes have drifted down, and now a few of them sift gently onto the place where Claire is buried. There have been mountaintops in Alaska and plains in Tanzania and swamps in Botswana; I've made a few good shots and missed more than a few easy ones, and I've stared into a lot of campfires, and every one is as good as the last. Sitting by the fire in Alaska one time, a fire that was built with wet alders and camp scrap and was more wishful thinking than anything else, a sheep guide said to me that he'd climb over an entire mountain range and down a dozen hanging glaciers if there was the chance of a big ram at the end of it, but he couldn't understand people who would do that just to get a photograph.

"It ain't the meat and it ain't the horns," he said. "I don't know what it is, but that's what makes it all worthwhile."

I don't know exactly what it is either, truth to tell, any more than Dale did, although actually I suspect we both knew, we just could not explain it.

One of the great things about big game hunting, more than any other activity known to man, is that one minute you can be poor as a church mouse, soaked through, shivering, with a thousand dollar rifle rusting into scrap before your very eyes, and the next minute you can be richer than Solomon—all because an animal walked out of the woods and threw his head back, and you made one of those wonderful miraculous shots that was as much luck as anything, but at least it was luck you made yourself. This is a fact that has been true since man first killed something to eat and hung the antlers in a tree over the campfire; it has been true since there has been a god of hunting (or a goddess, depending on who and what you are); and it will still be true long after all the other artificial pastimes we have invented to take the place of hunting are gone and forgotten. That is why there has always been a god of hunting, and why there will never be a god of racquetball.

It is why what you get will never be as important as what you gave to get it, and why sometimes you find, when the search has failed, that the search itself was what you were really looking for. That is when you look at a big Dall ram on the wall and remember what it took to get him back down the mountain, long since out of water with darkness coming on, and having to dig deeper into yourself than you ever did before. And why forever after you could say "No matter what happens, no one can take away from me that on that night, in that place, I did those things." That is why, looking at your cat curled up asleep on the bear skin, you can remember what that bear looked like when he came down off the hill at a dead and silent run. That is why the Cape buffalo will always be a memory of heaving shoulders and blowing blood and shooting from the hip, and to hell with how wide he was. He was plenty wide enough.

Then there are the times when a plan works to the letter, and the buck is exactly where he is supposed to be, when he's supposed to be there, and your pal drops him with one perfect shot as you come out of the woods, grinning. He's only a forkhorn, with one tine broken at that, but the plan simply worked too well to waste. The meat will be damned good, anyway, and those little antlers are just the right size to make a rattle. There's a buck just like that one hanging up outside my window right now, beside the woodpile. That hunt was 27 minutes from start to finish, like clockwork, but I'll remember it the rest of my life, just like the five-point bull in Colorado that Jim flushed out of the bush that time. Half the bunch went one way, the other half the other, but the one big bull came straight and nearly ran me down. I shot him at ten yards, in self-defense as much as anything. He was good meat, too.

It is fall again now, and last night for the first time we had those big heavy flakes. They covered the little buck where he hangs from the high branch, coated him like frosting, and I look at him every time I go out for more wood. He's high enough the wolves won't get him, but the shotgun is by the door anyway.

All of those are real things. The buck is real. The shotgun is real. God knows the wolves are real. None of it is magic, unless it all is. Claire was right all along: The magic lies just in being there.

AFRICA

2

❋

AND STILL CHAMPION

O N   T H E   T R A I L
O F   M B O G O

The Masai Steppe of central Tanzania is home to some of the
largest Cape buffalo on earth. Its miles of rolling grassland are cut
by brush-filled dongas and dotted with huge old baobab trees. A dry
river bed snakes through the country and eventually forms the western boundary of Tarangire National Park.

This particular area is called the Lotolya Plain, and it
was here that professional hunter Gordon Cormack brought an
American client, Terrell Shelley, in 1993. They had already taken
one buffalo when Shelley wounded a big bull with a running shot.
The buffalo made off, accompanied by a second bull, with Cormack
and Shelley hot on their trail. They caught up to the pair in a brushy
donga.

"I knew they'd be in there," Gordon recounted later, "and I
went in very slowly. It was quite steep, and Terrell was a few yards
behind me.

❋

"At the bottom were two buff spoors going into long grass along a sandy path. I was following them, just inching along, when there was a terrific crashing in the grass about 20 yards away. The trackers were up on the bank and they shouted down to us. They could see the bull in the brush, and he was coming straight for them!

"I was lower down, and the buff hadn't seen me. The boys scattered—very wisely—and Terrell jumped onto higher ground for a better shot. I could hear the buff coming, and I could see the top of the reeds shaking, but I couldn't see the animal himself. He rushed up the edge of the donga and caught sight of me just as I saw him. As he swung his head to come, I shot the top of his heart off; Terrell fired right after and broke his neck.

"Great stuff! He's down! Or that's what we thought, until we got a good look at him and realized he wasn't our wounded bull! That one was still in there…"

As they stood talking, the wounded bull broke cover from the same spot and dashed up the opposite bank, then turned and faced them. Terrell Shelley got another chance to show how well he could shoot, which was very well indeed. A bullet in the chest and a finishing shot, and it was over.

"The game scout accepted the shooting of the first bull as a genuine case of self-defense and did not deduct it from our licence," Gordon said. "But it was the strangest thing—the unwounded bull came for us, and he meant business."

❋

Read two stories about the Cape buffalo and you might think you were reading about two different animals. In one, the buffalo succumbs like a tired old milk cow; in the next, the beast the natives call *mbogo* is the devil incarnate with horns like railway ties and the disposition of your ex-wife's lawyer. On my shelf I have an encyclopaedia that completely dismisses stories about the Cape buffalo's ferocity: "Hunters' tales at one time indicated that the buffalo was one of the most dangerous of African mammals," it says, but "investigators now describe it as a peaceful grazer."

Even some writers who should know better, especially those who have never hunted Cape buffalo, tend to downplay the stories. They will say outright that the Cape buffalo is overrated, that left to his own devices he would rather run than fight, that a .30-06 is plenty of rifle for buffalo if you place your shot right. Stories of buffalo soaking up bullet after bullet and still coming at you, they insist, just prove you were not shooting very well. They point to professionals who have spent time on game control, killing hundreds of buffalo with a light rifle and no problems. This, they say, proves buffalo are not hard to kill, and a light rifle is more than adequate in the hands of a good shot.

The difficulty in sorting out these conflicting stories is that most of them are, to some extent, true. Many professionals have killed hundreds of buffalo and never been seriously charged, and often they do use light rifles for the purpose. Left to himself, even an old bull would sooner quietly depart than start a fight with a hunter. And if you place the first shot right on an undisturbed animal, you could drop a buffalo like a pronghorn antelope. But, there is always a *but!*

Run into an old bull that has had mix-ups with hunters before, that has a poacher's bullet in his shoulder or a snare cable around his neck, and you've got a horse of a different hue. Fail to place your first shot right, then let him get into some cover and have a few minutes to get good and mad, with adrenalin pumping like water from a hydrant, and you are in for the experience of a lifetime—yours or his. Or open hostilities with a lone bull, on his own turf away from the herd, and you may find you are dealing with a different beast entirely.

I once read that old hunters like to see young hunters get into a scrap with a Cape buffalo early in their careers. Nothing permanent, mind you; nothing maiming, just something serious enough to get their attention. The thinking runs this way: If you go through life bowling over one buffalo after another without a hitch, you lose respect for them and start to take them for granted. When that happens, you are begging to become a casualty in the buffalo wars. Better to take a bit of a hit early on and then go through life according Cape buffalo the respect they deserve.

Much the same holds true for sport hunters on safari. If you take your first one or two buffalo with no problem, you begin to dismiss the legends as the whining of incompetents. I know of one man who went to Africa all keyed up to battle to the death with *mbogo*, primed with stories about their ferocity and determination and strength and cunning. What happened? One-shot kill. Same with the next one, and the next. He doesn't hunt buffalo any more. Says they're boring. Now his passion is lion. He messed up his first lion, had a close call, and now he practically worships them.

For the record, my first Cape buffalo fell to one shot through the heart at 11: 00 o'clock on the first morning I ever hunted in Africa. I fired, and he dashed 40 yards in the other direction and died without a murmur. That was waist-deep in a swamp in Tanzania. Nice buffalo, 43-inch horns, but the whole thing was hardly what I expected. Two weeks later, in the sand and thorn thickets of Botswana, I had a somewhat different experience. That time the bull was facing me, and I pulled the shot. It broke his back leg and smashed an artery. We trailed him through the bush for half an hour, with the wound spraying blood all the way. When we caught up to him, I managed to anchor him with a spine shot and then finished him with five more into the lungs and heart. He died bellowing and trying to get at me. Seven shots in all, and except for the first, every one was a perfectly good, killing blow—from a .416 Weatherby, no less. But that bull did not die easily. If he had not been anchored by the spine shot, we would have had a sticky time.

The Cape buffalo is the most Jekyll and Hyde beast in the world, partly, I think, because he is a herd animal with all the herd-animal instincts for survival. Buffalo herds have leaders, and they put out sentries when they rest or feed; when a sentry sees or scents trouble, the herd departs. Although they may seem to be stampeding, they generally withdraw in good order, like an outnumbered but well trained army. They do not dash madly like wildebeest. When dealing with a herd of buffalo, it is definitely a battle of wits.

Hunting buffalo in a herd is considerably different than stalking a lone animal. First you have to get to within shooting distance. Then you have to pick out a good bull, get a clear shot, and pull it off. None of these is easy to do, but all are easy to botch up.

Buffalo come to water at dark and stay through the night. At dawn they head back into the thick brush to spend the heat of the day. One way of hunting them is to leave camp before sunrise, hoping to cut a fresh trail. You then creep along, trying to stalk up to the herd. This usually ends with you on your belly in the sand and thorns, peering through a thick screen of brush at a constantly shifting mass of horns, legs, and tails. Then one animal gets wind of you, the heads come up, the earth shakes, and dust rises in a cloud. Only then does the sound of their hoofs come to you, and by that time they are gone. At which point you climb to your feet, scrape the dust off your forehead, and trail off after them hoping for a better break next time. This can go on for days.

Once the herd is alerted the first time, your chances diminish rapidly. The buffalo dash off farther each time they're spooked and they put out more sentries. The big bulls, knowing full well which way is up, usually manage to put the rest of the herd between themselves and you. They do not reach bigness through dumbness. By noon, with the sun scorching overhead and the safari car ten miles away through scorching, bone-dry sand, most of us are ready to give it a rest.

To add spice, sometimes you will be stalking the herd just as some lions are trying to secure one for lunch. This happened to me in Botswana. We would spook the herd toward the lions; then the buffalo would scent the lions and come back our way. Once, a whiff of lion sent them running just as I was about to take a shot through a screen of branches at what we thought was the shoulder of a good bull. We felt the ground shake, saw the dust rise, and heard them departing for no good reason we knew of at the time. Around noon we gave up on them for that day. Trudging back to the safari car we came across two lions, a female and a big male, lying under a tree. They looked as disgusted as we were. I saluted. The lions sneered. Their loss, of course, was greater, since we at least had a chop box full of goodies back in the Land Cruiser. After draining a half-gallon of water in the shade of an acacia, a cold impala chop with Colman's mustard tasted awfully good.

If you do get a shot at a bull in a herd, however, the equation changes. The herd will dash off, and your quarry, wounded, will dash with them—up to a point. A wounded bull does not take comfort in companionship. He soon separates from the group and goes off on his own. At that point, it is up to you to find him. If you are lucky, you will be able to pick up a blood trail, but that is far from assured when hundreds of hooves have churned up the ground. It is at this point that you are no longer dealing with a herd animal: You are dealing with a wounded Cape buffalo bull, on his own and looking for trouble.

❊

Of all the species on earth, the Cape buffalo is one of the most successful in terms of evolution. Buffalo are tremendously prolific and resilient. Around the turn of the century, a plague of rinderpest swept the continent from the Cape to the Rift Valley. The buffalo were wiped out in some areas and severely reduced everywhere else. When F.R.N. Findlay hunted Mozambique in 1906, buffalo were still scarce, and various authors have written of hunting in East Africa in the early decades of the century at a time when you had two elephant on your license, and unlimited lions, but were allowed only one Cape buffalo—if you could find even one!

The last 75 years have not been kind to Africa's game herds, especially the big mammals. Elephant and rhino have suffered the most, but lion and leopard have also seen their ranges severely reduced. The only one of the Big Five that is really thriving is the Cape buffalo, which bounced back from the rinderpest and now outnumbers all other dangerous game put together. There may be as many as five million buffalo alive today, from the swamps of Tanzania and Zambia to the thornbush of Zimbabwe and Botswana, in thick forest and on high, lonely mountainsides. No animal is more adaptable.

You would think, being a species of wild ox and living on grass, that the buffalo would soon see its range turned into pasture for the mushrooming populace of Africa. This has happened in some places, but in others the buffalo has been saved by the presence of Africa's finest game warden, the tsetse fly, which makes huge areas untenable for domestic animals. As long as the tsetse fly survives, so, in all probability, will the buffalo. As well, the idea is gradually taking hold that Cape buffalo, in huntable numbers, present a more sound economic use for land than raising cattle does, in terms of both money and meat.

If the buffalo is successful as a species, it is because it is, individually, one of nature's engineering masterpieces. A big old Cape buffalo bull will weigh up to a ton—2,000 pounds of thick-skinned, steel-muscled wild ox. His only natural enemy is the lion, and even a lion will avoid tackling a mature bull. Buffalo and lion exist side by side, the buffalo living off the grass and the lion living off the buffalo. But there is more to the buffalo than size and strength. He is also deadly quick and agile. For all his bulk, he can spring like a hare, jump over fences, and leap across chasms that would defeat a horse. His senses are all excellent—sight, scent, and hearing. But even this is still only part of the story.

What makes the Cape buffalo so formidable is that he combines all these attributes with a cool intelligence, immense courage, and, when roused, a sheer determination that dies only with the buffalo himself. It is this determination that is the single most frightening aspect of him. He is absolutely relentless. When he has decided upon vengeance, one or the other of you will die. There is no third option.

You frequently read about the wounded bull who circles back and waits in ambush for his pursuers. This has happened to so many hunters over the years that it is impossible to deny it. Some argue it is not a deliberate ambush so much as a case of an animal watching its back trail, just as a fox or white-tailed deer would do. This may be so, but no whitetail leaps out at you with murder in his heart. Whether the ambush is deliberate or the pursuer is a target of opportunity is academic if you happen to be on the receiving end.

This happened to Tony Henley many years ago when he was hunting in East Africa. Tony was a licensed professional hunter for 50 years, the last 30 or so with Safari South in Botswana. Before that, he went the classic route of professional hunter, game warden, and game control officer in Kenya and Uganda. He estimated he saw 1,500 buffalo killed, either by his own rifle or a client's. One day, Tony and his client were following a wounded bull along a dry *donga*. There was a high bank on the left. Tony heard rustling and looked up in time to see the buffalo come over the bank straight down on top of him. All he could do was swivel his big double rifle and fire. He was carrying a .577 Nitro Express that once belonged to the famous elephant hunter, James Sutherland. The impact of the huge bullet actually deflected the buffalo enough that he missed Tony and landed, dead, at his feet. "Of course," Tony told me, "I fired both barrels..."

Ever afterwards, Tony was a great admirer of the .577 for Cape buffalo. With so many to his credit, as hunter, PH, and game control officer, Tony was in a position to speak with some authority on buffalo rifles. The last years of his career, he shot a Holland .500/ .465 double and was no promoter of light rifles or high velocities for *mbogo*.

After my first two buffalo I decided that, much as I liked the .416 Weatherby cartridge, the Mark V left something to be desired as a dangerous game weapon. As well, my companions that first trip, who included Finn Aagaard and Jack Carter, developer of the Trophy Bonded bullet, all favored at least a .45 caliber and 500-grain bullets. I came home and started work on a .450 Ackley and, later, a .458 Lott. This is no reflection on any of the .416s, which have a great record on heavy game, but the arithmetic is simple: A 500-grain .458 is 20 per cent heavier and has 20 per cent greater frontal area than a 400-grain .416, and that makes a difference not only in shocking power but in penetration. The extra weight gives you more penetration, shot for shot, and that is crucial with Cape buffalo.

When you start doing penetration tests, you learn a few things. For instance, a 500-grain .458 that starts out at 2,000 feet per second will out-penetrate a 400-grain, .416 bullet of considerably higher velocity, simply because the extra weight gives it momentum. If it is penetration you are looking for, bullet weight is your biggest ally. Velocity, on the other hand, is a mixed blessing. It can cause a bullet to expand too much, or even fly apart, and stop short of the vitals. These are general rules, and anyone who cares to refute them is welcome to try.

While on the subject of light rifles for big game, my friend Patrick Mmalane, who also hunted for Safari South, once took on four crop-raiding elephants with an FN-FAL (.308 Winchester) military rifle, with army-issue ammunition. He got them all, but it was pretty sticky for awhile. This was when he was a young army officer. Would he use a .308 on elephant today? "Are you insane?" he asked.

Yet, the FN semiauto is standard equipment for large-scale culls in Zimbabwe. The difference is, those boys approach it like a military operation, shooting in teams and eradicating entire groups. And they always have some heavy ordnance in the lorry if a bull gets off into the bush alone. In no way does this support the idea that the .308 or the .270 Winchester is an adequate Cape buffalo rifle, even in the hands of a good shot. The best marksman in the world has the odd bad day, and if you do not put a buffalo down with the very first shot, you should expect to pump him full of lead in order to drop him. No .308 or .270 is up to that task. Roy Weatherby once killed a Cape buffalo with one shot from a .257 Weatherby. What does that prove? I am one of the .257's great admirers, but I would not hunt buffalo with it even as a stunt.

Getting back to penetration, some say you can solve that problem by always using a solid. This is not very good advice, for a couple of reasons. One, a solid does not do as much internal damage as an expanding bullet; two, a lot of buffalo hunting today involves herds of animals. Solids tend to penetrate too much, skipping right through an animal even as thick and tough as a Cape buffalo if they are not stopped by a bone. In a herd, the bullet can emerge on the other side and wound a second animal. Then you really have problems—legal, logistical, and otherwise. The only real application for solids is a going-away shot on a departing animal (and not always even then) or a buffalo in full charge when you need to penetrate the skull.

The difficulty here is having the right bullet up the spout when you need it. Hunting situations can change dramatically from split second to split second. Fumbling around with ammunition, trying to get them in the right order in the magazine and then remembering which one is where is an exercise that I, personally, find unsettling. When there is a wounded buffalo around, I do not wish to be unsettled.

93

Anyway, the problem with most buffalo is not over-penetration but under-penetration—soft-nosed bullets that expand too quickly and fail to get to the vitals. Factory bullets like the Winchester Silvertip are about the last thing I would want to use on Cape buffalo—in any caliber. Soft bullets get you into trouble faster than anything except lousy shooting. The answer is a good premium soft-nosed bullet that holds together and gets where it is supposed to go, while at the same time expanding to do maximum internal damage. My favorite is the Trophy Bonded Bear Claw, especially in the newer "solid shank" configuration, but Swifts are also good and the A-Square Dead Tough has established a solid record. I am sure other premium hunting bullets perform well, too, but most of my experience is with the Bear Claw. My seven-shot kill in Botswana was done with Bear Claws, and all expanded perfectly, held together, and penetrated extremely well. One travelled through two feet of spine and still retained 69 per cent of its weight! Another entered one flank and came to rest under the chest hide, a full Cape buffalo-length away. All came out perfectly mushroomed.

Bullets like these give you the virtues of a solid combined with the advantages of an expanding bullet. George Hoffman, professional hunter and developer of the .416 Hoffman, says that since Jack Carter introduced the solid shank Bear Claw bullet, he no longer bothers with solids at all because he feels they are unnecessary. The advantages of hunting with just one type of bullet cannot be overstated, and anything that simplifies things when hunting Cape buffalo is fervently to be desired.

As Tony Henley found, the legendary penetration of the .577 is no myth, and he favored big calibers and heavy bullets that penetrate evermore. I, for one, am not going to argue. I do not deny that buffalo have been killed with smaller rifles. I know of one American who hunted in South Africa with a friend of mine and knocked off something like 30 animals with 30 shots, including two Cape buffalo. He was using a .270 Weatherby with 140-grain Bear Claws. It was very impressive for all concerned, but I wouldn't try it. Too many things can go wrong and leave you trying to fend off a locomotive with a pea shooter.

Even if you have inhuman confidence in your own shooting ability, in Cape buffalo country you have to be ready for the unexpected. When Gordon Cormack and Terrell Shelley took on their buffalo, they were armed with a .375 H&H and .375 Weatherby respectively—fine cartridges but certainly the minimum for that kind of work. The last I heard, Gordon had a new .416 Rigby coming, a rifle "more suitable for close-range charges."

※

People hunt Cape buffalo for two reasons, mainly. The goal with your first buff is a good set of those wide, black, wicked horns. From then on, however, diehard buffalo hunters are looking for the experience.

By consensus, the widest horns come from Tanzania, although some big lads also come out of Zambia and northern Mozambique. The Rowland Ward minimum is now 45 inches, which is one big *mbogo*. If a listing in Rowland Ward is what you are after, then Tanzania is your best bet. But width alone, regardless of Rowland Ward, does not make a great trophy. A great Cape buffalo head has horns that dip deeply, curl, and sweep back. The bases of the horns should form a thick, wide boss over the skull, with little or no gap in the center. The world record is 60 inches plus, side to side, and today anything over 50 inches is phenomenal. Depending on where you are, though, a good trophy can range from 35 inches up. And, as I say, width is not the only criterion for a great trophy.

My first Tanzania buffalo was 43 inches wide, but when you look at the horns from above, they are straight across rather than angling back. As well, there is a wide gap in the center of the boss, indicating a youngish bull which had not reached his real potential. A fine trophy, but the one I took a few weeks later in Botswana, while not as wide, had a wider, thicker boss, a more classic shape, and longer tips. He was a really old bull.

In terms of horns, Cape buffalo reach a peak and then begin to decline: Their horns get worn down, the boss becomes smoother, and sometimes they rub one horn completely away, leaving little more than a thick skull cap. These are the bulls you find living off by themselves, what they call *dagga boys* down Zimbabwe way. Stalking the mean old *dagga boys* is the purest form of Cape buffalo hunting. An old bull living in solitary retirement has pretty much shed all his herd instincts. He no longer depends on others to be his eyes and ears and takes no comfort in numbers. Instead, he depends solely on his own strength and senses to survive lions, poachers—and you! He becomes even more wary and alert, highly attuned to the game of cat-and-mouse that constitutes this kind of hunting. This is where you gain the experience that quickly becomes, for most dedicated Cape buffalo hunters, the real addiction.

Some say Tanzania buffalo are more vicious and ready to fight than buffalo in Zimbabwe and Zambia. Robin Hurt, who has hunted *mbogo* in Kenya, Tanzania, Uganda, Botswana, Zaire, the Sudan, and the Central African Republic, says the only difference he's ever seen is the terrain, not the temperament.

"The East African buffalo has a worse reputation, but I think it's purely because of the habitat," he insists. "When a buffalo starts charging from 30 or 40 yards, as they do in the south, you have lots of time to react. When they charge from three or four yards, as they do in the thick stuff up here (Tanzania), that's no joke!"

Tony Henley said the most vicious buffalo he ever saw were in the thick forests of Kenya and Uganda, but he felt the difference in temperament was due at least partly to the herd mentality.

"In herds they behave much like cattle," he said. "Lone buffalo are more vicious no matter where they live. Another major factor is poachers. Many buff you find here (Botswana) have poachers' bullets in them, old Martini-Henrys and so on. Up in Uganda, I once had a game scout killed by a buff that had a cable snared around one leg. When the scout went to investigate, the buffalo came for him and killed him. You get so much of that kind of thing these days, I don't wander anywhere in buffalo country without a rifle— a big rifle."

A few months after his experience with Terrell Shelley, Gordon Cormack and I hunted down around Tarangire. We set out at dawn, hoping to cut a track. We found the spoor of three bulls and soon caught up to them, but they spooked before we got a shot. We lost them, but spotted a fourth bull on a hillside across a shallow ravine. Just as we started our stalk on him, we flushed a fifth bull from the long grass about 60 yards out. Just a glimpse, but enough to tell Gordon this was a big one.

I took a snap shot and wounded him. We then followed his blood trail for six long hours. At one point we thought we had caught up to him in a donga when we heard the usual thundering hooves, and we braced ourselves for an attack, but it turned out to be yet another bull. We finally lost our wounded bull when he crossed into Tarangire National Park just before dusk. The bitterness of that defeat was tempered somewhat by the knowledge that he could not have been badly wounded, because he never weakened all day, nor did he stand and fight. For action, though, that day would be hard to beat—flushing buffalo like grouse and carrying a .458 like a bird gun.

"I don't ever want to shoot another one," Robert Ruark told Harry Selby after his first Cape buffalo, and Selby replied, "You'll shoot another. You will always hunt buff. It's a disease. You've killed a lion and you don't care whether you ever take another. But you will hunt buffalo until you are dead, because there is something about them that makes intelligent people into complete idiots."

A few years ago, Robin Hurt told me much the same thing. "They are my favorite dangerous game animal," he said. "If I didn't hunt anything else, I'd still like to hunt them."

Finn Aagaard feels likewise :"I'd hunt buffalo until they buried me—and if it was a buffalo that buried me, that'd be fine, too!"

It is not the usual formula for happiness, dying of thirst and sunstroke, scraping tsetse flies out of your eyes, following a blood trail that never ends. But now, home again, I wish nothing more than to be back there with the heat and the flies, the dust and the buffalo, and a spoor in the sand that leads...where? Selby was right. It is a disease.

VENGEANCE

The border post at Namanga comes up suddenly as you climb through the heat haze from the Tsavo plain of Kenya toward the sweeping highlands around Mount Kilimanjaro. Namanga itself isn't much. A collection of ramshackle buildings, a scattering of trucks, a lopsided bus, and everywhere, like shifting flocks of tropical birds, the bright-beaded Masai in their crimson robes. There are a few trees, and under every tree in the dust is a seller of something: Beads. Pens. Pots. A few have board *duccas* thrown together—a two-foot counter fronting a one-shelf store. Those who aren't selling are begging. When they crowd around, it's hard to tell one from the other.

Years ago, every safari passed through Namanga, hot and dusty and two days out from Nairobi, heading for Arusha to draw licenses and have a cold beer at the Greek's. Nobody does that anymore. Today the safari trade is airborne; sleek six-seaters whisk you from Nairobi's Wilson Airport to Kilimanjaro in an hour; pay the bribes, pick up licenses, and continue on west by air. By sundown you're in camp with a cold one in your hand and Tommies prancing on the plain. You don't even hate the safari car. Not yet.

The border post at Namanga, deprived of the high-rent safari trade, has been reduced to shaking down busloads of package-deal tourists, who stand there looking helpless as they are deftly disencumbered of their loose belongings by the bony fingers of the crimson-clad crones who trade on their Masai appearance to ply city-bred skills. The old Africa hands avoid making eye contact, stride purposefully, and snarl *hapana* as they wade through the crowds to get their passports stamped. Sometimes it works. By the time you finally roll out of Namanga with Mount Meru looming in the distance, you truly feel you are in Tanzania—land of great beasts and grubby beggars, and more than enough of each.

When Tanzania gained its independence in 1963, the new government embraced a philosophy of crackpot socialism that over the next 30 years managed to undo what little economic progress the country had made in the last 100. On the social front, the newly minted politicians with their pseudo-Oxonian accents and Savile Row suits found their less enlightened brethren rather an embarrassment, and none more so than the Masai. The Masai, with their spears and their buffalo-hide shields, their crimson cloaks and elaborate beads, their herds of cattle and lion-mane headdresses, were great for the tourists but bad for the image of a socialized society. In quick order, the Masai had their spears confiscated, their red robes banned, and their children locked up in school. In far-off Dar es Salaam, the politicians and United Nations do-gooders congratulated each other over cool ones on the veranda and discussed whose lives they could screw up next.

For 30 years the Masai in Tanzania lived under proscription. Their entire way of life—all the things that made them Masai, and hence made life worth living—had been legislated out of existence. The old men crouched in the dust and drank beer, and the lions went unhunted.

Then came the end of the old government. Julius Nyerere, darling of the aid agencies, retired to reflect on his accomplishments, and a new crowd took over a country that had become an economic basket case. Disenchanted with socialism, they unleashed free enterprise (or tried to) and backed it up with a more or less blanket endorsement of the old ways. Not many Masai would return to their traditional way of life anyway, they reasoned. Not after 30 years. What harm can it do? And so the proscription was lifted. Announcements went out.

Within days the spears had come out of mothballs and every scrap of red cloth had been swept from the ducca shelves. The elaborate, blue and white and red beads and headdresses sprouted from every Masai head, and the school desks sat empty. The smiths on the plain stoked their forges to begin once again making the long-bladed spears and *simis*, the short swords that, together with shield and spear, announce to the world that this red-clad dandy is a blooded Masai *moran*.

It's a funny thing about Tanzania: You can pull the Land Cruiser over to the side in the middle of nowhere, with nothing in sight for miles across the plain except dust devils, and within five minutes there will be a couple of urchins crowding around the truck with their hands out. Give it a couple more minutes and there will be a half-dozen locals begging for handouts. Even if you don't pull over, when they see you coming in the distance they lock their eyes on yours and stand by the road with their arms straight out, palms upward, gaze unwavering as you roar on by, muttering. In Tanzania, begging at the personal, regional, and international level has been elevated to the status of national pastime.

But just when you think you've got that figured, you round a bend and see a Masai by the road. His hand is not out. It's holding a spear, or fingering a *simi*, and if he stares at you at all it is down his long, straight nose. The Masai—the *real* Masai, not the sheep in wolf's clothing that infest Namanga—asks nothing from anyone except to be left alone with his herds and his flocks and his lion scars.

About 20 miles south of Namanga you are in the heart of Masai country. Mount Meru looms in the distance, and on the other side lies Arusha, the metropolis of the north; but here the plain stretches away with only the occasional spiral of smoke to indicate a dwelling. Off to the southeast, Kilimanjaro drifts in and out of its constant clouds and haze. As you drive, a line of hills appears on your left, rising starkly from the plain. It is not really a line of hills, though; it is the rim of a long-extinct and worn-down volcano called Mount Longido, which rises 3,000 feet from the Masai plain.

Eroded to a stump, Longido is dwarfed by its sisters, Mount Meru and Mount Kilimanjaro, and is now little more than a high crater encircled by steep, rocky hills. The crater is several miles across and grown over with trees. The name comes from the Masai *Ol Donyo Ngito. Ngi* is a type of black rock found on the mountain, and for centuries the Masai have climbed Longido to sharpen their spears and simis on the black rocks. The highest remaining point of Mount Longido is a sheer rock pinnacle like the prow of a ship. It is usually obscured by clouds, and on the higher slopes the thick brush turns to rain forest. From the upper reaches you can see all the way to the border post at Namanga, 20 miles north, and into Kenya as far as Amboseli National Park.

There is a Masai village, also called Longido, at the base of the mountain. It consists of a few buildings, a ducca, a police post. Under the spreading acacias, two saloons grace the main drag, which is nothing more than a wide spot in the dust. One establishment is called the Lion, the other the Vatican. The Lion is the more up-scale of the two, which is to say it has a door. Right now the door to the Lion stands open and beckoning, and inside a stack of beer crates reaches to the low ceiling. The bar is a plank, and the seats are planks that run around the edge of the one small room. Two Masai moran in blinding red robes sit with a glass of ale, their spears leaning against the wall, discussing stock prices. They nod as we enter and do not stare overlong.

Ever since the army I have not been a lover of warm beer, but sometimes it isn't bad. This was one of those times. Then we continued on out of town and around the base of the volcano and into our camp, on the southern slope facing Kilimanjaro far out across the Ngasarami Plain.

❋

The plan was fairly simple. Mostly what people hunt around Longido are lesser kudu and some plains game. Sometimes they venture up the outer slope in hopes of a klipspringer, but mountain climbing in the heat is not a lot of fun, and as you get higher the going gets rougher. Like most mountains, it looks a lot easier from a distance.

Longido is shaped like a huge bowl. There are one or two passes where you can climb up over the hills and down into the crater, and in some spots these hills rise higher and higher, eventually simulating real mountain peaks, shrouded in cloud with rain forest and heavy mists. The crater is several miles across; a few Masai live up there and raise crops in the crater, carrying on a running battle with the baboons who raid from the forested hillsides. The Masai run their cattle on the hillsides as well, sharing the sparse grazing with a few dozen Cape buffalo. Rumor had it that high on Mount Longido there lurked a few buffalo bulls, too old to breed, too cantankerous to associate with, living out their lives alone. A few people had been

❋

up there and seen tracks. That was all. But they were big tracks. I had hunted Cape buffalo waist deep in swamp water and dry as dust in sand and thornbush. Why not on a mountain top?

Cape buffalo hunting today consists all too much of roaming around in a safari car. No one we knew of had ever climbed Mount Longido looking for a big old bull off by himself on a distant mountainside, but preliminary investigation suggested there might well be a good one up there if we were willing to sweat. Jerry Henderson thought that hunting such a bull would make good publicity for his new-found safari company and reminded me in his soft Texas tones that I like mountain hunting.

Sure enough, I do. And sure enough, I will. The company had a small group of very good professionals from Zimbabwe—Gordon Cormack, Duff Gifford, and a third I will just call Frank. Frank was a youngster of Afrikaner stock, and he was to be my PH when Jerry and I went off up the mountain. Jerry had dispatched him earlier to go up and look around, and Frank had returned determined that once was enough, although he did not say it in so many words. Instead, he decided the best way out was to discourage me from going up there. One conversation with Frank was enough to persuade me that I wanted no part of hunting Cape buffalo with someone I didn't trust, and it was obvious, as he lectured me on the perils of mountain hunting, that he himself did not want to go up that mountain.

"I'll go," I told Jerry. "I *want* to go. It can't be any steeper than the Chugach, or any thicker than coastal Alaska. But I ain't going with *him*."

Frank, to his relief, was out. Duff Gifford, to my relief, was in. The next morning we rolled out of camp and edged along the base of the mountain toward the winding trail up and over the hills to the Masai settlement in the crater.

Our party looked, as we made our laborious way up the mountainside, much like those porter safaris from Teddy Roosevelt's day. In addition to Duff, Jerry, and me, we had our cook and camp boy, both laden down with equipment. A couple of Masai retainers trailed along as well. Then there was the government game scout, Swai, a grinning citizen of legendary corruption who was based in Longido. By law we had to have him along; by custom he surrounded himself with his own retinue of flunkeys, including a gunbearer, a gunbearer's assistant, and who knows what all. Altogether, we had a dozen people strung out along the dry watercourse that cut through the thick brush on the mountainside and afforded the easiest route over the hills and down into the crater.

We reached the Masai huts around noon with the sun directly overhead and overbearing as only the equatorial sun can be. We flopped down under an acacia while Swai went off to negotiate with the locals. While we waited they brought us tea and maize, scorched by the fire and not half bad. When Swai returned, he brought with him three Masai to guide us. They wore their working clothes—gym shorts and spears. Ceremonial garb is fine for standing around wowing the tourists, but climbing a mountain in search of buffalo calls for something a little more practical. We divided up the baggage, formed a line, and swung on up the mountain.

To anyone accustomed to the Chugach, or any of the mountains of the American West, the going was not that hard. It was steep in places, and stony, but there were trails through the thorn brush where generations of goats and cattle and buffalo had browsed. The worst part was the heat. The sun was a physical weight on our shoulders as we struggled upwards, panting and sweating. The Masai suffered not at all, moving ever upwards in a loose, swinging gait, bare feet oblivious to rocks and thorns, bare shoulders shrugging off the sun.

Below us the Masai settlement was soon reduced to a few dots and postage-stamp fields, and we were high enough to look out across the crater. The peaks still loomed above, but the ancient volcano had lost its shape and unity, and we felt as though we were climbing among jumbled hills. There were ravines and gullies overgrown with a jungle of tangled brush. There were boulders that blocked our path as we wended our way back and forth, ever upward toward a high meadow that bordered a patch of rain forest just below the peak. There we would camp and, with luck, glass the hillsides below for a glimpse of buffalo.

We reached the meadow in late afternoon and made camp—a couple of small tents and a fire pit. Dinner was a laudable effort under the circumstances, eaten around the fire in the chill brought on by the sudden darkness of the equatorial night. Then our cook produced a precious few ounces of Scotch—barely enough for a sniff apiece, but it lent the illusion of a safari camp—and Duff and Jerry and I sat around our cheerful little blaze talking guns and buffalo and mountains.

That night was one of the coldest and most miserable I can remember. With darkness the temperature plunged and the rain came. We had no bedding—a slight mixup—and I spent the hours huddled on the damp plastic of the tent floor with the stock of my Model 70 for a pillow. I didn't know it at the time, but the sheer misery of that cold, wet night on the mountain was to prove a great benefit to us.

As soon as the sky turned grey I crawled out into a soupy mist that swirled and drifted and soaked the air as the rain had soaked the grass. Everyone was gathered around the fire, which smoked and hissed as it tried to produce enough heat to boil water. A more forlorn looking group I have never seen in a hunting camp. Swai, the game scout, huddled close to the tiny flame wrapped in an army blanket with his teeth chattering and his retainers bunched close around. Duff handed me a coffee and smiled his wolfish smile. The wet misery of the mountainside had robbed him of none of his assurance.

"Shall we go take a look?"

"In this stuff?"

"It'll clear. We want to be out there when it does."

Duff said a few words to Swai, who mumbled in response but made no move to leave the warmth of the fire.

"Is he coming?"

"Not right now. I told him we're just going to glass. No need to disturb himself." The wolfish smile again.

Duff and Jerry and I gathered our rifles and binoculars and picked our way through the grass along a ridge to a rocky promontory. The fog was shifting now, swirling gently at first, then a little stronger. Somewhere up there the sun was rising and bringing with it a breeze, and soon that breeze would become a wind and clear the fog away for good. Meanwhile, we could see little and do nothing but wait. But at least we were waiting alone.

For those who have not had the pleasure, hunting in Tanzania is, by law, a group activity. By law, you must have a game scout with you at all times. By the letter of the law, that means *all* times. No self-respecting game scout, however, goes out alone. He needs at least as many retainers as the professional hunter has, to show his equality. So if the PH has two trackers and a boy to carry the water jug, the game scout needs at least three flunkeys and preferably four. That adds up to a hunting party of ten, traipsing through the bush and scaring the wildlife.

In hunting, one is company and two is pushing it. Hunting with a cast of thousands, all arguing about what the tracks mean and debating whether we should go left or right, critiquing *bwana's* shooting and generally having a hell of a time, is not my idea of a perfect hunting scenario. If the game scout insists on coming, though, you don't have much choice.

Now we found ourselves, thanks to that blessed, wonderful, beautiful mist and rain and cold, allowed to leave camp unencumbered while Swai the Ungodly attempted to thaw himself out. And if Swai did not need to venture forth, neither did anyone else. For us, it was like being let out of school early.

The slopes of Mount Longido are cut by dozens of ravines carved by centuries of torrential rains. Some are so deep they could be called canyons, others are just dongas, but all are overgrown with vegetation and jumbled with boulders. We found a lookout and settled in, each watching a different valley. It was like being high up in an enormous stadium—or would have been but for the thick, shifting fog. We shivered and waited. A sporadic wind began to blow. The clouds came and went, clearing one minute, enveloping us the next. It was during one of these brief clear moments that I happened to catch sight of a grey-black object disappearing into some brush on a far hillside. Just a quick glimpse, and then the fog rolled back in.

"Duff, I saw one," I said, not quite sure I really had. Maybe all I had seen was a rock. But when the fog drifted away again, there was no grey rock right there. It must have been a buffalo. He had shown himself in a clearing for a split second at the precise moment a window had opened in the fog, and I just happened to have my binocular trained on the spot.

We sat and willed the fog to clear. By now it was 9: 30; the sun was well up and the rising wind made short work of what was left of the clouds. The slopes and the crater were all in plain sight, and for half an hour we studied the hillside across the valley. For Duff and Jerry, I pinpointed as best I could where I thought I had seen the buffalo disappear. There was the bare face of a large boulder just to the right of the spot. That was the only real landmark in the hodgepodge of brush. As the minutes passed, I became less and less sure. Had I really seen a buffalo? Had I really seen *anything*?

"What'd you see, exactly?"

"Just the back end, and just for a second."

"Which way was he moving?" Duff is from Zimbabwe, and his Rhodesian voice was clipped and military as he gathered information. But he seemed to have no doubts.

"Along the hillside, from left to right. About halfway up."

Half an hour went by. By that time I was almost convinced I had been hallucinating. When the buffalo did not reappear, Jerry wandered back to watch the other valley.

"I've got an idea," I said to Duff. "Let's have Jerry stay here to spot for us, and you and I go down and look for him." Duff grinned. "Sounds good to me," he said, and padded off to get Jerry.

"We'll cross straight over to the hillside and use that tree as a start line," Duff told him, pointing to a bare-trunked acacia that rose taller than the others. "When we get there, we'll work straight along toward the big boulder on the right. If you see us get off course in that thick stuff, signal. Or if you see the buffalo…"

Jerry nodded a quick assent, gave me a clap on the shoulder, and a soft Texan "Good luck." Then we dropped down the steep hillside with Duff leading. Almost immediately we came upon a scraped-out hollow. The musky urine smell of buffalo hung in the air, and we found hoof prints the size of dinner plates. "Well, we know there's one here," Duff whispered. "Big old boy, too."

We continued down along one of the bull's established trails. There was a wart hog skull under a bush and, a few feet away, one of its ivory tusks, slightly rodent-chewed. I put it in my pocket for luck.

We were across a creek bed and climbing again. Now we could look back and see Jerry perched high on the rock opposite, watching us. Through the binocular, he gave a thumb's up. We were on course and almost immediately found the bare-trunked tree. A clearing stretched along the slope in front of us, and at the far end I could just make out the big rock face.

It was approaching 10:30. The sun was high, and the air had warmed. I was sweating in my goosedown shirt. Worse, it was noisy, catching on every thorn and twig. I tore it off and stuffed it into my belt. Duff, in shorts and khaki vest, moved through the brush like a leopard, and his cropped hair and compactly muscled shoulders reinforced the image. We were edging along the clearing now, a few feet apart, communicating by signs and instinct as if we had hunted together for years.

He was watching for tracks and I was looking past his shoulder when the bull stuck his head out of the bushes about 150 yards in front of us, right beside the boulder. I hissed and pointed. We froze. The buffalo had not seen us. He swung his head from side to side, and the boss of his horns was so big it made his horns look stubby, but they were not. His boss was heavy and black and met on the top of his skull without a gap. He was, indeed, a big old boy.

The bull looked around, then slowly withdrew into his sanctuary. We breathed again and melted into the thick brush out of sight.

"He's big, he's wide," Duff whispered. "You want him?"

"I sure do."

We crawled along inside the screen of brush until we came up against a large rock, then crept back up to the clearing. We found ourselves on the edge of a deep donga jammed with a jungle of scrub.

On the other side, 60 yards away, was the rock face where we had seen the bull. This was as close as we were going to get.

"Can you shoot from here?"

I nodded, found a clear spot to sit down, jacked the scope up to four power and wrapped the sling around my arm. Just as I leaned forward the big buffalo came out again, right on cue. He seemed to be going somewhere. I put the crosshair on his shoulder and squeezed. As the .458 bucked up into my face, the bull hunched and roared and dashed down into the donga, deep into the thickest of the thick brush.

"Shoot again," Duff yelled, but there was no time, and then the bull was out of sight. We could hear him, moving around down in the donga a few yards away. Then the rustling stopped and all we heard was his breathing, heavy and rasping. We stood together on the lip of the donga, looking down into the undergrowth. I replaced the spent cartridge in the magazine of the Model 70 and turned the scope down to one. Then we waited.

"He's hard hit," Duff said. "He blew blood out his mouth as soon as you shot. Hear him?"

From the brush, the sound of heavy panting came to us. He was no more than 15 yards away, maybe less.

"Hear him? Can you hear him? He's *kuisha*," Duff said. "Finished. That was a good shot, bwana. You got him in the lungs. We'll give him ten minutes, see what happens."

We stood side by side, trying to pierce the brush with our eyes, listening to the harsh breathing, waiting for the long, drawn-out bellow that would signal the end. But the only sound from the donga was the rough grating of each painful breath, in and out, in and out, in and out.

❊

The old bull had lived alone on the mountainside for many years. There was a small herd of younger Cape buffalo up there, too, cows and calves and bulls, maybe a dozen in all, but they wanted nothing to do with him and they avoided his valley. He bedded on a slope over-

looking the crater and each day visited the creek that bubbled down the mountain, then browsed up and along his favorite hillside as he made his way toward his own special place.

There was a boulder there, and some thick acacias, and in the shadow of the boulder it was cool for him to doze through the heat of the day. On one side was a donga and a narrow trail that led down into it and back up out of it. He crossed through that donga each day. Although the brush looked as solid as a wall, with his four-foot horns he could force his way through.

On this day, as the clouds cleared (cleared as they did almost every day up here, away from the plain, away from the big buffalo herds) the old bull sensed there was something wrong. He caught a whiff of something—smoke, perhaps—but there was no smoke on the mountain; the Masai stayed down in the crater, and the smoke from their fires rarely drifted this far up.

But there was something, something; once or twice he emerged to look along his backtrail before withdrawing back into his hideaway. Finally, he decided he would climb the hill to a better vantage point. As he came out he caught it again, that scent—not leopard, not Masai—a scent he had known only once or twice before in his long life, and just as he quickened his pace he was slammed in the ribs and a tremendous roar slapped his head and a cough was forced out of his lungs by the impact of the bullet and blood sprayed from his mouth.

Involuntarily he bucked and sprang. His trail was at his feet, the familiar trail down into the donga, and he let it carry him into the friendly gloom. Once there, he paused. His head was reverberating from the crash of the rifle and he could feel his breathing becoming heavy as a huge vise tightened on his chest. From the embankment above came the murmur of voices, and his rage began to build as his lungs filled up with blood.

The bottom of the donga was a tunnel through the vegetation, scoured clean of debris when the heavy rains came. The old bull slowly walked a few yards up the creek bed, then turned and lay down facing the trail. On each side of him were high earthen banks, and over his head was a roof of solid vegetation. They would have to come down that trail. He fixed his eyes on it, six feet away. Now let them come.

And there he waited as blood spurted out the bullet hole, his heart pumping out a bit of his life with each beat. Each breath came a little shorter, and the pool of bright red blood under his muzzle spread wider, and his rage grew inside him like a spreading fire. He heard them whisper "kuisha..."Well, not just yet. And he heard them say "give him ten minutes..."Yes. Ten minutes. He was old and he was mortally wounded. But he was not dead yet. The old bull fixed his gaze on the trail and concentrated on drawing each breath, one by one, in and out, in and out.

The minutes ticked by: Three, four, seven, eight.

Duff and I waited on the bank. Only the wounded buffalo's rasping breath broke the silence on the mountainside.

"I know you want to see..." Duff whispered.

"Not me, *bwana*," I answered. "I can wait here forever."

"When you hear him bellow..." he began.

The old bull watched as the pool of blood grew and he felt himself growing weaker. Ten minutes. They weren't coming. Not much time left now. He heaved himself to his feet and a gout of blood poured from his mouth.

The bull could have eased silently down the donga and died, off by himself. But he did not want to go quietly. He wanted to take those voices with him. And since they would not come to him...

He bunched his muscles and sprang, charging up the trail. His horns plowed through the brush and shook the trees. He could not see them yet, but he was coming hard. There was not much time, and he had to reach the hated voices.

"He's moving, get ready!" Duff yelled.

We saw the brush trembling and his hoofs rocked the hillside, but we could not see the bull. Not yet. He was only yards away and moving fast, but where would he come crashing out? We couldn't see a damned thing. And then a black shape burst from the bushes five yards down and to my right.

"*Shoot!*"

I tried to get the scope on him, but all I could see was black. I fired, hoping to catch a shoulder, then worked the bolt and Duff and I fired together.

As we did, the bull turned his head toward us. His murderous expression said, "Oh, there you are!" and his body followed his head around. I was between Duff and the buffalo, and the buffalo was on top of me, and all I could see was the expanse of horn and the massive muscles of his shoulders working as he pounded in.

No time to shoulder the gun now—just point and shoot and hope for the best. I shoved the .458 in his face and fired as I jumped back, and the bull dropped like a stone with a bullet in his brain, four feet from the muzzle of the rifle.

"Shoot him again!" Duff shouted, "In the neck!"

"With pleasure," said I, weakly, and planted my last round just behind his skull.

Duff and I looked at each other.

"We're alive..!"

✳

We gave the meat to our Masai guides, and they brought the skull and cape down the mountain for us the next day. It took three hours to skin him out. They built a fire, and we roasted chunks of Cape buffalo over the flames as the skinner worked, carving off bites with our belt knives and tossing the remains to the Masai dogs. The meat was tough, but juicy and rich tasting. Duff and I ate sparingly and chewed long. If you are what you eat, we were one mean bunch of bastards when we came down off that mountain.

Then the reaction set in. For two days I did little except stay in camp, sometimes talking, but mostly just off by myself. I set up a camp chair in the shade where I could catch the breeze through the day and look out across the plain to the smoke rising off the slopes of Kilimanjaro. I had a well-worn copy of Hemingway that has travelled with me around the world, and it was then I discovered that there are times when you cannot read. Mostly I just sat and stared at Kilimanjaro in the distance, or rose and walked to the edge of our camp and looked back up the slopes of Mount Longido.

In the first split second when my buffalo burst from the bushes, I thought he was the most wonderful creature that ever lived, and when he dropped at my feet with a bullet in his brain and his eyes still open and fixed upon me, at that moment I knew a thousand times more about Cape buffalo than I had even minutes before.

✻

We were driving back into camp late one afternoon when a brightly clad Masai elder flagged us down. A roving trio of lions, two young males and female, had killed a cow that afternoon. The dead animal was in the brush, guarded by four morani who had driven them off the kill with spears. Could we help them get the cow back to their village?

By the time we got there, nosing gingerly through the brush with Duff at the wheel and me riding shotgun with my now thoroughly beloved .458, it was pitch black. Our headlights picked up a Masai, waiting for us in the bush beside the dirt track to guide us in. The Land Cruiser forced its way through and over the thorny acacias to a tiny campfire beside the dead cow and four heavily armed Masai, standing in the darkness with three hungry lions somewhere nearby.

They hauled and heaved the carcass up into the back, and Duff put the Land Cruiser in gear. As the headlights swung in an arc, they picked up three pairs of eyes in the bush not 20 yards away. The lions had not gone far. As we pulled out onto the track, we met two Masai youngsters swinging along the road, armed like their elders with tiny spears and scaled down swords, driving two donkeys ahead of them, coming to start ferrying the beef back to camp if we had not shown up. Two little boys with two little spears, driving two tiny donkeys through the darkness, with three hungry lions lying up somewhere in the bush nearby. Three hungry and bitterly disappointed lions who, to the best of our knowledge, never did get a meal that night. Standing up in the back with the .458, I suddenly felt a little foolish.

❋

The door of the Lion was still open and beckoning when we pulled into Longido the next day. Beer crates still reached to the ceiling, and the propane refrigerator was still not working. We had a beer anyway.

Three Masai in full regalia sat in the bar with their spears against the wall, drinking Tusker and discussing stock prices. We bought them a beer, and they gravely returned the favor. A few days later, bribing my way back out of the country at Namanga, a scarlet-robed native pawed at me and begged for alms, all the while proclaiming, "I am Masai!" To which I replied, "Like hell you are, bucko."

❋

Epilogue

About a year later, an envelope arrived in the mail with a Houston postmark. Inside was a newspaper clipping from The Daily Telegraph *with the headline, "Peer's Son Killed By Charging Buffalo," and the story of how Andrew Fraser, the youngest son of Lord Lovat (of World War Two commando fame) had been charged and killed while on safari near Mount Kilimanjaro.*

"Mr. Fraser shot and wounded the buffalo, but it took cover in thick bushes from where it made its charge, tossing him and causing severe injuries," it read. The clipping was dated March 17, 1994—one year to the day after our encounter on Mount Longido.

In the margin was a note: "Terry, does this sound familiar? Jerry."

❋

CORRIDA

A Short Story

They stumbled across the blood trail as they returned to the safari car. It lay in broad bright splashes on the sand, leading away at an angle from where the rest of the Cape buffalo had disappeared among the thorn trees. The trackers, neither smiling, were leading the way back across the trampled sand when there it suddenly lay like an invitation to a dance.

Selilo and Kiloran, the two trackers, whispered among themselves, and the musical Setswana was harsh and clear in the absolute stillness of a late Okavango afternoon. The professional hunter knelt by the blood and then looked up at Robert Woods with the first hint of a smile he had shown in many minutes.

"Artery."

It was a shocking red, not dark like heart blood or milkshake pink like lung, either of which it could have been given the angle of the shot.

"He's bleeding good," said Patrick. "Lots of blood."

He turned to the trackers, now silent and waiting, and spoke quickly in Setswana. Selilo turned away, taking the lead, the prerogative of the senior tracker when the chips were down.

Robert Woods slid back the bolt of his rifle, far enough to count the rounds in the magazine, far enough to ensure the fat .416 cartridge in the chamber was live, then pushed it slowly home and down and pulled the safety catch back. The dust from the stampede hung all around in the sunlight and turned the air faintly amber. It gave everything a halo—the trees, the thorn bushes, the giant abandoned anthills. The silence was loud against the background buzzing of tsetse flies. The blood trail led off across forty yards of sand and melted into the thorn bush.

Selilo was on it now, whipping a thin branch in his hand. He had plucked it from a bush when they set out to follow the herd after the first shot. All the while they were searching each thicket for the wounded bull, as the hoofbeats grew faint in the distance, Selilo

The short story "Corrida" first appeared as "The Bulls" in Gray's Sporting Journal, May, 1992.

had slowly and deliberately peeled the branch until it was a clean white wand. Now, it danced about, pointing out each splash of blood, each red smear on a leaf, reading the sign like a newspaper and pointing out the relevant passages for the benefit of the less literate.

Kiloran, the younger one, carried the shooting sticks and followed close behind. Then came Patrick, his black face opaque. He was a stranger when stripped of his smile. A stranger now. He carried his .375 across his chest like a quail gun, and Woods did the same. The .416 now seemed the merest feather as he followed, casting eyes to right, and left, and right again. Cape buffalo were known to double back on their blood trail and lie in wait for anyone who followed. Or so the tales went.

There were many tales about buffalo, and he thought he had read most of them over the course of twenty-five years. Buffalo that lay in wait for their pursuers. Buffalo that died of thirst rather than abandon hopes of vengeance. He particularly remembered the stories about buffalo that licked the skin from the feet of hunters who took refuge in not-tall-enough trees, and the hunters then bleeding to death through their flayed feet.

The other night in camp, as hunters and clients gathered around the fire, Robert Woods had asked about that legend. Tony was an old Kenya hand who had hunted and game warden-ed all over East Africa and been in on the deaths of probably a thousand buffalo, and earlier that day he and Jack had made it a thousand and one. Now Woods was startled at his reply.

"It's rubbish," he snorted. "Absolute rubbish. I don't know who wrote it first. Cloete, I suppose. Then Ruark picked it up and wrote it again. Now everybody believes it.

"Now a lion might do that. They have a rough tongue, like a house cat. But if a lion was close enough to lick you, he'd just use his teeth, wouldn't he?"

After forty years of professional hunting, Tony had a brain full of the most arcane facts about animals, all of them learned first-hand. With all that knowledge crammed in, there seemed to be no room left for patience. Still, he was eager to share what he knew.

"There's a lot of claptrap about buffalo. Writers try to make them worse than they are. And you know what? They don't need it. They're jolly well bad enough. They don't need embellishing.

"Malibuko! *Chakula!*" he roared, using Swahili from long habit, and soon they were seated around the long safari table by the edge of the swamp. The hissing Coleman in the tree cast lengthy shadows across the white tablecloth as the steward appeared with a smoking tureen of Cape buffalo tail soup.

"Now you'll taste something right fine, Outlaw," said Jack, smiling his old Texan hunter smile. "There's two parts of a buff fit to eat, one at each end. The tail makes the best soup you'll ever taste. The tongue's the other good part. You eat that boiled and sliced cold with mustard. The rest of it, why, just cut it up and dry it for…what's that you call jerky over here…?"

"Biltong."

"…biltong, right. Dryin' it can't make it any tougher than it already is. When you get as old as Tony and me, you know you have to get your buff early so you can have some soup and give the cook time to boil that tongue tender. Now we'll be in camp for lunch tomorrow enjoying that tongue while you young fellas are wearing yourselves out chasing buffalo and living off sardines and swamp water."

Robert Woods could still taste the rich curry bite of the soup and see the shimmer of butter on its surface where he had dipped his bread, coarse and white and still steaming from the Dutch oven it was produced from every magical day. And the next day, when Patrick and Robert had found themselves back in camp nursing a bad clutch, they had all eaten the buffalo tongue for lunch under the shade of the giant ebony trees that ringed the swamp in front of their camp.

It came sliced cold on a platter, ovals of delicate brown meat, slightly pink in the centre, with Colman's mustard and chilled pickles and white bread whose oven warmth melted the squares of icy butter. Robert could not imagine that anything so tender could ever have given rise to such a legend. But of course, the tongue had been boiled for twenty-four hours to get the skin off, so maybe it was possible.

Now, on the blood trail of his own Cape buffalo—a day or

a decade later, he hardly knew which—he was not thinking of the rough tongues of buffalo, nor of steaming soup made from their tails. He was not even thinking of how tough they were. There was only the possibility of buffalo ambush, the immediate prospect he was being asked, for the first time, to deal with.

In any direction, he could see a clear twenty yards, and a further unclear twenty yards, and beyond that a darkening snarl of brush and branches. He studied the base of each thorn bush in turn, looking for the ground, seeking to assure himself that no bulky black mass lay in the tangle. Right, then left, then right again, his head swivelled in a rhythm, his feet feeling their way along as he tried to look in eight directions at once.

His swinging eyes took in the moving backs of the men in front—Selilo crouched low, his eyes on the ground reading the blood and the tracks, the wand flicking to each in turn. And then the second tracker, almost as low, noting the pointed messages and casting frequently up over Selilo's head, anticipating where the blood trail would lead and looking for black bulk in the bush ahead. And then Patrick, the old-young Sandhurst-graduated professional soldier turned professional hunter, whose eyes took in the blood and the wand but mostly concentrated on the bush in front and on both sides, anticipating what might happen at every moment in a situation which was evolving with all the tragic certainty and ponderous inevitability and glorious artistry of a bullfight gone wrong.

Robert Woods had taken his wife to such a *corrida* once, in Madrid at Los Ventos, when the bull cornered a picador against the *barrera* right below them and threw the horse. The picador tumbled over the barricade as the horse landed on its side, tangled in the stained and bloody protective armor it was forced to wear out of deference to the humanitarians, but which only condemned it to die a slower death from internal injuries, and the bull gored it as it lay on its side with its back wedged against the barrera and its unprotected belly exposed to the ivory-tipped horn.

"Not the horse oh not the horse," his wife cried out as the matador and the other, waiting matadors rushed in to draw the bull away, and the horse was hauled to his feet. The filthy rag bound around his eyes to blind him had come askew and long tendrils of saliva dripped from his mouth as he stood heaving and the picador clambered back on. Sawdust from the ring clung to the saliva and his lower jaw quivered and beneath the blindfold you could feel the eyes roll.

But that was early on. With the last bull of the day, the matador positioned himself directly in front of the *tendido* of the *aficionados* and took the bull *recibir*, the old way, the dangerous way, standing firm as the bull charged and going in over the horn, laying it all on the line with no way out if any slightest thing went wrong. But the sword slid in easily and well as the bull charged and the bullring erupted with flowers and that and the horse were all that Robert Woods really remembered of that Second of May in Madrid.

"He stumbled here," Patrick said, pointing to a broad splash of blood along a fallen log. "He's weakening."

Woods looked at his watch. Twenty minutes since they had picked up the blood trail; thirty minutes since he fired the shot which set everything in motion. The blood no longer stood out bright red, but sprawled in darkening rusty splotches, becoming crystalline at the edges, turning black in the sun.

"Where's he hit, damn it?"

"I don't know. That's artery blood, all right. He should have been down by now. He's gone a good half mile. That's a lot of blood. But they can go for miles even with half their heart shot away."

There was blood on the leaves of the bushes they passed, blood as high as their thighs. The bull wasn't just losing it, he was throwing it.

Over and over, Woods replayed the shot in the back of his mind, trying to recall the exact position of the crosshairs at the precise moment the big .416 had exploded and bucked up into his face. Behind the frontal lobes of concentration, he reviewed the scene searching for clues. He ran the film forward, stopped, backed it up, ran it forward again in slow motion. Stop. Rewind. Forward.

Over and over, he saw the bull as he had stood behind the screen of thorns, almost square on with other buffalo on each side and his head lowered. Between the head and the left shoulder there had been one small square of black hide, visible through the branches. In the centre of that square, beneath the inch-thick skin, lay the buffalo's heart and lungs and shoulder. And with the rifle wedged firmly into the cleft of the shooting sticks, leaning into it, bearing down with his left hand, centering the crosshairs on that square, deep breath, exhale, crosshairs there, almost there, there...now!

The rifle reared back and the dust from hundreds of hooves had appeared in the air as if by magic.

This was always the first indication of a buffalo stampede, seen long before you heard the sound of the hooves themselves. It had become all too familiar during his three days of buffalo hunting—the dust, the sound, the movement, and then nothing but empty thornbush and the prospect of another long walk beneath the Botswana sun with the sand sucking at your feet.

Their routine had become a ritual, too. Each day, they left camp before sunrise, driving out around the swamp and on toward the expanse of water where the buffalo drank at night. In the morning, early, the buffalo retreated into the bush, working their way steadily until they were miles from the water, deep in the thorns. Then, they would lie up during the heat of the day and slowly work their way back at dusk to water once again throughout the night.

Patrick's strategy was to find the fresh tracks across the makeshift road, leave the safari car and trail them on foot, Selilo leading, then the younger tracker, then Robert Woods, then Patrick. Following the fresh impressions in the sand, they crept through the thornbush, looking for the first telltale horizontal black line that said "buffalo." The sand was covered with crisp yellow raintree leaves that crunched beneath their feet, and with inch-long thorns that embedded themselves in the soles of their boots and in their knees and elbows as they crawled. On his belly, Woods could see the tiny raintree flowers like amethyst tears scattered on the ground, and see the drops of sweat evaporate as fast as they hit the sand, and smell the lingering buffalo smell of heat and dust and dung.

The first morning they had come up on the buffalo quickly, a few hundred yards in. Then, the trick was to pick out a good bull— a bull good enough to shoot—and then get a shot at that bull—a bull that was black as all the others were black, that wore horns as all the others wore horns, and which constantly changed places with others in the herd as they absentmindedly browsed in the early morning sun behind the protective, confusing screen of branches and leaves and grass.

And then a buffalo would see them, or see a movement, or the wind would change and carry their scent, or one would smell lion, and they would be gone. First, the cloud of dust thrown up, then the shaking of the ground, and finally the sound of the stampeding hooves would carry to them, and there would be only empty brush again. And they would slowly stand up and look at each other and set out once again in pursuit.

After the first time it became more difficult. The buffalo, once spooked, became defensive and wary. They set out flank guards, old cows and useless bulls who would run at the sight or sound or scent of them and send the others crashing off.

This went on until almost midday when, dusty-sweaty-itchy under the overbearing sun, they stood and listened for the final uncountable time to the hooves fading in the distance.

"It's no good," Patrick said. "They know we're here. They're spooking at anything."

The younger tracker offered Woods the water bottle and he gulped it down. The water was hot. It scalded like tea and did little for his thirst. They turned and started back. Two hours later, with the entire weight of the sun on his neck and his rifle barrel too hot to touch, they reached the safari car and Woods lurched down beside it in a gulf of nausea.

"Better wear a hat tomorrow," Patrick said.

They drank water from the big reservoir in the car, water faintly reminiscent of gasoline, but delicious in its cool wetness; they drank it down greedily, and drops rolled down their chins and onto their shirts. Then they ate lunch from the cooler, cold impala chops and pickles, hard cheese and mustard, bubbly cold mineral water and the wonderful bread with rock-hard butter from the green plastic dish. And then they dozed through the early afternoon, sprawled on the anthill in the shade of the raintrees, soothed by the buzzing of tsetse flies as the sun made its stately way across the top of the sky.

Finally, they roamed in the car looking for stray buffalo until late afternoon, when Patrick turned back to camp although the sun was still shootably high.

"There's only half an hour of good light left," he said. "It goes quickly when it goes. You don't want to trail a wounded buffalo in the dark."

The second day was a repeat of the first, and the third a repeat of the second. Cross the trail, stalk to catch up, watch as they spook, trail some more, watch as they spook quicker, and quicker, and quicker, and then turn back to the car with the sun high and six miles of thorn-strewn sand between them and the car and its treasure of water that tasted like petrol. After a while, with the sameness and the tension and the sun beating down, the hours and days swam together to become a never-ending succession of failed stalks and nagging thirst, with all the past and all the future running together in a long tunnel with no end.

Sometimes, Robert Woods would slip into a kind of heat trance. His mind would wander into the past as he slogged along mechanically behind Selilo and Kiloran, who seemed always to know where they were and never to suffer thirst or fatigue.

Only the car was a respite, as they drove through the afternoon when luck was more important than technique, and it was only by chance that you might come across a buffalo. The afternoon of the third day they cruised at Selilo's insistence, although Patrick put little faith in finding a good buff any time except in the morning.

As they nosed through bush with the trackers spotting up top, there was an insistent light tap and some urgent whispered Setswana, and Patrick looked at Robert Woods unsmilingly and said "Out. Load."

And that time, for once, it had all gone like clockwork—the stalk, using an anthill for cover, stepping out and setting up the shooting sticks at seventy-five yards, Patrick bracing them with his left hand while Robert Woods settled the fore-end in the 'Y' and held on the bull as best he could and finally, unforgivably, yanking the trigger.

So now here they were, on foot in the sand yet again. Only this time, it was not empty thornbush ahead of them. This time, it was a wounded bull.

As the herd evaporated into the bush, Patrick had gathered up the shooting sticks and dashed forward, searching for the exact spot the bull had been standing, and Woods followed, one round in the chamber and another in the magazine. He had a sick feeling in his stomach. The shot was not right. He wasn't even sure he'd hit it. Seventy-five yards. A ton of black beast. A firm rest, a good rifle and a standing shot. No one could miss. But Woods was almost sure he had.

The trackers did not look at him as they ran abreast of Patrick. This was their *shauri* now. His ended when he pulled the trigger and the buffalo had not gone down.

Patrick found the first blood, a few drops in the sand, a scattering of rubies that could as easily have not been found. A few drops in a line that ended in the churned-up sand where scores of hooves had fallen in the minute or so since the shot was fired.

"He went right into the centre of the herd," Patrick said tightly. "I saw him turn. He's hit. He turned and headed right into the middle of them."

The broad trail of hoofprints sprawled away into the brush, overhung by a cloud of fine dust, the talcum of centuries of pulverizing by millions of hooves.

Slowly, they followed along behind the dust cloud, adding their footprints to those of the buffalo. After a few hundred yards, their steps petered out and they stood, looking off into the distance.

The younger tracker chewed on a stalk of grass and kicked at the sand. Selilo slowly pulled another ribbon of bark from his switch. Neither looked at Robert Woods.

"Let's get the car," Patrick said. "We'll drive around slowly, see if we can pick them up. If he's hit bad, we should be able to spot him."

"What about looking for a blood trail?" Woods had asked.

"There won't be a blood trail. Not in the middle of a herd of stampeding buffalo. He went right into the centre, I saw him,"

Patrick said. And then, more quietly, "We've got a couple of hours. We should be able to pick him up."

Robert Woods opened the bolt of his rifle and pressed a second cartridge into the magazine. He closed the bolt on a third, and they trudged back over the hot sand toward the car. Nobody spoke.

And then suddenly, unexpectedly, no longer expected, like a long overdue letter from the only person you'll ever love, there was the blood trail.

In broad red splashes it led away from the herd's line of retreat at a deliberate angle.

The bull was parting from the others, separating his life from theirs.

He was no longer like them or even of them. He was no longer a wild ox, bovine in unwounded live-and-let-live complacency. He was now what the Spaniards called a *"toro de lidia."* He was that terrible creature of legend: A wounded Cape buffalo bull. And this trail of blood was the summons to join him for the *tercio del muerte.*

Robert's wife had not liked the bullfight in Madrid. She hadn't liked it about the horses, and even the patient explanations of the Colombian *aficionado* who sat on the other side of her and sacrificed the enjoyment of his long anticipated *Maio 2 corrida* attempting to explain the theory and the artistry and the tragedy had not changed that. Afterwards, when they went to drink sherry from stemmed glasses and talk in the smoky *bodega* of the wonder of the recibir, that "most difficult, dangerous and emotional way to kill bulls, rarely seen in modern times," a feat which even Hemingway himself saw executed only three times in three hundred bullfights, she sat in silence.

She hated hunting, too, Robert recalled, and they finally agreed simply not to discuss it anymore. She still ate the meat, but she avoided the heads and the hides and the horns, even though they hung mostly in his office away from the rest of the house.

And then came Africa, and that was wrong, too, and he got on the plane alone and the English steward suggested that he looked like a man who needed a drink and he said yes, he needed many, and the steward said, as soon as we take off, and he'd been as good as his word and Robert Woods had emerged into the early London morning viewing the world with diamond clarity through a crushing hangover.

But none of that entered the front of his mind now, because it was concentrating wonderfully on what was at hand, and what was at hand was the *ultimo*—the ultimo for the wounded buffalo, and for Robert Woods, the long awaited and long dreaded and long wondered about moment, twenty-five years' worth of wondering what might happen.

Patrick's hand shot up in front of his face and Woods froze. The trackers were motionless, Selilo peering through a tunnel of thorns. His hand came up a fraction and his finger curled. Patrick's bent slightly in response, drawing Woods forward. The professional's hand settled on his shoulder and drew him in.

"He's there," he breathed. "About fifty yards. Shoot quickly."

And then the hand propelled Woods up behind Selilo, and he peered over his head and into the brush.

The buffalo was facing directly away. He had no idea they were there. He was standing utterly motionless.

"Shoot," Selilo barely breathed. "Shoot now."

Woods brought the rifle up and let the crosshairs settle at the root of the tail and squeezed the trigger. He felt nothing and heard nothing as the bull's back end collapsed as if his feet had been pulled out from under him.

"Shoot again!"

The bull was still up on his front legs, his black body tossing from side to side, bellowing to bring down the gods. Again, the .416 crashed—or should have, Woods heard no sound but the roaring—and again.

The bull was still up, still tossing, as if his hind quarters were nailed to the ground and he was trying to jerk them free. Woods worked around to the side, fumbling with more cartridges. A jam. A curse. Shake it free, drive it in, aim for the shoulder, shoot. Behind him, he heard snatches of shouting in Setswana as he worked out to the side and closer to the bull, convinced that each shot must, must, *must* be the last.

A fifth shot and a sixth. Puffs of dust smacked from the bull's shoulder as the bullets hit. The great head sank slowly, then up a bit and tossed, then down again, always bellowing, until the chin reached the ground, his left eye still fixed on Robert Woods twenty yards to his side as he made one last supreme effort to get at him, one last lunge, and then his head settled and the moan expired into the dust.

Woods fired the seventh shot directly into the shoulder and that shot he heard and felt and he knew then that it was over. Patrick came up behind him and they sat for long minutes, watching the bull.

"They wanted me to shoot too, but I said no. You anchored him. He wasn't going anywhere."

"Thank you."

The trackers squatted beside them. Finally, Patrick said a few words and they carefully moved in. But the bull was well dead. He did not stir as Selilo reached out gently with his white switch and touched the open eye.

The sun was settling quickly now, and Robert Woods sat beneath a tree.

He had his back against the trunk, and was nibbling at a last, hoarded can of beer. It was still cool from the chopbox, and sweated gently in his hand. The froth bubbled up and ran down the sides and he carefully licked it away. He watched the vultures circle and settle into the treetops around them as the trackers worked at getting the skin off.

The first shot, the wounding shot, he had pulled badly. It missed the chest and would have missed the buffalo completely, but he was at a slight angle and the bullet caught his hind leg and smashed the bone and the artery with it. Artery blood. But his second shot, the spine shot that anchored him, that shot had been perfect at the base of the tail. And that made up for it. That shot he would remember. He had not killed the bull recibir, but it could have turned out that way. The edge of the can felt cool on his lips and the froth was deliciously bitter in his mouth.

The vultures drifted in until the trees around were heavy with obscene feathered blossoms. The sun was low now. Sunlight streamed through the trees and the air glowed with the warm lazy light of afternoon, refracted by the dust particles and turning it into golden unreality. All his life he had chased rainbows and....he wondered what it would be like to see this country with someone you loved above all things, and to have that person love it as you did.

It would be dark when they got into camp. He could see it now, the red campfire glowing and flickering across the swamp.

They would see it when they were still half a mile out, where the road touched the edge of the swamp before it swung back into the bush to come in from the other side. The dining table was set up in the open in front of the mess tent. As they ate breakfast in the morning, they could look out at the expanse of knee-deep water which always held herds of lechwe and tsessebe, sable and impala. Across the swamp, too, they could see where the road emerged briefly from the bush. And it was here that, at night, coming back into camp, they looked across the swamp from the east and saw the red welcoming campfire.

Robert Woods could see it already, although the sun was not yet down. He could see the campfire, and he could picture Jack sitting beside it, leaning back in one of the canvas camp chairs cradling the first good whisky, waiting for them to come in.

Jack always came to the safari car when it stopped behind the mess tent. He came to see what they had shot, to congratulate or commiserate in his low, slow Texas drawl, saying, "Well, now, how'd y'all do, Outlaw?"

And you couldn't stop smiling as you walked around to look at what was in the back, and he would hand you the first magnificent dust-cutting Scotch over ice that nothing had ever before tasted like.

And then you would go and collapse into the canvas chairs around the fire with everyone talking at once, a little too fast and a little too loud and laughing all the time, gulping your drink and calling for a second, and then asking for water to be heated for the shower in the enclosure behind your tent, and waiting for the quiet announcement that your bath was ready, and you would take the rest of the second whisky off with you through the darkness to your tent with its kerosene lantern and clean clothes already laid out on the bed, fresh smelling and still warm from ironing.

And later you would dress, deliberately and luxuriously by lantern light. You would push your feet into clean woolly socks and slippers and carefully comb your still-damp hair and pad back to the campfire, and there you would have another tall Scotch with big chunks of ice, and the main pleasure of that would be recalling the memory of the first.

He could see it and hear it and feel it and smell it, the blazing, smoking campfire and the jolting safari car and the burnt smoke smell of Africa; a good Cape buffalo in the back and everyone a hero again because no matter how it started out the final act had gone according to the script.

Robert Woods watched as the horns with the huge boss were manhandled into the back of the safari car, and he could see the campfire already off in the distance and feel the dust in the sweat on his forehead. He raised the can, and it felt cool on his lips.

"The hell with her," he thought. And then aloud, "The hell with her."

A SUDDEN SILENCE

A Short Story

*Sometimes it is not what happens
so much as what happens afterwards.*

The buffalo came in a rush of heaving shoulders, out of the thicket, head up, hunting. The bullets struck and his body followed his head around and down on top of me.

The bolt worked on its own, firing, ejecting, firing again as the buffalo came on with our eyes locked, and part of me loved him as the other part worked the rifle in a concentration of conscious effort and subconscious analysis, counting down the shots remaining...*three, two, one*...

We cut strips from his loins and blackened them over a fire as the skinners worked. The meat was rubbery-fresh and juicy, and we chewed and chewed and chewed in the silence that persisted in spite of the chattering voices and the breeze ruffling the trees.

Then a part of me withdrew. I would sit in camp and look out across the plain to the smoke rising from the lower slopes of Kilimanjaro. They were burning off the grass and the smoke mingled with the clouds that shrouded the peak. I stared at it for hours at a time. Sometimes I would walk to the edge of camp and look back up the mountain where the Cape buffalo had died with his eyes still fixed on me, muzzle to muzzle with my rifle. Then my other self returned, haggard but intact. It was very quiet in that camp, I remember. That part of it lasted two or three days.

3

✳

A Patch of Red

Ask a hunter to name the greatest trophy in Africa today and you will probably hear lion, or greater kudu, or perhaps elephant. He would be wrong. It is none of the three. Nor is it the elusive nyala, the ghostly leopard, or the fearsome Cape buffalo. The most sought-after trophy in the Dark Continent in 1998 is a spiral-horned resident of the deepest, darkest parts of Deepest Darkest. It is known by its Fanti name—*bongo*—and it has driven more hunters to the brink than all the greater kudu since Hemingway stepped ashore in Mombasa more than 60 years ago. The bongo is to African game what a 40-year-old single-malt Scotch is to whisky—expensive, and very, *very* hard to come by. But he is an acquired taste that, once acquired, seems to be slaked only by more of the same.

The bongo is known to science as *Tragelaphus eurycerus*. It is the size of a bull elk, the color of a red fox with vertical white stripes, and dwells in the thickest, most horrible, nerve-wracking, depression-inducing rain forest, jungle, or swamp that it can find.

✳

There are two races—the western bongo and the eastern (or Kenya) bongo. The western was discovered first and brought to the attention of scientists by the explorer and gorilla hunter, Paul Du Chaillu, who took some of the colorful skins back to Paris in the 1860s. Du Chaillu called his discovery the "broad-horned antelope" but the name never stuck. Others called it *bongo*, and bongo it remains. The eastern race, known to exist only in the highlands of Kenya, was discovered later, around 1909.

For many years, most of the bongo-hunting stories that lent the animal its mystique took place in the gloomy, wet, bamboo forests on the upper slopes of Mount Kenya, and in the Aberdare Mountains. Hunting the bongo under those conditions—upper growth that was impenetrable to sunlight, undergrowth impenetrable to man, and throughout it all a steady, drizzling rain—was a nightmare. Rare was the man with two bongo trophies, as most came back determined never to hunt bongo again.

The western race, on the other hand, lives not in the cold and wet highlands but in the hot, wet, low country of central Africa. Its range begins in the "White Man's Grave" of Sierra Leone, stretches 3,000 miles east to the southern Sudan, and includes the steaming swamps of the Moyen Congo, the forests of Cameroon, and the dreary brush of the Central African Republic, where midday temperatures can reach 125 degrees.

The bongo is one branch of a large family of spiral-horned antelope that includes the mountain nyala of Ethiopia, the nyala of Zululand, the sitatunga of the deep swamps, the bushbuck of the dark forest glades, and the greater kudu of almost everywhere. Of the bunch, however, the bongo is regarded as the greatest. Not only is it the most difficult to hunt, it is widely available and its numbers are holding their own in their traditional habitat without resorting to game ranching. The bongo is a worthy opponent for the best of hunters and will test you physically, mentally and morally.

At one time, Kenya was the most popular destination for North American bongo hunters. It had the safari industry out of Nairobi, it had the best-known professional hunters, and English was the spoken language. Few but the most ardent went to French-speaking central Africa. With Kenya closed to big game hunting since 1977, central Africa is today the only choice, and more and more countries are trying to attract bongo hunters and their (large) fistfuls of hard currency.

You can now hunt bongo in the Central African Republic, Cameroon, Congo Brazzaville, and a number of smaller west African countries. The price of a two-week bongo hunt begins at around $30,000, which puts it in a realm with even the most luxurious East African safari. But bongo hunting is, most assuredly, not luxurious.

After Kenya closed, the East African safari companies looked around for other places to hunt bongo, and most of them settled on the southern Sudan. It was familiar to them, accessible by road, offered a number of game animals not available elsewhere, such as various bushbuck and the Mrs. Gray's lechwe, and for one brief period, it was free of civil war. It is in the Sudan that this story really begins.

※

THE SUÉ BONGO

Robin Hurt is regarded by many as the greatest professional hunter of the modern era. Certainly, if you measure greatness by the number of animals his clients have placed high in the record book, Hurt has a legitimate claim. There is hardly a species under which you do not see his name, either as guide or as hunter, for unlike many of his colleagues, Robin Hurt is also a dedicated trophy hunter in his own right.

After a hard season guiding the rich and famous, Hurt's idea of relaxation is to spend three or four weeks hunting bongo in the central African thickets. He has one Kenya bongo to his credit, taken in the early 1970s, and several western bongo shot over the past 20 years.

Like most safari operators in East Africa, Hurt's company was forced to look far afield for hunting grounds when Tanzania

※

closed hunting in 1974, and Kenya followed suit two years later. Tanzania remained closed for ten years, but during that time the southern Sudan was free of civil war, and there Hurt established his company. Meanwhile, the Zaire government jealously eyed the revenue that was forthcoming from trophy hunting and, in the early 1980s, invited a number of professional hunters to extend their operations to that country as well, including Robin Hurt Safaris. These companies invested hundreds of thousands of dollars in equipment, moved it overland, and established safari camps across northeastern Zaire. Access was long and hard—poor roads across northern Uganda that crossed into Zaire at remote border posts, connecting with even poorer roads in a territory that has been isolated since the Belgians left and the *simba* terrorist movement died away. But the effort, it seemed, would be worth it. Zaire offered a number of species not found elsewhere, most notably the forest elephant, and it was generally believed there were some awesome tuskers to be found there.

In 1984, Jesus Yuren, a noted Mexican big game hunter, booked a hunt with Hurt to pursue the huge Zaire elephant. There were to be two hunters—Yuren and his friend Tony Riveira—and two professionals, Robin Hurt and his alter-ego, Danny McCallum. They flew into one of Hurt's camps in Zaire, and set off hunting.

The first day out, they struck gold: The tracks of a big old bull with tusks so long they ploughed a trail in the dust. With their hopes soaring, they began the long slog in the sun that is classic elephant hunting. Then disaster struck. A light plane flew in low overhead and set down at their bush airstrip. Since they were, as Robin Hurt puts it, "really in the middle of nowhere," there could be only one reason for a plane to come in. Figuring it bore an emergency message of some kind, they broke off the chase and returned to camp. There was, indeed, a message: Zaire had abruptly closed all hunting, and the safari companies had just 48 hours to pack their gear and get out of the country. The safari operations had interfered with the poaching activities of the locals, and the chiefs had prevailed on President Mobutu Sese Seko to put a stop to them. Zaire's experiment with safaris came to a sudden halt. Now the companies had to try, somehow, to rescue a bit of their investment.

It was an obviously impossible task. Distances were long, roads were bad, and there were swollen rivers in between and not nearly enough vehicles. What was worse, Hurt had a big-money, prepaid safari and nowhere to hunt. He was faced with the prospect of a huge loss of investment along with the need to refund a large chunk of cash to Yuren and Riveira.

Knowing he and McCallum could do little to help get the camps out of Zaire, Hurt left that task to a pair of junior hunters who were the camp managers, and began looking for a way to salvage Yuren's safari. The Sudan border was within a few days' drive; he suggested they repair there and look for a big elephant. Yuren agreed.

When they reached the southern Sudan, however, another shock awaited them. Poaching had been heavy, and everywhere they looked they saw carcasses of elephant with the tusks hacked away. The smell of rotting flesh filled the air, and the sight of so much wanton slaughter sickened the hunters. Feeling they could not, in all conscience, add to the elephants' problems by trophy hunting, the safari was once more at risk. Desperate to offer an alternative, Hurt suggested that since they were in prime bongo country, why not try for a trophy bongo instead? Again, Yuren and Riviera agreed to the change in plans.

At that time, Hurt's company had been hunting bongo in the southern Sudan for 11 years, and his group of professional hunters—McCallum, Franz Coupé, and Roy and Mike Carr-Hartley— were, as a group, the preeminent bongo hunters in Africa. The bongo were secretive, shy, and elusive, but there was little about bongo hunting they did not know.

The traditional method of hunting bongo is to look for a track, get on it, and stay on it, creeping through the undergrowth, desperately looking for a small patch of reddish hide at which to shoot. Hurt & Co. developed new methods. One was to conduct drives with native beaters through patches of brush where they believed a bongo might be lying up. The prelude to such a drive was classic bongo hunting—following tracks for mile after mile under a broiling sun. It was only when you thought you had come up close to the animal that you attempted a drive, and then it was, Hurt says, a tremendously exciting way to hunt. You never knew what was going to come boiling out of the bush.

"One time we flushed a very angry leopard," he said, "and another time one of the trackers was almost trampled by an elephant. My own tracker, Laboso, was bowled over by a yellow-backed duiker, of all things. You just never knew!"

In their collective 11 years, Hurt's bongo-hunting team had taken 104 bongo bulls out of the area, a phenomenal record that is unlikely ever to be rivalled. And now the Yuren safari was in the Yambio region on the Sué River, in the heart of bongo country.

The first thing was to find some sign. The locals reported a good-sized herd in the neighborhood, and the next morning they found fresh tracks. Hurt, Yuren, and Riveira began the pursuit and continued throughout the morning and into the afternoon. Late in the day, as the sun was sinking, they came up on the bongo herd feeding in a patch of dense forest. The brush was so thick they could see nothing, although they could hear the animals moving about and browsing. Bongo are very noisy when they feed, using their horns to pull branches down and break them so they can reach the leaves and shoots. The hunters waited patiently, listening to bongo sounds around them, creeping an inch at a time and waiting for an opening. Finally, they came to a tiny glade covered in new shoots. Hoping the bongo would eventually feed out into the open, they settled in as the shadows lengthened.

One by one, the bongo appeared inside the screen of brush and stepped gingerly into the clearing. Yuren motioned that Riveira should have the first shot—a very sporting gesture under the circumstances—and Hurt, Riveira, and Laboso crawled on their stomachs to within 30 yards of the feeding animals. Hurt spotted a larger, darker shape, screened by trees; when he stepped into the open, Riveira fired.

The bongo scattered, but the bull was obviously well hit. The hunters raced after him, and as they did so, out of the corner of his eye Hurt saw another form, even larger and even darker, still back in the trees. It was huge bongo bull, the largest he had ever seen. And then the bull was gone.

They pounded on after the stricken bull, picked up his blood trail, and found him dead just inside the trees as darkness cloaked the forest. It should have been a moment of triumph, and for Tony Riveira it was, but Robin Hurt had seen the big, *big* bull, the *huge* bull, and the image haunted him as they sat that night around the campfire, celebrating the victory.

"Never had I seen a bull like that," Hurt told me many years later. "He was huge, and his horns were enormous—much larger than anything I had ever seen before."

All that night, Hurt lay awake in his tent, thinking about

the monster bull and the flashing glimpse of his magnificent horns. The next morning, Hurt and Yuren decided they would hunt that bull, and that bull only, for the rest of the safari or as long as it took. If it meant that in the end Jesus Yuren went home empty-handed, well, so be it. But it would be the big Sué bull or nothing.

In *African Hunter*, James Mellon writes about hunting one particular greater kudu bull in Tanganyika. He draws differences, grades if you will, in trophy hunting. The first level is seeking a good, representative head; then there is seeking a truly magnificent head, one that will place high in the record book, and settling for nothing less. And then there is a third level. On that level, you hunt one particular animal, an old and wise beast that has eluded all other hunters throughout his long life. You learn his habits, you haunt his haunts, you imprint his hoofmarks on your mind like a signature. No other of his kind, no matter how large, will tempt you. And the pursuit becomes, like Captain Ahab and Moby Dick, an obsession. It is another level of trophy hunting altogether. This was the mission that Robin Hurt and Jesus Yuren set for themselves: to find the bull they now referred to as "the Sué bongo."

It was not going to be easy. Everyone knew that from the outset. The group had been extremely lucky finding the herd the first day and collecting the other bull. Sudan bongo, like their brethren in Kenya, have a survivalist habit that serves them well. That is, they are almost devoid of curiosity. They hear a noise, they depart. They don't know what you are, and they don't care. Startled, frightened, alerted, they leave the country and they don't look back.

The Sué bongo's herd had not been just startled; they had been shot at and one of their number had died. It was reasonable to assume they would put many miles between themselves and the death-dealing hunters. What was worse, overnight a steady pounding rain had washed away all sign. They did not even have the option of picking up the tracks and hoping they could cover enough miles to come up on them again. They were now looking at an absolutely clean slate, hundreds of square miles of brush and forest, and one bongo bull that could be anywhere. Doggedly they set out to comb the territory, hoping for the one chance in a million that they would cross a track, and that track would give them the thread.

For two weeks they searched. For two weeks they followed up each set of bongo tracks they came across. For two weeks they observed bongo cows and bulls and yearlings. They studied how they moved, quiet and graceful in the thickest brush, seemingly awkward when caught in the open, and how their gaudy white-striped fox-red coloring actually blended so uncannily with the deepest bush and rendered them invisible. Every day for two weeks they were out before dawn and dragged themselves back to camp after dark, only to rise and go out the next day to do it all again. They covered, Hurt says, vast distances, vast areas, but they found no trace of the Sué bongo. It was as if he and his herd had vanished from the face of the earth. "It was enormously discouraging," Hurt said. "Where could they have gone? There was nothing we could do but keep looking, and hope."

At the end of two weeks, with time now becoming a factor, they returned to camp one afternoon as rain clouds gathered once again. It rained throughout the night, washing the earth, cleaning the slate. In the early hours, Robin Hurt awoke and had a premonition. That morning they set out in the sparkling dawn and headed directly for the forest, and the glade, where they had first glimpsed the big bull two weeks earlier. And there, in the rain-washed earth of the burned-over glade, they found bongo tracks. Not just any bongo. *The* bongo.

"The tracks were extremely fresh—maybe minutes old," Hurt said. "I could hardly stand still, I was so excited. They were somewhere very close to us. Then I realized that it was still not going to be easy. The tracks led into some extremely dense forest. Tracking them through that, and coming up close enough for a shot without spooking them, well..."

As it turned out, the tracking itself was not difficult. The rain-softened earth made easy reading. But the forest, a maze of creepers and vines, made the going difficult indeed. Slowly they crept. Hurt always carries a pair of small clippers when hunting bongo, to cut vines out of the way. He needed them that day.

By midday they were deep in the forest. The sun was high

and it was hot; they knew the bongo would be lying up in the deepest shade they could find. It was only a matter of time until they caught up with them. An inch at a time, they crept through the bush, which was motionless in the still air. It was very calm, and very quiet, and then...

"There was a loud rustling in the trees overhead," Hurt said. "Colobus monkeys—bongo watchdogs. Bongo like to lie up with monkeys in the trees to warn them if anything approaches. If we spooked the monkeys, the monkeys would warn the bongo."

The hunters sank to the ground and prepared to wait out the little primate busybodies overhead. For two hours they waited, hoping the monkeys would lose interest and drift away. Eventually they did, and the hunters rose to their feet. They had moved barely a few yards when they heard rustling again. Thinking the monkeys had returned, they froze. But this time, it was not monkeys.

"I searched the treetops, but I couldn't see any of them," Hurt said. "But I did see a creeper moving up and down. Something on the ground was tugging at it. Bongo! It had to be!"

And it was. They were right on top of them, separated only by a few yards of impenetrable brush. They had stalked right into the middle of the herd, and now the bongo were all around them.

Gradually, as the bongo moved, the hunters began to pick out a patch of hide here, a white stripe there, now and then a flash of horn. Not the big lad, though. Not the Sué bongo. He was nowhere to be seen.

"We had been following his particular track, so we knew he'd been with them," Hurt recalled. "What often happens, though, is that when they lie up, the bull drifts off by himself. I figured that's what had happened. As the herd began to feed away from us, we prepared to go after them."

Just at that moment, with the herd gone and only the sound of scuffling hooves in the distance, the tracker Laboso caught a glimpse of movement through the trees, about ten yards off to their right. A straggler was hurrying to catch up. A very large straggler.

"I saw the horns moving through the trees, and they looked thin. I thought it must be a cow," Hurt said. "Then the whole horns came into sight, and I realized that what I'd been looking at was just the top halves. The bases were massive. Then the head appeared, then the neck. He had a neck like an ox, and the horns were absolutely huge!"

Hurt whispered to Jesus Yuren. Yuren said yes, he could see him. Then shoot, Hurt whispered. Yuren raised his rifle, an inch at a time, took careful aim, and fired. The blast broke the magic silence of the forest, and the bull stood motionless—untouched, perplexed by the noise as the rest of the herd crashed away through the undergrowth. Sure that the slightest sound would now break the spell, Yuren silently reloaded his rifle, raised it and fired again. This time there was no mistake. The Sué bongo dropped where he stood, shot through the neck.

They had known the bongo was big. They were not quite prepared for just *how* big. Back in camp that night, triumphant, Danny McCallum finally took a tape measure and walked over to the head where it sat, ivory tips dancing in the firelight. The horns measured more than 37 inches, beating the previous record for a western bongo by an unbelievable three inches! It was a new world's record, salvaged from a safari that from the outset had seemed to be doomed.

Epilogue

As it turned out, the hunt for the Sué bongo was fitting in more ways than one. Shortly afterwards, the civil war in the Sudan flared up once more and hunting was closed down. It remains closed to this day. As far as we know, Jesus Yuren's world record was the last bongo to be taken legally in the southern Sudan. The record did not stand for very long, however. Three years later, in the Central African Republic, Canadian Bill Clark took one with horns that measured more than 38 inches, to claim the number-one spot.

The adventure Hurt and Yuren shared in 1984, however, was a classic of trophy hunting, with every element that makes it the addictive pastime that it is—disappointment and despair, physical exhaustion, and great triumph. In 1995, Jesus Yuren was given the Weatherby Award, hunting's highest honor, in recognition of his years of trophy hunting and service to the sport. Not least of the accomplishments that led to the honor was the saga of the Sué bongo.

THE BIGGEST
BONGO EVER

Bill Clark was a successful businessman and lifelong hunter when, in the early 1980s, he says he "decided to get serious about trophy hunting." In 1984, he made his first trip to Africa, shooting, as he puts it, "the usual stuff." Having done that, he then set his sights upon hunting the glamor game. Afraid that other countries would follow the lead of Kenya and Zaire and close hunting altogether, Clark set out to collect the most prestigious species while he could still do it. High on the list was the mountain nyala in Ethiopia, and right beside it was the bongo. Once he had taken a mountain nyala, Clark booked a hunt with Eric Stockenstroom and in 1987 flew to Bangui, the capital of the Central African Republic, on the first leg of his search for a record-book bongo.

The Central African Republic (CAR) is one of the most remote countries in all of Africa—literally, the middle of nowhere. For trophy hunters, however, the CAR is a mecca, for it is home not only to the bongo, but also to the Lord Derby eland, one of the most coveted of all animals among serious trophy hunters. After Kenya closed hunting in 1977 (ending all hunting for the Kenya bongo) and the Sudan closed because of war in 1984, the CAR became the only game in town for bongo hunters. At that time, the other bongo countries (Cameroon, Congo Brazzaville, and a few others) were just beginning to realize the potential of trophy hunting. Until they actually opened on a serious scale, the CAR was the capital for bongo.

"The thing I noticed most about the CAR, really, was just how remote it was," Clark says. "You land in Bangui and then get in a small plane and fly, and fly, and fly to get to the eastern part of the country. It is just solid jungle, all the way."

The bongo of Kenya live high on Mount Kenya and in the Aberdare Mountains in some of the toughest, thickest, most inhospitable terrain on earth. The western bongo of central Africa most often inhabit the thick, swampy jungles of the Moyen Congo. In eastern CAR, the country is not as swampy as other parts of their range, nor as depressing as Kenya's rain forests, but it is not easy, either. It is thick (albeit dry) jungle with very little open space.

Bill Clark, his wife Peggy, and Eric Stockenstroom flew to the southeastern part of the country a few miles from the border of Sudan, and actually (in African terms at least) a stone's throw from where Hurt and Yuren shot their bongo three years earlier.

The regimen was reasonably simple: Up at 3:00 a.m., visit various salt licks or waterholes until you pick up the track of a large bongo bull, and then begin tracking. Like Robin Hurt, Stockenstroom used Azande trackers. The Azande tribe live on both sides of the border and down into Zaire. They are a large and diverse group, noted for their intelligence and ability as trackers, and also for their secret societies, superstitions, and interest in magic. One of their superstitions is that bongo meat is taboo, for it is reputed to cause leprosy. It is a belief that no professional hunter or client does anything to disabuse, for the last thing anyone wants is for the Azande to start poaching bongo for meat.

Tracking is the usual method of bongo hunting, and certainly the most demanding. For Bill Clark, it was a physically exhausting exercise, hour after hour, day after day.

"The tracking itself was not that tough, and fortunately it was not terribly hot," he says. "The real difficulty was moving through the brush. It was very dense, with low tunnels pushed through by animals. We would get on a track and follow it along these brushy tunnels, hunched over as we walked, hour after hour. That was the tough part."

While bongo hunting places a premium on stamina it is really, as Clark discovered, a game of stealth.

"Imagine trying to track a big whitetail buck through the woods, staying quiet enough to finally get within sight of him without him knowing you're there. What do you think the chances are? Well, bongo are just as wily as a whitetail—and just as wary."

For nine days Clark, Stockenstroom, and their Azande trackers trailed bongo through the bush, and for nine days they dragged themselves back into camp empty-handed. Clark had been told before he left home that it takes an average of three trips before you get a bongo, so he says he was prepared for failure. But that did not make it any easier. "What really began to get to me," he says, "was the monotony of moving through the bush hour after hour without making a sound. It is really wearing on you after a while."

Wearing and exhausting. The thick bush sheds its leaves constantly, and they lie on the ground as desiccated and crunchy as cornflakes. Each footstep must be carefully placed to ensure you do not spook every bongo in the country. Communication is by hand signals, low whistles like bird calls, and tongue clicks that sound like small animals. For ten hours a day. Every day.

The tenth day began like the previous nine—out of bed in the dark of night, a cup of tea, and on the trail long before dawn. Just as the sun was beginning to color the horizon, they reached a salt lick and fanned out, looking for bongo tracks. One of the Azande whistled and pointed: two sets of tracks. Two bulls. One big one. It was back to tracking, placing each foot with infinite care, studying every opening for a glimpse of red hide, and never, ever speaking.

For several miles the tracks meandered along, sometimes together, sometimes drifting apart. The Azande stayed on the big bull as Clark and Stockenstroom trailed behind, waiting for a sign. At one point Stockenstroom spotted a tortoise in the sand and picked it up, tossing it to one of the trackers. Without a word, he carefully cut a small chunk from the shell and placed the tortoise back on the ground. The tiny talisman went into a small bag he carried. Tortoise shell brings good luck, and since Stockenstroom had already confided that he was considering consulting a witch doctor, the episode with the tortoise required little in the way of explanation.

The big bull finally parted from the small one, wandering off on his own with the hunting party on his trail. By mid-morning they felt they were coming up on him and dropped to their knees, crawling through the undergrowth. At one point they paused, making no sound. There was not a breath of wind, and no noise whatever. But a sudden *whoof* split the air, and the big bull crashed away through the brush, alerted by...*what?*

"He must have a sixth sense, that bull," said Stockenstroom.

They resumed tracking. About 200 yards down the trail, they saw where the bull had paused in a most unbongo-like way and looked over his shoulder, back down the trail. This gave the hunters hope that just maybe he was not badly spooked and might not leave the country as is their wont when seriously frightened. Eric Stockenstroom decided it was a good time for a rest. Wait half an hour, he said, and see what happens. Give the bull time to settle down. They stopped and plastered red mud all over their faces, hands, and legs, looking for any camouflage, any advantage no matter how small, that might give them an edge.

It was now almost noon. The trail approached a large clearing, and Clark and Stockenstroom cut across it, leaving the trackers on the spoor and hoping to intercept the bongo on the far side, or that he might feed close to the edge of the jungle. When they were about 500 yards ahead, they crawled silently up onto a small wooded mound, staying well out of sight, and settled in to watch. They had been there only two or three minutes when, Clark says, "I saw a sight I'll never forget. About 30 yards away from me was the front quarters of a bongo. A *giant* bongo. He was browsing just where the jungle met the clearing, using his enormous horns to twist the branches down to where he could reach the leaves. He was so close I could see his black muzzle and the white spots on his cheeks, and even see his ears flicking."

Clark reached over to Stockenstroom. "There's a bongo," he breathed.

One look, an urgent "Shoot him!" and Clark raised his .375 H&H. The bullet took the bongo in the chest. As he charged out into the clearing, Stockenstroom put an insurance shot into him, and the bull dropped. The two hunters had not even reached the animal when Stockenstroom declared it had to be a new world's record. It was certainly the best trophy of any species he had seen in 17 years of professional hunting.

"Quit hunting, Bill," he said to Clark. "You will never equal this."

When it was finally measured, the left horn of Bill Clark's bongo measured 38⅜ inches—almost three inches longer than Jesus Yuren's, while the right horn shaded Yuren's by a quarter inch. Bill Clark owned the new world's record with a total of 97⅛ points. It was his fourth African safari, and his first in search of a bongo.

"That was quite a hunt," Clark says. "It was tough hunting. Hard work. I shot a mountain nyala, but this was a hundred times tougher. Sheep hunting? I shot a Marco Polo sheep in the Pamirs in 1988, and sheep hunting is child's play compared to bongo. With sheep hunting, in the end it boils down to the accuracy of the shot. Bongo hunting is *hunting*. That's the difference."

4

❄

LEOPARD IN THE ROUGH

In big game hunting as in war, the direst of consequences can flow from a decision that is routine, and even, seemingly, trivial. To an outsider, the big game hunter's preoccupation with detail (Bolt or double? How long a barrel? Softs or solids?) can seem obsessive, absurd, even childish. But to a professional hunter, this attention to every little thing, weighing each factor and guarding against anything that might go wrong, is what keeps him and his clients alive—safari after safari, beast after nasty beast.

Over the years, some theories of big game hunting have grown to the stature of accepted truth. One such is Wally Johnson's dictum on how to handle big cats when they are wounded and desperate. Both lions and leopards charge at astounding speeds, leaving the hunter only seconds in which to react and get off a shot before the claws and teeth are upon him. According to Johnson, in this situation, the only absolutely dependable weapon is a 12-bore shotgun loaded with buckshot. Armed with two barrels and two ounces of

❄

145

large buck, Johnson used to say, a cool shot facing a wounded lion was "as safe as a baby in its crib."

The only proviso was that you had to be cool—you had to wait until the cat was less than ten yards away to ensure that the shot hit in a clump, not a solid mass but not yet a pattern, the brief instant when it carries the maximum thump and does the most damage. What you had to guard against was shooting too soon against an incoming cat. There was not much consideration given to shooting too late. It was assumed that at cat's-breath range, the shotgun would work just fine. That was the assumption.

⁂

In more than 30 years as a working professional hunter, Robin Hurt has seen his share of wounded leopards and gone into the bush after more than a few. Altogether, he reckons, he has hunted leopard with clients perhaps 300 times; inevitably, given the nature of leopard hunting, at least once a year he had a wounded one to deal with, yet in those first 30 years he never received a scratch.

Hurt came to know leopards well, however, including the fact that when you have one wounded and in the bush, you are almost certain to receive a charge unless the leopard dies of his wounds before you get there. It is a matter of *when*, not *if*. Although leopard maulings are not uncommon, actual deaths are rare—at least these days. The leopard is not a huge animal; 150 pounds is a good size, and 200 is a monster. Part of the danger with leopards lies in the fact that, by preference, they feed on well-ripened meat. The rotting flesh gets between their teeth and under their claws; when they bite and rip at you, the danger of infection is extremely high, and that is one reason death by mauling was more frequent in the days before antibiotics.

A leopard is so incredibly quick that a few seconds can make all the difference between having a dead cat and congratulations all around, and having a dead cat surrounded by a half-dozen slashed and bleeding bodies. For this reason, it is important to stop a charging leopard all at once. Seconds count, and they can seem longer than a lifetime.

This is the factor that caused Robin Hurt to have misgivings about the buckshot-for-leopards rule. Granted, the shotgun is lighter and easier to handle. Granted, it throws a number of pellets and increases the chance of a hit when you have a split-second opportunity. But near or far, it just does not carry the devastating wallop of a big-bore rifle. And so, when Hurt has to go into the bush after a wounded leopard, he usually takes both, with a gunbearer carrying the second weapon. Robin then decides which one he will carry, depending on the circumstances.

Still, over the years, when the charge actually came, Robin usually seemed to be holding his old William Evans .500 Nitro Express, and he credits it for the fact that he never received a scratch in all those years.

❈

It was very early in Tanzania's 1992 big game season when Robin returned home from his annual North American tour of the Safari Club conventions and meetings. He had a European client who wanted to hunt leopard, and March was the only time he could come to Africa. It was not an ideal time, since the trees were in leaf and vegetation was thick from the rains. But it was the only time available. Hurt took his client into northern Tanzania, to the area around Monduli, not far from the town of Arusha and Mount Kilimanjaro.

"It is one of my favorite game areas because of the variety of animals," Hurt says. "There are rain-forest species—suni, duiker, bushbuck—and there are species from the semi-desert, such as gerenuk, lesser kudu, and oryx. You'll find large herds of Cape buffalo as well as plains game, so it is a fine place for a mixed-bag safari. And, of course, it contains some of the largest-bodied leopards I've seen anywhere in Africa."

The most reliable way to hunt leopard—in fact, just about the only way where you have more than a snowball's chance—is by baiting. Leopards love to eat well-aged meat—aged three or four days in the African sun. Knowing which tree a leopard might like to eat out of is one of those skills that the best professional hunters have, but which defies ready explanation. Why leopards will come consistently to one tree, yet steadfastly avoid another seemingly identical tree a hundred yards away, is one of those mysteries. But they do, and having a PH with an instinct for it is the first requirement of a successful leopard hunt.

Since leopards are nocturnal by nature, the hunters wait for them in a blind, within good shooting distance of the bait tree, but not so close the leopard will spot them. Once the bait is hung and attracting the kind of leopard you want, you either approach the blind stealthily before daylight, hoping to get a shot as the sky slowly brightens, and before the leopard abandons the kill to go and lie up, or you go to the blind in late afternoon and wait for darkness to come, hoping that hunger and over-confidence will bring the leopard to the tree while there is still a minute or two of shooting light. Under these circumstances, if you get a shot at all, then one is all you get. If you kill the leopard, good. If the shot is the slightest bit off, however, it means a wounded leopard in the bush, and you rarely get a second chance without going in after him.

Robin Hurt and his tracker, Tallo, set out a number of baits and sat back to wait. A few days later, they found a female and her cub dining royally on one of them, and left them to it. That same evening Tallo reported action on another bait.

"*Chui, bwana. Mkubwa. Mkubwa sana!*"

Chui. Mkubwa sana. A big male leopard—a *very* big male leopard—had fed once on a bait set out in one of the deep gullies leading down off Burka Mountain into the Rift Valley. If he had fed once he would probably feed twice, and the party decided to creep into position near the bait before first light and hope for a shot as the sun came up.

There were four men in the group: the client, Jacques; the trackers, Tallo and Samuel; and Robin Hurt. With exquisite attention to detail, Robin timed their approach to coincide with the brief minute or two when it was still dark, yet the birds would be awaken-

LEOPARD IN THE ROUGH

ing and their morning greetings would mask any noise the hunters made.

The bait tree was visible through a peephole, and Robin could clearly see the three baits hanging there, a zebra leg and the hindquarters of a lesser kudu. Big leopards have big appetites, and Jacques wanted a big leopard. Hurt could see that a large portion of the zebra leg had been gnawed off during the night. The question was, was the diner still nearby?

They sat in the blind in absolute stillness as the sky brightened. With so much meat gone, Robin feared the leopard would be full and not return until evening. Since they were already there, however, he decided they might as well wait a bit and see what happened. The chance paid off: After about 30 minutes a huge leopard appeared at the edge of the gully and ghosted up into the tree, pausing at a fork, silhouetted broadside against the bright morning sky. Hurt had a clear look: Massive body, enormous head; another Monduli monster leopard offering a brief opportunity for one clear shot.

Grasping Jacques by the arm, whispering as he pulled the grass plug out of the wall of the blind in front of him, Hurt told his client the leopard had returned. Calmly, smoothly, Jacques slid his .375 H&H through the opening and took careful aim. He was an experienced hunter and a good shot. Everything was going according to plan.

"I was watching the leopard through my binocular," Hurt says. "Something happened. He sensed something, because suddenly his head snapped around and he was staring straight at us. His eyes were a bright, piercing yellow."

The .375 went off with a terrific boom, deadening the morning air with its echoes, and the cat turned a complete somersault. He landed heavily on the ground, on his back and obviously well hit, but immediately leapt to his feet and made for the wooded ravine at a dead run. The dense vegetation swallowed him up, leaving only silence in his wake.

The thickly forested mountainsides of East Africa—Mount Kenya, Mount Kilimanjaro, Mount Meru—offer a strange and usually forbidding atmosphere, with the towering canopy of the rain forest, dark and brooding vegetation, and the distant calls of monkeys. The tall trees and thick cover are prime leopard habitat, where they can lie in ambush and stash their prey high in the branches away from hyenas and lions. The gully off Burka Mountain into which the leopard had disappeared was a dense tangle of *sansavera* (a kind of wild sisal), thick wait-a-bit thorn, and green *maswaki*, also known as "toothbrush bush." The ravine was about 100 feet deep, and visibility was measured in inches.

As the leopard made his escape, Hurt heard him making loud grunting noises, indicating a solid hit; now, as the hunters stood on the edge trying to pierce the foliage, they could hear the leopard close by. His breathing was deep and loud, but not, it seemed to Hurt, the breathing of a mortally wounded cat. It was not a death rattle. The sound continued to come from one spot as they tried to catch a glimpse of something through their binoculars. When that proved fruitless, they decided to wait for the safari car to come up, give the leopard half an hour to (with luck!) die of his wound, and then go in after him.

When the car arrived, it brought with it an elated game scout from Monduli, Israel by name, who thought from the single shot he'd heard that Jacques had his leopard. The news that the cat was still alive and in deep cover quickly killed the joyful mood.

The Tanzanian game department system of having a game scout accompany every safari has been roundly (and soundly) condemned by many writers as one more way of exacting graft. Quite often, that is the way it works out, but not always. Many of the game scouts are not only well-trained (they are all graduates of the game management academy at Mweika, near Mount Kilimanjaro) but also conscientious wardens and fine hunters besides. Israel was one of those scouts—a good and careful shot who knew his job. As Hurt knew, his client was also an experienced hunter and an excellent shot. Accordingly, he planned the next stage of the campaign very carefully.

"It was a time for some decisions to be made," Hurt says. "I knew from experience that Israel was completely trustworthy and fearless in such situations. There was a chance the leopard was not too badly wounded and that, as I went in on his tracks, he might break cover and make for a smaller ravine nearby. I placed both of them where they could cover the open ground and maybe get a shot."

Hurt then took the two trackers, Tallo and Samuel, and prepared to go in on the blood trail. As they started for the bush, Hurt was carrying his old William Evans .500 Nitro Express; Tallo carried a double-barrelled shotgun loaded with #00 buckshot.

The debate over proper loads for dangerous game in different situations has continued for a century, and will go on as long as dangerous game is hunted. No one questions that a .500 Nitro Express is one of the most deadly of all the British big-bore rifles; in fact, John Taylor suggested it was actually overpowered for anything except elephant, rhino, and Cape buffalo. Firing a 570-grain bullet at 2,150 feet per second, it starts with a muzzle energy of close to 6,000 foot/pounds. On a dead-on shot at leopard, the bullet would easily penetrate the length of the cat and come out the other end, and the chances of the animal doing anything further would be minuscule.

A standard load of #00 buckshot, on the other hand, has 12 pellets with a total weight of around 730 grains, with a muzzle velocity of almost 1,300 fps. When it leaves the muzzle it is still in a cluster, like a bunch of grapes, and has a total energy of about 2,750 ft/lbs., less than half the punch of the .500. Within a couple of feet of the muzzle, the cluster breaks apart and starts to spread. By ten yards it has opened up, depending on the gun, anywhere from six to 12 inches, and its impact now depends on how many pellets actually hit the target. Even if all 12 strike a leopard, however, they will have nothing even remotely approaching the penetration and sheer destructive power of the 570-grain jacketed softnose bullet of the .500 NE as it mushrooms and plows a devastating wound channel. Those are the ballistic facts as they relate to shotguns and rifles (or this shotgun, and this particular rifle) and wounded leopards.

The argument goes that it is better to hit the cat with a few pellets and less energy than it is to take the chance of missing completely with a single bullet. But the proviso has always been that you *must* wait until the cat is inside ten yards before shooting, to ensure that you hit him with the full load. That being the case, you would also, in essence, hit it with a single bullet, since the pattern does not become a factor unless the cat is more than ten yards away. One advantage of a shotgun that is undeniable, however, is weight. The average .500 NE double rifle weighs close to 12 pounds; a double shotgun weighs seven. It is much quicker to handle at close range and can even be managed, in a pinch, with one hand.

Robin and Tallo picked up the blood trail at the base of the bait tree, noting that the blood was "black as treacle," indicating a serious wound, but not one that would likely be immediately fatal. Hurt would have preferred it to be bright red and bubbly, indicating a lung shot, but at least the blood trail was substantial and easy to follow, and they entered the gully's thick vegetation with Hurt in the lead. The ravine got deeper and deeper, and the brush thicker and thicker. If ever a place was made for leopard, Hurt says, this was it.

They were slowly approaching the spot where they had last heard the cat breathing. When they were right below it, the trail changed and disappeared into a solid mass of vegetation. To get through it they would have to climb, using their hands to pull themselves up the rocky slope through the thick brush. Hurt turned and handed his .500 NE to Tallo, taking the shotgun himself instead.

"The cover was so thick and our position so precarious on the edge of the gully that I felt that with only one hand free to handle the gun, I had a better chance with the lighter shotgun," Robin said. "Also, the thought ran through my head that, if things did go wrong and the tracker had to shoot, there was less chance of my being hit if he was shooting the rifle. And, too, I never expected to get a clear shot in such thick vegetation. I thought that in the event of the leopard running away or charging, I would have a better chance of a hit with the pattern of the shotgun, rather than the single bullet of the rifle."

All were perfectly sound reasons for carrying the shotgun under the circumstances. And all, as it turned out, were perfectly wrong.

❄

Hurt, Tallo, and Samuel reached a small clearing close to the spot where they had last heard the leopard. The two trackers began to lob rocks into the thicket, pelting different areas in turn while Robin stood by with the shotgun ready. But nothing happened— nothing except a startled bushbuck that gave them a brief rush of adrenalin.

There was no other course than to resume following the blood trail, which at this point led into the dense brush along a game trail. The trail had created a low tunnel through the thick cover. Unwilling to risk going in on his hands and knees, where he would be an easy target for the leopard, Hurt told Samuel to hack a way through with his panga. The tracker began whaling away at a thick branch that was the first major obstacle, while Robin stood close behind. At that moment, he says, "All hell broke loose!"

"All I saw were the bushes erupt and spots coming fast," Hurt says. "All the time we were throwing rocks to flush him out, he'd been lying up not five yards away!"

Robin swung the shotgun and fired wide as Samuel dived to the side. Then Tallo fired the .500. Another miss. The cat sprang at Robin from low down just as he fired the second barrel directly at its head. Even though the muzzle was less than a foot from the cat's snarl, he was moving so quickly the shot missed the head and plowed into the side of his neck. The solid clump of shot had absolutely no effect. A split second later Hurt was on his back with the cat on top, long teeth clamped solidly into the right arm he had thrown up to protect his throat, and Robin once again found himself staring into the hard yellow eyes and smelling the breath that was almost over-powering from a lifetime of eating rotting meat.

Hurt watched, strangely detached, as the skin of his fore-arm split and blood spurted. In the surreality of the situation, however, he felt no pain. Then the cat released his arm and tried again for Hurt's throat, standing over him as the hunter fought him off. This time the cat's teeth sank into his shoulder and chest just inches from his throat.

"By now I was fighting for my life, kicking frantically and holding him off by his neck," Hurt says. "I remember noticing that his left side was completely useless (Jacques's shot had broken the shoulder), but he was still tremendously strong.

"He bit me again, this time my upper arm, which made it even weaker. I shouted to Tallo to shoot him, and I was trying to hold him far enough away from me that the bullet wouldn't hit us both. But for some reason, I didn't know why, there was no shot. I was completely on my own!"

As it turned out, the .500's heavy recoil had knocked the tracker off balance and he had fallen straight down the gully, about 15 feet onto some rocks, badly hurting his knee. Although he immediately tried to climb back up to help his professional hunter, it took precious seconds for him to recover and crawl back up the slope. Meanwhile: "I kicked as hard as I could and managed to throw the leopard off me," Hurt said. "He thanked me by sinking his teeth into my left leg and shaking me like a terrier with a rat, and my left calf started to bleed heavily."

Suddenly, as quickly as it began, the attack ceased. The leopard lay quietly at Robin's feet, resting his head on his paws and facing away from the gully. Hurt still had some buckshot loads, but no idea where his shotgun was. His only weapon was his belt knife, and he slowly moved his hand toward the sheath, fearing the movement might spark a new attack. But the leopard lay silent, as if sleeping. In a low voice, Hurt called again for Tallo to shoot the leopard with the one round remaining in the .500. Still no answer.

"I could not understand what had happened to him," Hurt recalls, "for he is a brave and reliable tracker. Then I heard him, crawling up the rock face to the ledge where I was lying."

As calmly as he could, Hurt instructed Tallo as he crawled forward, placed the rifle's muzzle against the leopard, and pulled the trigger. The rifle went off with a tremendous roar, but the leopard gave no reaction to the shot beyond a slight lifting of his head. He had died quietly of his wounds where he lay.

With considerable difficulty, Samuel, who had reappeared with his panga, and the injured Tallo helped Hurt back down the slope and out into the open. Jacques was distraught, although Robin assured him none of it was his fault.

"If there was any fault at all, it was mine," Hurt says. "I decided to use the shotgun instead of the rifle. If I had done differently, none of it would have happened."

The party was desperate to get Robin to a hospital, but he insisted they bring out the leopard's body and not leave such an admirable animal to the scavengers. It took Samuel, Israel, and the driver almost fifteen minutes to maneuver the huge cat through the underbrush. Meanwhile, Robin doused his wounds in Dettol, leaving them open to bleed and, with any luck, getting rid of the poisons the cat undoubtedly carried. He watched the men return with the leopard, and the very sight of him brought tears to Hurt's eyes—tears for the leopard as well as the memory of the attack.

"He was truly a noble beast who fought bravely to the end," Hurt said. "I had the greatest respect for him in his death, and I asked Jacques (who was understandably anxious to get his friend to hospital) to take photographs of him."

They then began the procession back to camp, hobbling along in silence. Usually, when a big cat is killed, the trackers sing a hunting song in his honor; this time they made no sound. "Why do you not sing?" Hurt asked. "We cannot," they told him. "We cannot sing when you are so badly hurt." "Sing," Robin said. "This leopard deserves it above all."

And so they sang all the way back to camp, with Robin and Jacques joining in.

Epilogue

Some stories cry out for an epilogue, and this is one of them. Where did Jacques's first shot go? Why was the shotgun so ineffective? Were the wounds, indeed, toxic? And if he had it to do again...?

"It was not Jacques's fault at all," Hurt says. "He actually made a very good shot. The bullet went about an inch below the heart and broke the shoulder. An inch higher and the leopard would have been stone dead."

The shotgun blast hit the leopard in the neck, missing the artery and plowing into his back. It entered as a single bullet would have, but did not do enough damage to stop the cat cold. If it had been the .500, it would have been a different story.

"If there was any fault at all it was mine, for changing to the shotgun when I did. I've always been a believer in double rifles of large caliber for dealing with wounded cats. The knockdown power of a shotgun, even loaded with buckshot, is minimal compared to a big-bore rifle loaded with softpoint bullets. If I had made exactly the same shot with the .500 as I did with the shotgun, it would have killed him instantly.

"It was a calculated risk. I was well aware of that when I made the decision, but it just didn't work out. But life is full of risks, isn't it? Hunting itself is the chance of the chase."

Hurt insisted on leaving his wounds unbandaged to allow them to bleed freely, and even though there was a lot of blood, he knew he was in no danger of bleeding to death. The drive into Arusha was agony, for although he felt no pain during the attack, now his arm, shoulder, chest, and leg burned with pain as they lurched over the rutted Tanzanian track.

When he reached Nairobi after an emergency flight from Arusha, Hurt was treated by a doctor who specializes in lion and leopard maulings. He was placed in a bath to wash the wounds thoroughly, then a drug called Dermazin was spread on them like butter. For four days, he was given intravenous antibiotics while his wounds were left open and treated twice a day with antiseptic baths and Dermazin. The treatment worked. There was no infection.

A fellow hunter, Gerard Ambrose, called the hospital from Arusha. He had just seen the leopard's skull, he said, and it had "the longest teeth I've ever seen!"

"You're telling me?" Hurt asked.

As he lay in his hospital bed, Hurt recalls, parts of the experience would come back to him with sudden clarity—the leopard's size, his speed, his ferocity. Again and again, he saw the hard yellow eyes, fixed upon them from the bait tree in the distance, and then up close—smelling the breath, seeing the blood spurt from his arm.

"I realized then just how lucky I had been. And you know what? The strangest thing is, it seems to take an age to tell the story. Yet the whole thing happened in so few seconds."

NORTH AMERICA

JORDAN BUCK

5

❄

OUR FAVORITE GAME

OVERTURE

The Boone and Crockett Club has been in existence for over a century, and has been keeping records of North American big game animals for more than 60 years. But never in all that time has there been a year to equal 1995.

The 22nd Boone and Crockett big game awards in Dallas, held to honor the best big game animals taken in the preceding three years, featured a stunning array of trophies. There were more entries than ever before, the 100 trophies sent to Dallas for judging were easily the equal of any previous program, and there were three new world's records. Overall, the quality was the highest in the club's illustrious history, but everything else paled in comparison with one head, a new world's record whitetail buck, shot in Saskatchewan by farmer Milo Hanson. The antlers scored 213⅝ points, and finally dethroned the legendary Jordan Buck, a whitetail killed in Wisconsin in 1914 by James Jordan.

There were many who thought the Jordan Buck could never be equalled, and more than a few who thought it never *should* be

❄

equalled—that it would stand for all time as the most magnificent whitetail ever taken in America. The fact that an even bigger buck should be taken in 1993 is evidence, not only that North America's whitetail population now is healthier than at any time since Columbus, but also that 108 years of work by the Boone and Crockett Club has paid off, not only for the whitetail, but for every big game species we have.

❊

The Boone and Crockett Club was founded in 1887 by Theodore Roosevelt when a small group of his friends gathered at his New York City home in December of that year. They were hunters and conservationists, although that term had yet to come into common use. It was fitting that they met around the time of the winter solstice, for the days were growing short for North America's big game animals. The bison were gone, and the elk had been eradicated from the eastern United States and severely reduced throughout the West. The whitetail population was dropping quickly. Pronghorn antelope, once as numerous as the bison, were on what seemed like a one-way journey to oblivion as the high-plains grasslands disappeared under the plough.

The formation of the Boone and Crockett Club did not have an immediate effect. Nothing could have. But it was the start, and although game populations continued to dwindle until 1920, by that time many of the programs and policies for which B&C was responsible, or in which it was involved, had started to take hold. If there is a turnaround point, 1920 is the year.

Theodore Roosevelt did more than found B&C. When he became President of the United States, he used the powers of his office to initiate policies that would have far-reaching effects. These included the establishment of dozens of national parks, forests, and wildlife reserves. Other Boone and Crockett members, such as Aldo Leopold, were either influential in the field of conservation or helped found related organizations like the National Wildlife Federation. Eventually, a combination of game laws and bag limits, the abolition of market hunting, and the establishment of parks and wildlife preserves would bring many species back from the brink of extinction.

At the turn of the century, however, the situation was critical for many species and subspecies. In 1906, fearing that extinction would rob the world of any trace of some animals, B&C established the National Collection of Heads and Horns. The goal was to create a museum collection to ensure that future generations would be able to see, at least, what these animals had looked like.

From there, it was a short and logical step to establish a permanent record book. The first edition of *Records of North American Big Game* was published in 1932, and an official measurement and scoring system was set up at the same time. Although the initial purpose was to record for posterity evidence of species that were thought to be disappearing, B&C members realized quickly that *The Book* was also a good way to document the health of different species as they rebounded throughout the country. One such species was that most North American of animals, the white-tailed deer.

The year 1900 is generally quoted as the low-water mark for big game. Certainly that was true for the pronghorn antelope, whose numbers were down to about 13,000 from an estimated 40 million a century earlier. Elk numbered only 90,000. Whitetails, while not hit nearly so hard, were still merely a shadow of their former selves and probably totalled no more than 500,000. Some estimates place the figure as low as 300,000.

When Columbus discovered America, there were at least 20 million whitetails on the North American continent, although the actual number could have been double that. They quickly became a favorite game animal, and over the next several hundred years their ranks were steadily reduced by a combination of commercial and subsistence hunting. The whitetail effectively disappeared from state after state.

In some cases, the eradication of the deer was not even a long process. The *Mayflower* landed in 1620, and the first permanent settlement was established in Rhode Island in 1636; just ten years later, whitetail numbers had dropped so dramatically that the authorities imposed a closed season to try to preserve what few deer were left. Other states were quickly forced to take similar measures, but they did little good. Deer were food, and deer hunting was a right. By 1900, New Jersey had but 200 deer left, and they were so rare in Vermont, New Hampshire, and Massachusetts that even the sight of a deer track in the snow made the local papers. The situation farther west was little better. By the early part of this century, whitetails were gone from Ohio, Indiana, Illinois, Iowa, and southern Michigan.

By 1910, the estimated whitetail population for the entire midwest was a mere 2,000 animals. That fact alone makes the story of James Jordan and his fabulous whitetail all the more incredible.

❋

THE JORDAN BUCK

For some reason, there is always a story surrounding the taking of a record animal, and rarely do the stories go according to the script. Through the years, tales of fabulous animals that were killed by a meat-hunting farmer, or by a settler wanting biltong, occur far more often than accounts of great trophies taken by serious hunters who approach the chase with science, determination, and self-denial. Other times, strange events happen after the animal is down: Great racks disappear for years, are remembered in song and story, then much later rediscovered hanging in a bar somewhere. The story of the Jordan Buck includes many of these elements: There is luck both good and bad, there is rank injustice followed by belated recognition, and most of all, there is an uncanny dollop of sheer coincidence.

In 1914, James Jordan was 22 years old—young, vigorous, and an experienced deer hunter. All his life he had hunted whitetails in Wisconsin and killed more than a few. He was primarily a meat hunter; when he shot a deer, it was to fill the larder, not to put antlers on the wall. Still, a big old buck carries more venison than a yearling, and like any other deer hunter, he was susceptible to the sight of a big rack.

It was a cold and snowy November morning when Jim

Jordan and his friend Egus Davis set out in search of deer. Fairly quickly, Davis downed a doe. Jordan gave him his knife to dress her out, and continued hunting on his own.

Near a set of railroad tracks, he came across whitetail sign— tracks of at least four animals, one of which appeared to be a monster. His hoofprints looked like a moose that had inadvertently fallen in with a bunch of deer. Jordan followed the tracks through the brush, anxiously peering ahead for any sign of the animals.

As he did so, he heard a train in the distance. On it came, its whistle splitting the air once, then twice. Four whitetails leapt to their feet in front of him. One of them was, indeed, a monster—the biggest buck Jordan had ever seen, silhouetted against the clear morning sky. He brought up his .25/20 and emptied the magazine at the big one. The deer scattered, showing no sign of being hit. Jordan raced after them, searching the ground for blood. Finally, he saw a trace of red in the snow. At least one bullet had found its mark. Unfortunately, he also discovered he had only one cartridge left, and his knife was back with his friend Davis. Still, he had no choice but to follow the trail and hope he could make his last cartridge count.

The huge buck was heading for the Yellow River, a stream that forms the dividing line between Wisconsin and Minnesota near the town of Danbury. He swam the river and was climbing the opposite bank when Jordan reached the edge of the woods. The buck stopped to look back. Jim Jordan took very careful aim, drew a deep breath, and dropped the buck where he stood with his final shot. He then plunged into the freezing water himself and made his way across.

What he found on the far bank was a huge deer—big in body, but even bigger in antlers. Later estimates placed his undressed weight at 400 pounds, but even on such a large body the antlers looked huge. Seeing that the deer appeared to be dead, Jim Jordan crossed back over to the Wisconsin side and went in search of Davis to retrieve his knife and to get help dragging out his deer.

When the pair returned, however, they were in for a shock. The buck had been down but not out. With his final ounce of strength he had kicked himself down the bank and into the Yellow River, and been carried away by the rushing water. Seeing the story written in the snow, Jordan and Davis began to search, hoping for a miracle. Again they were in luck: At the first bend in the river, the deer was held fast against a rock by the midstream current. Again Jordan waded in and dragged his prize to shore. By rights that should be the end of the story, with only honors and accolades for an epilogue. In many ways, however, it was only the beginning.

Knowing that this was a head among heads, Jordan decided to have it mounted and took it to a local taxidermist. He dropped the antlers off—and unwittingly said goodbye to his buck for 50 long years. What happened next appears to be a series of misunderstandings, although no one will ever know for certain. The taxidermist left town with no forwarding address, but left the antlers in storage in Minnesota. When Jordan went to claim his deer he was told the taxidermist had moved away, and his attempts to make contact failed. To all appearances, the Jordan buck was gone.

In 1958, 44 years after he was shot, the Jordan buck resurfaced. At a rummage sale in Sandstone, Minnesota, the mount, tattered and black with age, sold to a man named Bob Ludwig for three dollars. A few years later, Ludwig read an article about the Boone and Crockett Club and decided to have the mount measured. The final score was 206⅛ points—a new world record.

Thrilled at his find, Ludwig wanted to show his prize to a distant cousin, an old man who, in his day, had been a noted deer hunter up in Wisconsin. Incredibly, unbelievably, ironically, the cousin was none other than Jim Jordan, now a man of 72. He took one look at the head and recognized the buck he had killed 50 years earlier.

Understandably, Bob Ludwig was skeptical. This was his head, bought at a rummage sale, and now this ancient relative was trying to claim ownership! In fact, however, Jordan was not doing that at all. All he wanted was recognition. Not the head, not any money—nothing but acknowledgement that the new world's record was a buck that he had killed so long ago.

Unfortunately, there was little to go on except Jordan's word. All the other participants were dead or gone. There was no solid evidence, much less conclusive proof. His claim soon grew into a full-blown controversy, with the states of Minnesota and Wisconsin dragged into it for good measure. For years, Jordan struggled to have his claim accepted, and for years he drew a blank.

In 1968, the head changed hands again. Ludwig sold it to a collector for the sum of $1500—a tremendous amount of money for the time, and certainly a fair return on his three-dollar investment. Then, finally, in 1978, Jordan's claim was recognized, and he was confirmed as the hunter who had shot the world's record white-tailed deer. As you might expect with such a star-crossed story, however, even that came too late: James Jordan had died two months earlier.

Interlude

The Jordan Buck is distinguished by more than mere size. Many people regard it as the ideal of what a whitetail should be. The antlers are almost perfectly symmetrical—heavy but not too heavy, enough points (five on each side) for impact, but not so many that it looks cluttered, and with each point long and defined. It has weight, but is not so heavy that it looks squat, and so on. When you look at the Jordan Buck, and someone asks how you might improve on it, there is no obvious answer. It has no flaws.

This was a major reason so many thought it would never be equalled, not just in size, for given the right combination of genes and vitamins, a bigger head was always possible. But short of a grotesque super-whitetail along the lines of the extinct Irish elk, possibly as a product of controlled breeding in an artificial environment, the chances of nature herself creating a buck to eclipse Jordan's were remote at best. Also, there was the fact that while the whitetail has bounced back to pre-Columbian numbers in the last half century, they are also heavily hunted by men in search of trophies. Trophy animals require years to reach the caliber of the Jordan Buck, and the odds against a buck surviving to reach that level are very high. Over the past 20 years, there have been many, many large bucks taken. The upper levels of the record books are constantly changing, but the pinnacle—ah, the pinnacle! That record appeared safe—as safe as the Chadwick Ram atop the Stone sheep lists.

❋

As it has rebounded, the whitetail has taken different shape in different areas. Southern whitetails, while numbering in the millions, tend to be small, with Texas whitetails probably the smallest of all. They have antlers that are large relative to their body size, although a Texas 10-pointer looks like a big deer in miniature, and a 100-pound buck is quite large in some parts of the Lone Star State. Often, hunters will shoot a whitetail that can be carried out of the woods like a large jackrabbit. Impressive though they are in many ways, the whitetails of Texas are unlikely to pose a threat to the Jordan Buck.

Farther north, the whitetails are much bigger in body but, surprisingly, generally smaller in headgear. In Ontario, for example, a 250-pound buck is fairly normal and you do not start discussing body size seriously until an animal tops 300 pounds. Yet the antlers are often almost stunted. Put the average Ontario antlers on a Texas deer and they would not even bother to shoot him. This has been attributed, in part at least, to the harsher winters and shorter growing season. If a buck is hard-pressed to eke out enough food when the snow is chest-deep right into April, he is not likely to sprout much in the way of antlers. As well, there is the question of minerals in the soil, which has at least as much to do with antler size as the animal's genes do. As you move into the hard-rock regions of the North, mineral content changes dramatically and in the coldest regions, you find that the body size of many animals becomes generally larger. A Barren Ground caribou of the Northwest Territories is larger in body than a woodland caribou of Newfoundland, and an Alaska-Yukon moose will dwarf a Shiras. Similarly, it seems, with whitetails.

But there is a middle ground, and the middle ground exists in middle America—the rich crop-growing regions of Illinois, Minnesota, Wisconsin, and of course, southern Saskatchewan. There, the winters are long but the food supply is good, and the snow does not drift in deeply and reduce the deer to eating alder twigs. There are cornfields and wheat fields with browse aplenty—forage with a very high food value, not the shrivelled cedar buds that many eastern whitetails are reduced to in the deep-snow days of February. Midwest deer also have the genes as some of those, at least, must be descendants of the Jordan Buck and his relatives.

In the 1980s, stories began emerging of a new super-strain of deer to be found in the rich flatlands of the Canadian prairies. For a few years Alberta was the destination of choice for serious trophy hunters, as one big buck after another was brought out of the Alberta foothills. Soon, there were waiting lists for the best outfitters, and Alberta whitetail guides began wearing ostrich-hide boots and hanging out in Cadillac show rooms. Still, there was nothing to threaten the Jordan Buck. Nothing that big, that spectacular, that inherently *sound*. In Michigan, deer *aficionados* founded The Sanctuary, to raise whitetails in controlled conditions, applying the scientific breeding principles that produced Secretariat to the goal of creating the ultimate whitetail. Trophy "hunters" who could not bear the thought of a wall without a 12-pointer paid up to $10,000 for three days of stalking fenced-in paddocks to dispatch a "bragging buck."

And meanwhile, in far-off Biggar, Saskatchewan—*"Biggar is Better"*—the whitetails nibbled and bred and roamed the river bottoms and a doe gave birth, sometime in the 1980s, to one husky male fawn who would one day prove that nature still does it best. Period.

❊

THE HANSON BUCK

Biggar, Saskatchewan is a dot on a map where two roads and a railway line converge, 50 miles due west of Saskatoon and 100 miles north of Swift Current. In the vast sweep of the Canadian prairie, with its die-straight roads and monotonous vistas, Biggar is indistinguishable from a hundred, two hundred, five hundred similar settlements. The one thing you can count on is, if there is a railway line, the town's grain elevators will be visible from miles away, out on the prairie. That is Biggar, Saskatchewan.

In 1968, Milo Hanson moved to Biggar with his wife, Olive. They took up residence on Olive Hanson's family farm. Shortly thereafter they had a son, and settled down to the regular cycle of life of a farm family. Farming around Biggar is mixed, for the prairie. There are cattle as well as wheat, barley and oats, which means there are also alfalfa fields. Rapeseed (canola) is a major cash crop. The flatlands are interspersed with aspen bluffs and river bottoms, which provide cover for the whitetails. When Hanson first moved to Biggar, he says, there were few whitetails in the area, but a combination of circumstances—the decline of cattle markets (and, consequently, fewer cattle), milder winters, and easy access to good forage in the form of grain and alfalfa—caused the whitetail herd to grow steadily. Instead of migrating into the hills to escape the winter, the deer began staying around the farms, venturing out into the fields at night to browse. The sight of deer became common, and the taking of a good trophy buck was no longer occasion for amazement.

From the time he came to Biggar, Hanson was a hunter. His wife was also a hunter, and they hunted together every year. Although they are a working farm family (five sections and a hundred head of cattle), they always found time to take two or three weeks in the fall and travel the West, hunting for whitetail, mule deer, moose, and elk.

In rural Saskatchewan, as with remote farm communities anywhere, hunting is a communal activity. It is an excuse for people to get together. In the weeks leading up to the season they can talk hunting and plan what they're going to do; in the weeks afterwards, they can talk about what happened and why, while they grill venison steaks and get ready for curling season. Always, they look for deer and deer sign, studying antlers off in the distance.

Since Milo and Olive Hanson were avid hunters and all their neighbors were just as enthusiastic, the Hanson farm became a gathering point, and often they would go out in groups to hunt. With open spaces and brushy river bottoms, and enough people to make it work properly, a drive is a natural way for them to hunt deer.

On the very last day of the 1992 deer season, the local school

HANSON BUCK

bus driver reported sighting one monster buck feeding in an alfalfa field. News of the big deer made the rounds of Biggar's coffee shops, and everyone kept an eye out, hoping for a glimpse even though it was too late to hunt him that year. The following summer, one of the Hansons' neighbors saw him, this time close to the farmyard, and again later in a pea field. Obviously, the buck was a wise old lad who knew his way around and knew where to find the best forage.

Rifle season opened on November 15, 1993. Shortly before that, the big buck was spotted again, this time near a highway several miles north of town. By dawn on opening day, every hunter in Biggar knew exactly what he was looking for when shooting light came.

There had been some snow about a week before, and then the weather cleared. By opening day, there were tracks everywhere but no way of knowing what was fresh and what was not, and for the first week of the season the hunters came home empty-handed. Then, on the evening of November 22, it began to snow once again. Hanson and his hunting partners, John Yaroshko, Walter Meger, and Rene Igini, conferred on how best to approach it the next morning. Nature was presenting them with a fresh start, and the best time to put it to use would be first light.

Early the next day Hanson and Yaroshko drove to meet the others as they had arranged. When they found them, Meger and Igini were excited as only one thing could excite them: They had seen the big buck. He had gone into an isolated patch of willows. And he had not come out.

There is no feeling in hunting that can quite compare with approaching a stand of bush, knowing there is game in there, yet not having any idea what might happen, only knowing that something—something—definitely will happen. Every step becomes a vital part of it, and the feel of the ground underfoot; time is compressed into an unbearably vivid succession of instances in which a rustling leaf, a flicker of breeze, a crunch of ice, carry meaning beyond meaning.

Hanson, Yaroshko, and Meger arranged themselves around the willow copse to cover every escape route, while Rene Igini gently followed the buck's fresh trail into the thicket. Within a few seconds the buck dashed out. Shots were fired. None connected. And the buck disappeared in the distance.

They stayed on the trail, Rene Igini following the tracks until they were swallowed up in a maze of milling hoofprints. Unlike the Jordan Buck of 80 years earlier, this one did not have noticeably large hoofs, and it was impossible to distinguish his tracks from the others. Still they kept on, knowing the deer was in the area and hoping they might get lucky. As they drew blank after blank, however, they were on the verge of calling it a day when the big buck made his big mistake. Instead of sitting tight, he made a last dash from the aspen bluff where he was holed up and dived into a willow thicket on Milo Hanson's land. The hunters had been given one more chance.

Again, they surrounded the thicket. Again, Rene Igini went in on the trail.

This time the buck burst out at a flat run, 150 yards from Milo Hanson's post. Both Hanson and Yaroshko shot at him as he ran, but both missed. A touch of buck fever, Hanson later commented, and they watched him disappear into another willow run. This time as they approached, the huge whitetail broke out running dead away from Hanson. The first shot brought him to his knees, but he struggled back up and into another clump of aspens. Hanson ran up the hill to where he had had his last glimpse of him and there, below him, was the wounded buck. He was standing, waiting. Hanson took careful aim and the buck went down. And then another shot, just to make sure.

❋

Milo Hanson and his friends are not trophy hunters in the conventional sense of the word. Not in the sense of carrying a tape measure into the field, and pulling it out as they run up to a downed animal. Not in that sense. So it is not at all surprising that Milo Hanson and his friends were not sure exactly what they had taken and did not have an inkling until a week later. Having hunted the district year after year for a quarter-century, Hanson was confident that this buck was one of a kind—for that area. It would win the trophy at the big-buck night held every year in neighboring

Sonningdale, and he was pretty sure it would win the prize at the local wildlife federation competition in Biggar. But beyond that…?

A week after he killed the buck, a neighbor came over and measured it. He could scarcely believe the numbers and asked Hanson to go over them. They couldn't be right—that would make this a new world's record!

Which, of course, it was, and it was confirmed a couple of days later by a Boone and Crockett certified measurer, and then re-confirmed officially by a measuring team after the mandatory 60-day drying period. The buck's final score, and the one by which he will always be known, is 213⅝ points—surpassing the Jordan buck by more than six points! This is a victory akin to winning the Kentucky Derby by eight lengths. And the wonderful thing about it is, the Hanson Buck, like the Jordan Buck, is a beautifully symmetrical head, not perfect like Jordan's, but in no way freakish. The Hanson Buck is a fine, representative 14-point whitetail that just happens to be the biggest buck on record.

❋

BRUCE EWEN'S
CURIOUS BUCK

Whitetails are curious animals. Curious because they like to know what's going on. And curious because, more often than not, we can't figure them out. One buck will be so predictable you could set your clock by him, while another does not seem to know from one minute to the next what he is going to do. The predictable ones generally do *not* live to a ripe old age, so they are unable to pass their life-shortening traits on to future generations. The bucks that do pass on the best survivalist genes are those who know that the way to see tomorrow is to not do today exactly what you did yesterday.

If the previous paragraph seems a mite confusing, it was intentional: I wanted to emulate the convoluted thought processes of a devious old buck with grey hairs on his chin and a great rack on his head.

There is one whitetail trait that has probably cost more of them their lives than any other over the years, and that is their irresistible desire to stop and take one last look behind them. And quite often it is, literally, their last look. Jim Jordan shot his buck when it stopped on the far side of the river to look back. Milo Hanson caught up to his when it had paused in its flight.

Bruce Ewen, on the other hand, found a buck who just could not conquer his curiosity, and that curiosity cost him.

❋

Bruce Ewen is a Saskatchewan farmer who lives near the Barrier Valley town of Archerwill, coincidentally, not many miles from Biggar. Ewen is a lifelong hunter of the same stamp as Milo Hanson—not a trophy hunter *per se*, but not inured to the charms of a good set of antlers, either. Like most farmers, he carries his rifle in his truck everywhere he goes during deer season.

In November of 1992, the year before Hanson shot the new record, Ewen was out doing his morning chores with the cattle and spotted a small buck running with the herd. He returned to the truck for his rifle, but by the time he got it out and loaded, the little buck had disappeared into a willow run. Ewen circled around, looking for him, but without success. Knowing the run came close to the road and was a regular passing point for deer, however, Ewen finished his chores, confident he would be able to head the deer off on his way home.

When he got near the willow run he parked his truck, pulled out his rifle, and waited. Only a few minutes had gone by when he spotted another deer using the run. Not the little one, though. A big one. A *huge* one!

"He was so big I thought at first it was a small elk," Ewen said. "He was really huge. I watched him and watched him, and finally realized this was no elk, it was a really big whitetail. I mean *really* big."

Ewen put the ammunition clip into his rifle and fed a round

EWEN BUCK

into the chamber by hand. He was using an old Remington Model 760 pump he had bought, used, a dozen years earlier. It had seen hard use but still functioned well. Usually.

"I brought the rifle up and pulled the trigger, but nothing happened. The buck had stopped about, oh, 200 yards away and was watching me."

When the rifle did not fire, Ewen figured he had not pushed the slide all the way forward. He worked the pump, ejecting the cartridge, and this time the slide would not close at all. The buck stood there, watching him, and even came a little closer, all the while peering intently.

Ewen, meanwhile, was trying to get his rifle to work. The cartridges were piling up in the snow as he worked the slide, trying to get it to close properly. He removed the clip and replaced it a couple of times, hoping it would seat properly and solve the problem. Meanwhile, the big buck stood and watched.

"I knew the clip was wearing out, but I'd never had that much trouble with it before," Ewen said. "There was something wrong with the lip of it and the catch that holds it in was so worn it wouldn't hold the clip in position. Finally, the whole thing just fell out in the snow."

And still the big buck stood there, watching, curious. He came a few steps closer, looking bigger all the time.

Desperate now, Ewen picked a cartridge out of the snow. His hands were shaking with excitement as he wiped it off on his jacket, fed it into the chamber, and pushed the slide forward.

The buck was now only 150 yards away, watching as if he'd paid admission. This time there was no mistake. The buck stumbled at the shot, but recovered and ran. Picking another cartridge out of the snow, Ewen reloaded his rifle, lined up on the departing buck, and piled him up. By this time, he says, he was shaking so hard he had to rest for a moment before going over to see, up close, the curious buck who was curious no longer.

❋

Bruce Ewen was down at the farmers' cooperative in Archerwill, showing his prize to his wife, Elaine, when it struck him that this might be more than merely the biggest buck he had ever seen. The deer drew a crowd of about 20 people, all *ooh*-ing and *ah*-ing.

"It was at that moment I knew I'd have to get him measured for Boone and Crockett. He seemed to get bigger the longer I looked at him."

The curious buck carried a total of 17 points—nine on one side, eight on the other—and rated a total score of 202⅝ points. He was a shoo-in for B&C's top award, until a year later when Milo Hanson shot the biggest one of all, near Biggar.

The two heads are remarkably similar in some ways; Ewen's buck carried three more points, but the beam lengths are almost identical to Hanson's (about 28 inches each). Ewen's is slightly heavier and more compact. The only criticism of the Hanson Buck is that it does not have as much mass as the Jordan—or Ewen's rack either, for that matter.

The deer that Bruce Ewen took in 1992 is as fine a buck as any of us are ever likely to see, good for No. 6 all-time, and for one brief year the best whitetail ever taken in Saskatchewan. Ewen sold the rack to a collector and received a replica to put on his wall. As for the recalcitrant rifle...

"No, I didn't buy a new one. I bought a new clip, though." I'll bet.

Finale

The 1995 Boone and Crockett awards were certainly whitetail-rich. In any other year, Bruce Ewen's beautiful animal would have been a sensation, falling just short, as it did, of the Jordan Buck. As well, Boone and Crockett gave honorable mention to a whitetail from Alberta that scored 188⅜, and certificates of merit were awarded to deer from Illinois and Minnesota.

An interesting aspect about both animals is that they seemed to appear out of nowhere. Milo Hanson's buck was noticed for the first time in 1992, and taken a year later. As far as we know, Ewen's had never been spotted before. Yet both bucks lived among farms where everyone is a deer hunter and everyone notices racks, even if they do hunt mainly for the freezer. Both of these Saskatchewan monsters could have been spectacular trophies for two, or three, or even five years before they were finally taken. Yet they lived their lives with a reclusiveness, anonymous and unpredictable, that would have done credit to Howard Hughes.

Since whitetails, by and large, do not stray too many miles from their home ground unless they are part of a seasonally migrating herd, the Hanson and Ewen bucks obviously had (until their last year, that is) survival instincts of a very high order. They both passed those genes on, which is why, needless to say, the professional outfitters in Saskatchewan are now the ones wearing the ostrich-skin boots and visiting their local Cadillac dealers.

6

✻

APACHE GOLD

"For a few years rumors of existing bands of elk, always in very remote places, continued to filter out. Shed antlers were occasionally found. Now and then a prospector or cowpuncher reported seeing very old beds or dried dung. On rare occasions an excited hunter claimed to have seen a big bull. . . Then even rumors of their existence died out. . ."

Jack O'Connor
Game in the Desert
1939

✻

※

PRELUDE

In 1902, the American Museum of Natural History published a bulletin containing a momentous announcement. In an article by E.W. Nelson, the museum revealed the discovery of a new subspecies of North American elk. It was much larger than other elk, and it was found only in an isolated area in the mountains of Arizona, New Mexico and Texas and, sparsely, down into Mexico itself.

The specimen from which Nelson concluded he had found a new subspecies was the skull and antlers of a bull elk, collected in 1886 near the head of the Black River, in the White Mountains of Arizona, at an altitude of almost 9,000 feet. In every way the specimen was larger than comparable skulls from other elk—Rocky Mountain, Roosevelt, Tule, or Manitoban. The skull was wider and longer, while the antlers appeared to be both much longer and straighter, and with a greater interior spread, than antlers from any of the other subspecies.

Nelson named his new subspecies *Cervus merriami* in honor of Dr. C. Hart Merriam, organizer of the U.S. Biological Survey which, in 1885, had set out to study and document the native species of North America. It was later reclassified as *Cervus canadensis merriami*, and finally, in 1973, as *Cervus elaphus merriami*. Merriam's elk, as it came to be known, was obviously the king among North American wapiti—but not for long.

Barely had it been classified when it disappeared, seemingly forever, under a barrage of gunfire from market hunters and settlers. Merriam's elk were plentiful in Arizona and New Mexico in the 1880s, scarce by the 1890s, and gone forever sometime between 1902 and 1906.

For a few years thereafter, ranchers and hunters continued to find bleached skulls and old shed antlers, and many of these were added to collections, placed in museums, or nailed up over old barn

※

doors. Then those artifacts too were gone, and the Merriam's elk wandered out of history and into myth.

Elk Song

When the Europeans came to North America, the elk (or more properly, *wapiti*, from the Shawnee meaning "white deer") was the most widely distributed of all the deer species on the continent—as widespread as the ubiquitous whitetail is today.

There were elk in northern Mexico and had been for centuries. When Hernán Cortés and his *conquistadores* jack-booted into Mexico City in 1519, the Emperor Montezuma showed them several huge sets of antlers. They were similar to the familiar red stag of Europe, but much, much larger. They were, in all probability, the antlers of Merriam's elk gathered in the Sierra Madre.

There were also elk in the far northwest of British Columbia, and northeast to New England; there were elk in New York, in Pennsylvania, and in Virginia. The Canadian provinces of Quebec and Ontario had elk populations, they roamed the Great Plains, and were found throughout the mountains of the West. One by one, however, the wapiti herds were killed off. The last elk in Vermont was shot around 1800, in New York in 1847, Virginia in 1855 and Pennsylvania in 1862. The last elk disappeared from Quebec sometime in the early 1800s. As the white man moved west, he drove the elk before him, wiping out one herd after another.

The extermination of the vast bison herds on the Great Plains is a well-known story, overshadowing other equally sorrowful examples of game animals driven to extinction or near-extinction, including the pronghorn antelope, the big horn sheep—and the elk. The bison were killed off for their hides, for political expediency to subdue the Plains Indians, for their meat to some extent, and to make way for farmers. Elk, on the other hand, were killed for their meat and for their tusks, the otherwise useless upper canine teeth which were highly prized around the turn of the century by members of the Protective Order of Elks—a misnomer if ever there was one.

Elk were on the slippery slope downward when C. Hart Merriam initiated the biological survey in 1885, and it was a race between taxonomists and market hunters as to whether all the game animals would be classified for posterity before they were wiped out. In some cases the taxonomists won; in others the market hunters did, leaving the biologists to draw conclusions from fragments of bone and horn. In the case of Merriam's elk, it appears they were killed off in Mexico not long into the 16th century, or very shortly after the conquest by Cortés, and their range shrank steadily until they were reduced to a few pockets in New Mexico and Arizona.

In the early 1800s, naturalist Alexander von Humboldt travelled through Central America and later wrote about the enormous "stag horns" he had seen preserved in the viceroy's palace. Humboldt assumed they came from California, but he was then unaware that a much larger elk dwelt in the mountains of New Mexico; that is where scientists now believe those antlers—possibly the very ones Cortés saw three centuries earlier—originated. By that time, however, it was largely conjecture. E.W. Nelson classified the Merriam's elk just as it was killed off, arriving only in time to leave a record of a great animal—and a minor mystery that teases us still.

❈

Jack O'Connor was born in Arizona around the time the Merriam's elk disappeared from its last stronghold in the eastern part of the state, near New Mexico. As a boy growing up, and later as a hunter and writer in Arizona, O'Connor saw firsthand how elk were reintroduced, and he participated in the first legal hunt of the transplanted elk in 1935. Four years later, O'Connor published his first book, *Game in the Desert,* and devoted a chapter to the rejuvenated elk of Arizona.

Some authorities early in this century suggested that the Merriam's elk ranged from Arizona and New Mexico into Texas, and even up as far as Oklahoma, but scientists today largely discount that theory. It must be remembered that what we know, or think we know, about Merriam's elk is partly speculation and partly deduction, a puzzle pieced together from clues gleaned from the study of skulls and antlers. In taxonomy, two and two do not always add up to four. The case against Merriam's elk in Oklahoma rests not on a study of specimens, but on a piece of logic: Merriam's elk were mountain critters; why would they brave the vast flats of northern Texas, with little food and less cover, to reach Oklahoma? At any rate, it is generally accepted today that the Merriam's occurred in eastern Arizona and southern New Mexico, across the Rio Grande in the mountains of western Texas, and down into Mexico itself.

Sometime between 1902 and 1906, the last of the Merriam's elk disappeared and were presumed to be victims of over-hunting by man and over-grazing by cattle. As O'Connor points out, however, as he roamed the deserts and mountains of Arizona throughout his youth, he repeatedly heard reports—rumors, hearsay, gossip—of sightings of native elk in remote parts of the state, country where no farmer or rancher would normally stray and only prospectors and hunters were likely to venture.

Undoubtedly, skulls and antlers and ancient sheds were being picked up by cowboys and many of these found their way into museums. It is not such a long step from there to the finding of old elk beds and droppings, and from there to actual sightings. And the rumors of elk persisted.

Meanwhile, various bodies were busy with plans to reintroduce the wapiti to Arizona and New Mexico. The state game departments, often working with chapters of the Protective Order of Elks (now intent on making the name a reality), brought in Rocky Mountain elk from up north. The first were released in New Mexico in 1911—nine cows and three bulls purchased from a rancher in Colorado. These were followed by 50 more animals from Wyoming's Yellowstone herd in 1914. Initially they were released on private ranch land in the Pecos Mountains, and by 1934, the New Mexico herd had grown to 3,500 animals.

The first release of Rocky Mountain elk in Arizona occurred in 1913. The Winslow Elks Lodge provided the impetus, Jackson Hole, Wyoming, provided the elk, and the Arizona game department handled the logistics. Eighty-six animals were released in the neighborhood of Cabin Draw in the Sitgreaves National Forest. This was followed by several other transplants.

By 1937, according to O'Connor, the elk had established themselves in three separate herds. The largest was on the Mogollon Rim, another was in the chain of volcanic mountains south of the Grand Canyon, and the third was in the White Mountains of eastern Arizona near the New Mexico boundary—the original range of the huge Merriam's elk.

❄

"Back in the early nineteen thirties, I camped late one September afternoon on the Mogollon Rim, that gigantic fault across half of Arizona..." O'Connor wrote, many years later, in his book *The Big Game Animals of North America.*

He went on to tell how he made a dry camp, far from water, just for the joy of having a magnificent view out over the Tonto Basin. As he cooked his supper, he kept hearing a high, thin whistle. At first he thought it was a bird, but when he took his binocular and crept out to the head of a canyon, he watched a big six-point bull elk come out and start viciously attacking a small tree. Every so often the bull would pause and bugle, and the high-pitched braying sound would bounce back and forth off the canyon walls. It was on that same Mogollon Rim, a couple of years later, that O'Connor hunted elk for the first time, in Arizona's first legal sport hunt.

Since the reintroduction program began 20 years earlier, elk in Arizona had made a tremendous comeback. Given even minimal protection, elk will increase in numbers at a strong rate, and all over the west a combination of reintroduction programs, effective protection, and changes in habitat were having their effect. Forest fires and logging that wiped out mature forests and replaced them with new growth provided food, and the elk moved in. From southern British Columbia all the way to the Sonora border, elk were on a roll and the annual harvests mounted up.

American elk populations generally hit their low point around 1900, with the remaining sizable herds holed up in the mountains of Montana, Idaho, Wyoming, and Colorado, and a few pockets near the Pacific in Oregon and Washington. Since then they have bounced back, through transplants, protection and proper management, and today Colorado is without a doubt the major elk state in terms of overall herd size, the number of elk taken, and total number of hunters.

As an example, while many states limit non-resident bull elk tags to a draw system, a hunter from out of state can walk into any hardware store in Colorado, show his hunter safety certificate, hand over $300, and walk out with a bull elk license. This is not to say you are likely to take a huge 6x6 bull on public land in Colorado, because you are not. The elk are there in quantity, but the quality depends on where you hunt, and your best chance at a big trophy is on private land—the same as virtually everywhere else.

There is no more spectacular game animal in North America than a mature bull elk—nothing more majestic, no more impressive trophy. As elk hunting became more popular, trophy hunters began to get really serious about collecting record-class antlers. Recognizing the potential market, a few of the vast ranches in Colorado, Wyoming, Montana, and elsewhere began to manage their resident elk herds with an eye to growing spectacular trophy bulls. These were not breeding programs; elk are free-ranging animals, wards of the state, with licensing and bag limits set by state game agencies. What landowners could do, however, was post their land and limit those who were allowed to hunt. As long as the elk stayed on the private land—and elk, like deer, are very cognizant of where it's safe and where it's not after opening day—they could expect to lead long and fruitful lives.

Gradually a two-tier system of elk hunting evolved: There were the average guys who hunted on a shoestring, prowling public land in competition with hundreds of other hunters. And then there were those who paid ranchers big money, slept on clean sheets, and could pick and choose from a dozen or more six-pointers in a given morning without worrying about other hunters horning in. On public land, the state game departments managed for quantity, while on private land the ranchers managed for quality.

❋

Apache Gold

But there is private land, and there is *private land*.

There are the 200,000-acre ranches owned by individuals, and the 500,000-acre ranches owned by corporations. And there are the tracts of private land that are even more vast, including some of the most remote and wild country left in the West, that belongs to the Indians. Indian reservations are private land jointly-owned, and it did not take long for some of the tribes to realize that, game-wise, they were sitting on a gold mine. If there was money to be made from big game hunting, who better to make it than North America's original big game hunters?

Which brings us back to the Mogollon Rim of Arizona and the White Mountains, spiritual home of the Merriam's elk, and since the end of World War II, the range of one of the finest elk herds in North America:

> *A word now about the Mogollon Rim country,* wrote Jack O'Connor in 1939. *It is the best elk country in Arizona, and one of the best all-around game countries I have ever seen. The rim is the tipped-up edge of a great plateau, and the Tonto Basin below it came from a great fault which has left tremendous cliffs from 1,000 to 1,500 feet high—cliffs which extend for over a hundred miles...*

> *The top of the rim supports spruce and fir. It is a land of tiny lakes, thick timber, icy trout streams deep in the canyons. Here the elk find their summer home, and the whole country is tracked up by them. As the altitude decreases, the spruce and fir are replaced by yellow pine and Gambel's oak, still lower by the piñon and cedar of the upper Sonoran zone. So here, by moving a few miles, the elk can find ideal summer and winter range.*

In the 1870s, a huge area of the Mogollon Rim and White Mountains was given over to the Apache and became the Fort Apache Indian Reservation. For devotees of the American West, the very names *Mogollon Rim* and *Tonto Basin* ring with history. This is the country of Cochise and Geronimo, of the Chiricahua and the Mescalero Apache of western New Mexico. Directly south of Fort Apache is the San Carlos Reservation, where Geronimo led the Chiricahua Apache in a running battle with the U.S. Army that lasted, sporadically, almost a decade.

The Fort Apache Reservation was the scene of much of the fighting as well, including the Battle of Cibecue Creek. On August 30, 1881, the military moved out from Fort Apache to arrest the Indian mystic Nakaidoklini, a White Mountain Apache who was preaching a new religion in which the dead would return to rid the West of the white man. In the ensuing skirmish Nakaidoklini was killed; in retaliation, the Apache attacked the fort. The army brought in more troops, the violence escalated, and the isolated skirmishes grew into a full military campaign.

In 1882, General George Crook, a competent soldier and successful Indian fighter, was brought in to sort things out, but matters just got worse. For the next four years, Crook fought the Apache. He called them "tigers of the human species"—and he was in a position to know. But if so, he was a poor tiger hunter. By 1886, one small band consisting of Geronimo himself and 23 other Apache had proven so implacable and elusive, and such an embarrassment to the army, that Crook was replaced by General Nelson Miles and the army fielded a force of 5,000 men to bring the two dozen Apaches to bay.

The Apache Wars, which began, like so many others, with a false accusation against Cochise in 1861, and dragged on for 25 years thereafter, were just lurching to a close when someone killed a big bull elk in the White Mountains near the Black River—the very heart of Apache country. It was this bull that E.W. Nelson later came to examine and classify as the Merriam's elk.

Exactly what someone was doing dragging antlers out of the White Mountains while the Apache were at war is a subject for some rather delicious speculation. Obviously, they don't make hunters like they used to. The wonder really is not that the Merriam's elk was discovered so late but, under the circumstances, that it was discovered at all.

At any rate, with the Apache confined to the Fort Apache and San Carlos Reservations, ranchers moved in and the Merriam's elk moved on, right into oblivion. Or so everyone said.

❊

Since its first legal elk hunt in 1935, Arizona's state game department had managed its growing elk herd as a public resource; its primary aim was to provide as much elk hunting as possible for as many hunters as possible. Quantity was the goal, not quality.

On the Fort Apache Reservation, hunting and fishing were regulated by Arizona Fish & Game. Hunters from outside were allowed onto tribal land, the state set the bag limits and collected the fees, and a "nominal amount" was paid to the tribe. This arrangement continued until the mid-1970s, when the White Mountain tribe said "enough." Joe Jojola, the chief wildlife biologist for the White Mountain Apache, says his people simply decided they had had enough of seeing their resources regulated by an external agency and consumed by outsiders while they got little in return.

"So the tribe ordered Arizona Fish & Game off the reservation. We said, 'it's our land, our resource, and we'll run it.' Fish & Game took us to court, but the tribe took a stand and won," Jojola says.

The White Mountain Apache got some assistance from a similar battle being waged at the same time between the Mescalero Apache in New Mexico and that state's wildlife agency. The dispute ended up in the United States Supreme Court, which ruled in favor of the Indians. Seeing the writing on the wall, Arizona withdrew its opposition and the White Mountain Apache took control of their own wildlife resources, including management, setting bag limits, and licensing outside hunters. "One of the first decisions we made was to manage the elk herd for quality of trophies, not for quantity," Jojola says.

With elk, as with any antlered species, great trophies depend on two factors: the right genes and proper nourishment. Assuming the elk have both those requirements, a third vital factor is age. You simply have to let the bulls grow *old* enough to grow *big* enough.

Kevin Lackey, who is now conservation programs director for the Rocky Mountain Elk Foundation, worked previously as a game manager on Vermejo Park Ranch, a property of more than 600,000 acres near Vermejo Park in New Mexico. He says a bull begins to reach serious trophy status between seven and ten years of age, continuing until they are about 12, at which point the antlers usually begin to decline.

"A lot of wildlife managers will say that a six-year old is a mature bull, and sexually they are right, it is mature. But it's not likely to be a great trophy animal at that age," Lackey says. "That is the difference between the trophies that come off one managed ranch, and another a few miles away. The genes and habitat may be identical, but if you are shooting six- or seven-year olds, they will simply not be as big as they would be if they were left to grow for a few more years."

For many years, Wyoming has been the dominant state in terms of big trophies, partly because of the Yellowstone Park elk herd. Big bulls which grow to trophy-class maturity wander outside the park boundaries during hunting season, and the Yellowstone herd generally serves as a reservoir of elk. More recently, eastern Oregon has emerged as an area for big trophy elk, and there are a few other spots scattered throughout the West.

For consistently big bulls, however, the Fort Apache Reservation in the White Mountains of Arizona has become a major producer. At the Boone and Crockett Club's 22nd Big Game Awards in 1995, White Mountain elk took several of the top places, including both first and third for non-typical heads. The number-one non-typical was an 8x8 monster that scored 422⅜ points, just 25 points shy of the world's record. It was a triumph for the hunter, John

LoMonaco, but it was an even greater triumph for Joe Jojola, the guides, and the people of the White Mountain Apache.

❈

The Fort Apache Reservation stretches west along the Mogollon Rim, from the Tonto Basin to the White Mountains, and is bounded on the south by the Black River. It has a resident Apache population of about 15,000 and a resident elk herd estimated at 12,000 in the summer. The elk migrate on and off the reservation according to the seasons. Altogether, the reservation encompasses 1.6-million acres of diverse habitat that suits the elk just fine, ranging in altitude from 3,000 feet all the way up to 11,400 feet.

The range of wildlife on the reservation is as diverse as the habitat. Fort Apache is also home to desert mule deer and Coues' whitetail, pronghorn antelope and wild turkey, black bear and mountain lion. Traditionally, the Apache hunted the two deer species, and today they reserve those for themselves. All the others, however, are managed for trophy hunting and outside hunters are permitted— under strict controls—to hunt them. The elk, however, are the star attraction. Joe Jojola attributes the success of the tribe's elk program over the last 20 years to a combination of factors.

"We have a unique situation in that we can manage both the elk and the habitat," he says. "State fish and game agencies may cooperate with agriculture departments and environment departments, but they cannot control habitat like we can. That's an important point."

The other factor, as Kevin Lackey emphasizes, is age.

"A bull elk becomes a real trophy animal around the age of eight years. During the 1980s, we were shooting bulls that were six-and-a-half to seven-and-a-half years old; now, in the 1990s, we are averaging bulls that are seven-and-a-half to eight-and-a-half. This shows in the number of Boone and Crockett animals we are taking. More B&C elk have come off the reservation in the last five years (1991-96) than in all the years before that."

From the beginning, the tribe aimed for exclusivity among

hunters as well as quality among their trophy animals. As more and better bull elk were taken from White Mountain (as the reservation came to be known among hunters), word spread and demand for the limited number of permits increased. Soon there was a waiting list to get on the reservation, and the waiting list grew. And grew. And grew.

The system now in place at White Mountain is almost like a club with limited membership. There are 60 to 70 permits sold each year; in 1996, there were 70 permits, at $12,000 each. Those who hunted last year are given first chance to come this year, and those who hunt this year will get to come back next year—all at $12,000 a crack. If you miss a year, you are out of the loop. In a given year, there are five to ten new hunters brought in to replace those who drop out.

At one point, the waiting list grew to more than 400 names—at that rate of turnover, a 40- to 80-year wait! To reduce the list, the tribe instituted a $500 waiting-list fee; that cut the number down to about 125, while raising some very useful cash, but feeling that even that number was too many, they finally closed off the waiting list altogether. And there it stands.

"We will open it up again when we feel it is getting short, I guess," Jojola says. "But I have no idea when that will be."

For hunters who are not on the waiting list, or who simply cannot wait 30 or 40 years, there are four permits sold each year by sealed-bid auction. The last few years, the average price for these permits has been $24,000. That money buys you a completely out-fitted, all-inclusive hunting trip for elk on the Fort Apache Reservation. It may get you a Boone and Crockett elk and it may not. Just as important for most serious elk hunters, however, is the fact that this fee also buys you the opportunity to come back next year, and the year after, and the year after that. The amazing thing is that so many hunters do come back year after year. The reason is, the hunting on the reservation is like no elk hunting anywhere else in North America.

"The thing about White Mountain," says Kevin Lackey, "is that you may see more real trophy bulls there in one morning than you would see in a lifetime of hunting, say, the Selway-Bitterroot in

Idaho. You can go out backpacking in really rough country in Idaho or Montana, country where there are very few other hunters, and you still might go a week without seeing anything more than a spike bull. At White Mountain, you go out and see one big trophy bull after another."

For hunting purposes, the reservation is divided into territories. There are three camps, and they run about ten hunters at a time out of each camp. Once you leave camp, however, you see no one else until the end of the day; each guide has his own area, averaging about 25,000 acres, all to himself and his client. The hunt itself can be as rough or as gentle as the client wants to make it, because the terrain ranges from vehicle-smooth all the way to backpack-vertical.

Meyer's Elk

Herman Meyer had already hunted the reservation 11 years running when he left Maverick Camp one September morning in 1992. Two weeks earlier, John LoMonaco had taken his monster bull from the reservation's Paradise Camp. Although they did not know it at the time, that bull would win the number-one Non-Typical award at Boone and Crockett three years later. But all that was in the future. Having taken many fine elk from the reservation already, Meyer was looking for something really special.

Meyer and his guide, John Caid, left camp in darkness and climbed into thick timber. Almost immediately they found themselves among elk—big elk, rutting elk, bulls and cows, running, fighting, bugling, mewing, thrashing the timber, and paying no attention whatever to the hunters who had crept in among them.

"We had eight or ten bulls around us, within 15 or 20 yards," Meyer recalls. "But we were in dense timber and we never saw them all at once, although we heard them. New bulls appeared every few minutes, obviously attracted to the fighting and the deafening roar. We wanted to be behind trees to keep from being run down. If I hadn't seen another bull the whole time I was there, that would have been worth the trip."

The uproar lasted about ten minutes. During that time Meyer estimates he saw 25 to 30 bull elk, of which at least five would have qualified for Boone and Crockett (360 B&C points). Then the cows moved away, and the bulls moved with them. That was opening morning—a tough act to follow. And true to form, the next day was not quite in that class.

Again, they left camp early and set out walking in a different area. They looked over five bulls, but saw nothing special. Off in the distance, however, they heard a pair of bulls bugling back and forth in a canyon. They were in a crosswind with one bull on their left and the other on their right, hidden from sight by clumps of scrub oak. They crept on, hoping to catch sight of them, and finally settled in behind a log. The one bull was close—within 50 yards—but still well hidden from view.

At each whistle the hunters strained to see through the brush, to catch at least a glimpse. Finally John Caid caught a slight movement. The bull was bedded down and rocking his head back when he roared. Although his antlers were screened, they could make out that he was more than the usual 6x6. *Much* more.

"We tried every cow sound we knew, hoping he'd get curious," says Meyer. "But he stayed right there, bedded down in the brush."

Finally, Caid told Meyer to get ready. He was going to try all or nothing—a full-out bugle that was almost sure to get the bull moving, for better or worse. At the sound of the guide's roaring challenge, the bull jerked his head around and stood up. They could see a lot of antler through the brush, but exactly how much? Caid's judgement was quick and final.

"You need to shoot this bull," he hissed, as the elk stepped out from cover about 30 yards away, searching the log for his presumptuous rival. As Meyer prepared to shoot, however, the bull sensed something. He stepped back into the brush and down over a knoll out of sight. The hunters again crept forward and made out the elk's form another 50 yards away, once again bedded down in thick cover, once again offering no shot where he lay. Again, Caid bugled. Again, the bull rose to face the challenge. But before Meyer could get a shot this time, the huge elk caught a glimpse of something that should not have been there.

"The last I saw of him, he was tearing off into one of the steepest canyons on the reservation," Meyer said.

Another hour's tracking led to nothing. Finally, worn out and dispirited, they gave up the chase for that day. Not really wanting to hear the answer, Meyer asked Caid what he thought the bull would score. "Maybe 410 points," Caid answered. "I swallowed hard and kept walking," Meyer said.

After that there was no reason to try hunting anywhere else. There was a big bull in that section and they knew it. All they had to do was find him. "We searched for him the next two days and found nothing," Meyer said. "I was just about convinced we'd never see him again."

On the fifth day of the hunt, they set out to look over a mesa where John Caid thought the bull might have been heading when they spooked him that first day. As they methodically worked the mesa, they heard a lone bugle a few hundred yards away. Over the past three days they had looked over many bull elk, and this one did not sound like anything out of the ordinary. But, as they crept to the top of a rise and Caid peeked over he said, "This is him!"

There was no need to explain to Meyer who "him" was. As he chambered a round, the bull spotted them and trotted off. Caid let out a gentle cow-like "mew" and the bull froze in his tracks, standing broadside and looking back at them. With no hesitation, Meyer put the crosshair behind his shoulder and pulled the trigger. The bull netted 408 ⅝ B&C points, with beams 57 inches long and eight points to a side, good for third place in the Boone and Crockett awards in 1995.

⁂

Sunrise, Sunset

Herman Meyer hunted the Fort Apache Reservation at the height of the rut in late September, 1992. When John LoMonaco had arrived there three weeks earlier, however, the rut was barely underway, and warm, dry weather had left conditions on the reservation considerably less than ideal.

On their first morning, LoMonaco and his guide, Dave Kitcheyan, climbed through the aspens to a ridge that overlooked a grassy meadow. As the sun rose, they spotted three bull elk down in the meadow, sparring half-heartedly and checking out a small herd of cows. As dawn turned to day, the elk disappeared into the brush.

"During the next few days we looked over quite a few bulls, but didn't see anything that really turned our crank," says LoMonaco. "The weather had a lot to do with it. The season had started earlier than usual, and the rut wasn't really underway, so the bulls were skittish and wary. We noticed that they went into thick cover shortly after first light, so there was little opportunity to really look over many bulls."

LoMonaco and Kitcheyan hunted day after day, looking over a few bulls each morning before they went into cover and more in the late afternoons when they emerged once more onto the *cienegas*— the high grassy meadows. Finally the weather broke, beginning as a drizzle one evening and turning into a full-scale downpour by morning. It cleared late in the afternoon, and as so often happens in hunting, a change in weather heralded a swift change in animal behavior as well. Once again they headed up Sunrise Mountain to the high ridges where they had started on opening morning.

They worked the ridges through the afternoon, bugling periodically to try to rouse a bull, but got no response. The elk were "deathly quiet;" the frenzy that Herman Meyer was to see a couple of weeks later was still a few days off.

Working their way down the ridges as the shadows lengthened, it looked like another fruitless day. Being men of experience, however, both guide and hunter knew how right Yogi Berra was when he said "It's never over 'til it's over." Kitcheyan continued to toss out tantalizing bugles, and near the bottom of Sunrise Mountain he finally got a response.

"At the edge of some thick aspens, we picked up a lone bugle from far below us," LoMonaco said, "and then a second bugle from the same general direction. Things were picking up!"

The bulls were on the move, bugling back and forth, and LoMonaco and Kitcheyan kept pace with them, moving on down the ridge while staying in the cover of the timber, trying to close the distance as the light faded. They came to a *cienega* and worked their way around to the lower edge, which ended at a ridge overlooking a patch of second-growth timber. The two bull elk were somewhere in there, and the hunters moved cautiously along the ridge, searching the brush below.

Suddenly Kitcheyan ducked in behind a deadfall and motioned LoMonaco down. "Cow!" he breathed. They crouched under cover, afraid to spook the cow and effectively pinned down by her presence there below the ridge. And the bulls beyond, still bugling, were moving steadily, steadily, away from them.

As they hid behind the fallen tree, Dave Kitcheyan tried another bugle to see where the bulls were, and the answer he received indicated they were well out of range. With the light fading fast and the cow elk still browsing along the edge of the timber, it looked like the end of the line. Then Kitcheyan bugled again and a roar "like an angry domestic bull" split the air—a low, deep, short bray, right there in the timber. *Right there!*

Kitcheyan's call had definitely started something. LoMonaco eased a round into the chamber of his .300 Winchester and watched the cow through his scope. The light was going fast, and time was short, but if the bull with the hoarse bugle happened to come out of the timber and tried to herd the cow...well, it was possible!

"As if on cue we heard the distinct rolling bray, but this time it was much closer to the edge of the heavy growth," said LoMonaco.

"He's coming out," Dave whispered. LoMonaco was scanning the edge of the clearing when the bull stepped out from cover, not 20 yards from the cow. He stopped, looked around, then began walking slowly toward her. Watching through the scope, LoMonaco hissed at the guide. "Seven by eight?"

"No, he looks like a clean 8x8," Kitcheyan whispered.

The bull circled the cow, and they began to move back toward the timber together. Studying him through the scope 125 yards away, LoMonaco saw the magnificent heavy antlers sway from side to side. "I couldn't believe the weight of the beams and the dimensions around the burrs. There were heavy ivory tips sticking out everywhere."

The decision to shoot, the whispered order to shoot, and then the shot itself, all came in a sudden rush of action and noise. The bull shuddered and pitched forward into a clump of underbrush, and then all was stillness once again as darkness fell on Sunrise Mountain.

Merriam's Mystery

John LoMonaco's bull elk scored 422⅜ B&C points. Joe Jojola, who was guiding hunters out of Paradise Camp at the time LoMonaco shot the monster, says it was the biggest bull elk he had ever seen—alive or dead—"and believe me, I've seen a lot of them!"

Given the excellent management and strict controls on the elk being taken, it is reasonable to assume that trophies from the Fort Apache Reservation will have a significant impact on the record books for the foreseeable future, starting with the next Boone and Crockett Awards in 1998. In fact, the elk coming off the reservation for the past decade have been so good that they have raised some tantalizing questions. Why, exactly, should they be so spectacular? Could it be...? Naw, the Merriam's elk died out long ago. We know that. Don't we?

"Actually, that's a legitimate question, although if you raise the possibility the taxonomists will laugh at you," said Kevin Lackey. "Generally, the explanation given for the size of those elk is that they have good genes and they have been transplanted into an area where the climate and the habitat are just right to encourage great antler growth."

There is no question about the genes. The elk from Yellowstone have been renowned for many years for having great antlers, and there are still spectacular elk being taken from the fringes of Yellowstone itself. When Yellowstone elk were transplanted into a region like Arizona, with a mild climate and abundant food supplies, it is only natural that the state would start producing some tremendous bulls if they were allowed to grow to full maturity.

In recent years, Arizona has been producing top-notch trophies of other species as well—the pronghorn antelope springs immediately to mind—and the usual explanation is the easy living conditions in parts of the Southwest compared with eking out an existence in windswept, wintry, Montana, and similar locales. Logical as that explanation is, however, there are still a few points uncovered. For one, says Joe Jojola, the elk of the Fort Apache Reservation are not merely bigger.

"The elk here are a little different from elk in other places," he says. "It's not just their antlers; their bodies are more massive, too. If you have seen a lot of elk, you notice the difference right away."

The theory that there may have been a few Merriam's elk that survived, and that they intermingled with the newcomers to create a hybrid with many of the characteristics of *Cervus elaphus merriami*, is not so farfetched and even attracted the interest of biologists who proposed a study to try to confirm it. The tribe got as far as collecting tissue samples for testing, but the study never went beyond that. Now, however, they are looking at a proposal for DNA testing, comparing tissue from reservation elk with samples from Merriam's elk bones still in existence.

When you consider it, the possibility is not that outlandish at all. As Joe Jojola points out, the Fort Apache Reservation is a huge area—1.6-million acres—sparsely settled and much of it very remote. If some isolated bands of Merriam's elk were going to survive anywhere, it would be here.

What's more, being Indian land, it was not as vulnerable to uncontrolled market hunting and overgrazing as cattle ranches were. The Merriam's elk disappeared, ostensibly, sometime between 1902 and 1906, and the first transplants of Rocky Mountain elk occurred in 1913. Although they were not released on the reservation itself, the transplants took place along the Mogollon Rim, and the elk quickly established themselves in the White Mountains—as Jack O'Connor pointed out, one herd on the rim overlooking the Tonto Basin, the other in the White Mountains near the New Mexico boundary. Given those circumstances, who is to say the Rocky Mountain newcomers did not meet up with the last of the Merriam's elk in those secluded canyons? And, considering their size, it would only be logical to expect the Merriam's to dominate the others and leave their mark on the herd. Finally, as O'Connor pointed out, there were all those rumors of elk, and reports of sightings...

Jack O'Connor, an unapologetic romantic, was intrigued by the possibility that the Merriam's elk might somehow have found a way to survive, but also being a realist, he finally decided it was unlikely.

"It is pleasant to imagine that somewhere in the remote mountains a few scattered bands of Merriam's elk were still left to mingle their blood with that of the newcomers, but beyond any doubt this is but a romantic fantasy," he concluded ruefully.

Maybe so. But if O'Connor had seen the elk that are now coming off the Fort Apache Reservation, he might well have come to a different conclusion.

7

✳

BIG SKY, BIG HORNS

The horns of a mountain sheep are unlike any other big game trophy, for they are the living record of the ram's life and times. He sprouts them when he is little more than a lamb and they adorn his head until the day he dies. Over the course of ten, or 12, or, at the most, 14 years, his horns get scraped and chipped, battered and worn. They crash together in battles over ewes and they are deliberately rubbed against rocks; the odd time the ram loses his footing and falls, they are chipped and gouged and tip-broken. Throughout it all, they continue to grow, adding annual rings like an old oak—thin and hard in times of famine, thick and full in times of plenty. By the time a bighorn—or a Stone, or a Dall—becomes trophy size, his horns are a walking version of the Dead Sea Scrolls. And, they are just as fascinating and no less mysterious.

An elk, whose antlers spring forth anew every year, may have a magnificent rack, larger than the one he had a year ago, and larger even than it will be a year hence if he is past his prime. But antlers

✳

are ephemeral. Shoot a great elk trophy, or a whitetail or a caribou, and you have captured a moment in time. Shoot a mountain ram, on the other hand, and you capture a picture of time itself.

❋

It is difficult to separate the modern cult of sheep hunting, with its organizations and pecking orders, from the old magic when a handful of enthusiasts tackled the high peaks alone, for their own sake. Now it is mostly scorekeeping, and even a grand slam—bighorn, Dall, Stone, and desert bighorn—is no longer enough. Today you need a slam with a gimmick to get any attention at all. You don't need to read about too many of these ventures—about sheep hunters seeking to take all four in the shortest time, chartering helicopters and bribing outfitters, or to take all four with the same oddball rifle, or to shoot them all using the same rifle, in record time, while mixing the perfect dry martini. Pretty soon, you come face to face with the stark realization that we've lost something here—something valuable.

I know more than a few sheep hunters, and some very *serious* sheep hunters at that. Some have three of the four species and want desperately to get drawn for that one last tag so they can fill the gap on their wall and then never go near a sheep mountain again. Then there are the others, who will put in for sheep tags until Hell freezes over. For them, Heaven will be a lonely mountain side in a blowing rain, with a scattering of white dots two valleys over and only one way to get there.

Sheep hunting is not for everyone, nor should it be, but it is highly unfashionable to confess that you are not a Jack O'Connor clone and that, quite frankly, chasing sheep among the drifting mists of the high peaks leaves you cold. To admit that you don't like climbing, that you never met a horse you didn't want to shoot, and that your idea of a great time is riding in a Land Rover through an Okavango afternoon, is not politically correct, hunting-wise. It's too bad. What the world really needs is fewer sheep hunters, not more.

❋

Or, to put it another way, what the world needs is more sheep hunters the likes of Mavis Lorenz and Eugene Knight.

❋

The grand slam cult, love it or hate it, is not to blame for the perceived current shortage of sheep. In fact, on balance, any objective observer would have to admit that it has done the sheep of all species far more good than harm. That there are not enough sheep to go around has nothing to do with trophy hunting and everything to do with the market-hunting binge of the last century—to hungry railroad crews that devoured sheep meat like popcorn and mining camps in the mountains that kept professional sheep hunters busy 12 months a year. Throw in the encroachment of domestic stock and a few other factors, such as disease spread by farmers' sheep and feral horses taking over waterholes, and you have quickly (if simplistically) summed up the wild sheep's woes.

Like the Rocky Mountain elk, the bighorn was not always a denizen of the peaks and the high basins. Bighorns were once found lower down, populating large areas that are now ranch country, and it is the encroachment of man that has driven them into the remote regions. Ernest Thompson Seton estimated there were once as many as two million bighorns in the American and Canadian West, but modern studies suggest there was never anywhere near that many. Even so, by the late 1800s, as with elk, pronghorn, and just about everything else, bighorn numbers were dangerously low.

Management programs began in the early 1900s with the institution of closed seasons and ram-only laws. Many of the bag limits were incredibly generous under the circumstances—Alberta allowed six sheep per hunter, any sex—but still, it was a good start. National parks, wildlife refuges, and predator control also played a part, and by the 1920s, game departments had begun live-trapping and transplanting bighorns to try to reestablish herds in traditional ranges. Gradually, the numbers began to bounce back, but the bighorn's recovery suffered from periodic, catastrophic setbacks—die-offs which occur every so often, and for which there is no really

❋

satisfactory explanation.

In the early 1970s, Jack Reneau, now with the Boone and Crockett Club, graduated from university with a degree in wildlife biology. He recalls that the prevailing mood as it related to bighorn sheep was all doom and gloom. "The numbers were down in those days, and it just seemed that with all the pressures on them, sheep populations would never recover. The trend looked to be steadily down."

Reneau went to work for B&C and was involved in the 16th Big Game Awards in 1976. That program accepted animals taken during the period 1974-76. For the three-year period there were exactly nine bighorn rams entered in the competition. Nine!

Flash forward to 1995 and the 22nd Big Game Awards: Altogether, there were *121* bighorns entered in that competition. What is remarkable, however, is not just the increase in numbers, but the increase in quality. Boone and Crockett normally invites the top five entries to attend the awards program, but they also invite any entry that would make the current Top Ten list for the species (that is, any head better than the current holder of tenth place). In 1995, seven bighorn trophies qualified to participate. Of these, five managed to make it to Dallas. The result was the "most spectacular bighorn sheep display we have ever had," said Jack Reneau. "Every head on display scored more than 200 points."

When you consider that the number-one bighorn of all time is 208⅛ points, a year in which every entry is so close to that level is remarkable indeed. Of even more interest is the fact that all four heads that received B&C awards in 1995 came from Montana, and three of them, including James Weatherly's first-place entry at 204⅞, were from the Rock Creek herd in Granite County.

If any evidence is needed that reestablishment programs work, consider this: the Rock Creek herd is a transplanted offshoot of Montana's Sun River herd, a group that does not produce many Boone and Crockett heads, and those it does produce are usually older rams—ten or 11 years of age. The record heads coming out of the Rock Creek herd, on the other hand, are reaching these levels at the age of six or seven years! The Montana game department has, through a combination of good luck and better management, done an outstanding job of matching genes to habitat.

For the record, of the 121 rams that were entered in 1995, 70 came from Montana; the next largest group, 19, was from Alberta; Idaho and British Columbia contributed eight each, and the rest were scattered among Oregon, Washington, Utah, Colorado, Arizona, and New Mexico. Clearly, Montana is the preeminent bighorn region in North America today.

⁂

Although there are considerably more "sheep on the mountain," as the Foundation for North American Wild Sheep likes to phrase it, the fact remains that today there are more people who want to hunt sheep than there are sheep available to be hunted. There are far more sheep hunters, and would-be sheep hunters, in 1999 than there were in 1979, and a hundred or a thousand times more than in the 1930s. As a result, sheep hunting is both expensive and hard to come by; tags are either difficult to get or very expensive or both. And while the Foundation for North American Wild Sheep is undeniably one of the finest conservation groups in the world, firmly focused and intelligently run, there is also no denying that the same sheep hunters who founded and support the group are also the ones who have made so much of sheep hunting a rich man's game.

Because sheep hunting is such a cult thing, because "getting your slam" is so desirable in some circles, the cost of hunting the rarer two species—desert bighorn and Stone—have gone only two directions: high and higher. Bighorn tags in the lower 48 are mostly apportioned on a draw system for both residents and non-residents, while in Alberta, British Columbia, the Yukon, and the Northwest Territories, tags are issued in quotas. Nowhere on the continent is sheep hunting an open activity in the sense that whitetail hunting is. Every sheep gets counted, and allotments for next year are carefully controlled, whether through quota limits or entry draws.

Even for residents of states with viable bighorn populations, getting a sheep tag is usually a once-in-a-lifetime dream, something you put in for year after year, paying the fee, hoping against hope. When the fateful notice finally arrives in the mail—usually the one year when you really cannot afford either the time or the money—you don't have a choice. You go sheep hunting. It's now or, in all probability, never.

※

Them's the Breaks

For Eugene Knight, time presented a different problem. He did not sweat out year after year, missing the draw. In fact, he was drawn the very first year, 1991, that he applied for a tag. The difficulty was, Knight is an outfitter in Montana and was fully booked for the year, with clients coming in and going out and more coming in all through the season. He could not just pull out and go sheep hunting for himself, leaving his clients on their own.

During the whole season, the only time he could get away was three measly days in mid-November. Hardly the ideal time to go bighorn sheep hunting, but you play the cards you are dealt. Knight resolutely set about figuring how he could make the most of his once-in-a-lifetime opportunity in the space of just 72 hours.

Knight's tag was for a section of Blaine County, north of the Missouri River in the Missouri Breaks. This is on the extreme northern edge of traditional sheep range and is rarely thought of as bighorn country today. In the weeks leading up to his skimpy three-day opening, Knight studied maps and talked to anyone he could find who knew the area; when morning broke on November 10, Eugene Knight was rolling up to a ranch house on the north side of the river to get permission to cross the property into the breaks.

The ranch was owned by Milan Pavlovick, a friend of a friend who had made arrangements in advance for Knight to hunt there, so stopping on the way in was a courtesy. It was also a request for assistance. As a guide, Eugene Knight knew there is just no substitute for local knowledge, especially when time is short. Pavlovick volunteered the services of his son, Cody, to take Knight in on the road and show him the territory. Barring a stroke of luck, the first day would probably consist mostly of scouting, but as we all learned in the infantry, time spent in reconnaissance is never wasted. It would have been better to do it beforehand, but there was just no time beforehand. The whole thing was packed into three days—scouting, hunting, everything—and that was all there was to it. Together, Knight and Cody Pavlovick set out in Knight's Blazer to see the lay of the land.

The Missouri Breaks are aptly named—a jumble of cuts and creeks and arroyos and coulees and all the other terms from a half dozen languages that attempt to convey the nuances and subtleties of a churned-up, weathered-down country. Breaks are almost always great for game, though, and thus good hunting country. But they can be rough, and that day they were even less hospitable than usual. The temperature was running just around freezing with a foot of snow on the ground, and the going was tough.

Knight and Pavlovick followed the track as it wound hither and yon. As the day warmed up, the snow began to melt and the frost went out of the ground, turning the mud into a thick gumbo and pretty well confining the truck to the road, wherever it led. Where it led was up the creek bed, which it crossed and recrossed.

"By actual count, we crossed that creek 14 times," Knight recalled. "The water was up three or four feet in places, but Cody said not to worry, the bottom was rocky. He lived there, so I figured he knew."

That is a textbook example of why you seek local knowledge. Textbook. And just to be letter-accurate, they crossed the creek 13 times. The fourteenth time Knight coaxed his truck down into the swift water, he found that his guide was not quite right about the rocky creek bed. The Blazer wallowed into the soft bottom and sat there with the creek flowing around it, leaving Knight and Pavlovick to make a three-mile trek through the mud back to the ranch house for help. "By the time we crossed that creek 13 times on foot on the way back, we were pretty wet," Knight said.

It was too late that day to go back for the Blazer, and Knight went to bed with one precious day gone, a recovery job to look forward to before he could start hunting the next morning, and having seen no sheep. Sleep did not come easy.

The next morning, Milan Pavlovick took him back out to where the Blazer was mired and hauled it out with his pickup. Then they went back to the ranch and Pavlovick began making calls, trying to find out if any of the other ranchers had sighted any big rams. Nothing. And time, as time is wont to do, was marching on. Pavlovick suggested they just head out and try glassing. This time they took both vehicles, in case one got stuck. "With only a day and a half left, I really did not want to spend any more time walking back for help," Knight said.

With Pavlovick leading, they followed an old Jeep road deep into the breaks. A few miles out, the rancher's pickup disappeared over a ridge, then suddenly reappeared, backing up. Pavlovick motioned Knight forward. They turned off onto a sideroad and pulled to a stop overlooking a coulee. Milan told Knight he'd seen a big ram cross the road about a quarter-mile in front of him, heading towards them. There was just a chance he would come down that coulee. And all of five minutes later, that's exactly what happened. Knight spotted the lone bighorn trotting along about 300 yards away.

"He looked respectable so I knelt, put the cross hairs behind his shoulder, and pulled the trigger," he said. "We heard the bullet hit, and the ram burst into a dead run with his head thrown back and his horns on his shoulders."

Knight's rifle, a .270, was sighted in for 400 yards. He shot a second time—high—and a third time—also high. A fourth shot, as the ram rounded a point, nicked one horn. High again! But the ram never paused or stumbled. He just kept going.

Then he popped into sight again, coming down a side coulee, before he finally stopped and put his head down. Knight fired a fifth time and the ram "dropped like a brick." Milan Pavlovick tried to get Eugene Knight to his feet so he could shake his hand, but Knight's legs were not up to it in the excitement.

As Pavlovick went back for his pickup to try to get to within winching distance of the ram, Knight recovered his breath and legs and struggled across the coulee through ankle-deep mud to where his bighorn ram lay on the ground. Three days, as it turned out, was more than enough time.

They wrapped the ram in a plastic tarp to protect it from the mud as they winched it slowly up out of the coulee to the waiting truck. The mud made the slope a slippery mess; impossible to get a footing, treacherous and difficult. When they finally got the ram up to the truck, half an hour later, it was all they could do to lift him into it. He was that heavy.

Soon they were churning their way through the mud and snow back to the ranch house. But the adventure was not quite over. Just as Knight was getting ready to pull out, a neighbor arrived with the breathless news that five of Pavlovick's cattle had broken through the ice and were mired in a pond. They raced to the scene and found the five in deep, freezing water with only their noses sticking out. They managed to get a lasso on them and tried to pull them out with pickups, but the trucks themselves sank deep into the mud. Finally they winched the cattle out one at a time using Knight's chain-saw winch. That winch saw a lot of work that day. Two of the cattle died, but the other three survived, and the rancher was so relieved he told Knight that he had a place to hunt from that day on. "By that time, we were pretty good friends," said Knight.

His ram, which had "looked respectable" trotting across the coulee that morning, certainly turned out to be when they got around to measuring it. Knight's 36-inch tape was not long enough. The ram finally scored 200⅝ Boone and Crockett points, good for third place in the 22nd Big Game Awards. They don't happen like *that* very often.

Before the Storm

For Mavis Lorenz, the pressures of time were very, very different. A resident of Montana, she had applied for a bighorn tag year after year for 18 years. And, for 18 years, she came up empty. Now, on her 19th attempt, her name was drawn and she knew this would have to be it: If she did not get a ram this year, she would not be eligible even to enter the draw again for another seven years, by which time she would be well over 70 years of age. Even if she defied the odds and was drawn a second time—and what were the chances of that?—she felt she would be too old to backpack into the mountains alone. So it was 1993 for Mavis Lorenz, or no sheep.

In the months leading up to the season, she took a cram course in bighorns. She read masters' theses from the University of Montana that dealt with sheep studies in her permit area, Granite County. She studied videos on sheep behavior and how to judge trophies on the hoof, and talked to biologists and sheep hunters—everyone she could find who was knowledgeable about sheep and would answer her questions. And very carefully she made her plans.

Mavis Lorenz may have been a novice sheep hunter, but she was not new to hunting, nor to backpacking. Going into the mountains alone with her home on her back held no particular terrors, and she made provision for three days on the mountain living out of a spike camp. The first day she would hunt the high benches on the northwest side of the mountain, the second day hunt the south side, and the third she would work her way back to the bottom, down a long ridge, hunting all the way.

She drove to the foot of the mountain in the predawn darkness, left her pickup, and began the 3,000-foot climb to the camping spot she had chosen near the top. By nine the sun was well up, and the day, October 6, was bright and warm. On the point of a ridge, she set up her spotting scope and began to glass the openings on the slope above.

Almost immediately she picked up four rams feeding away from her toward some high benches. One of the rams looked like he deserved a closer look. The best way to do that, she decided, would be to make a mental note of where they were heading, then get herself into position to look for them later in the day. Carefully she pulled back from her lookout into a fringe of trees and continued on up, pausing to rest by a downed fir. The day was warm by this time, and the climbing already hard. As she sat with her back to the log, there came the sound of feet rattling the leaves behind her. Fearing it was another hunter, but careful in case it was not, she looked from the corner of her eye as a bighorn ewe picked her way around the end of the log and stopped, not 40 feet away. The ewe bleated softly, then insistently, and the leaves rattled again. A second ewe appeared and joined in, and then a third. Together, the three moved calmly down into some timber. Mavis Lorenz watched them all the time; they had no inkling she was there.

She gave the ewes half an hour to get well away so she would not spook them, then put her pack on again. As she did so, five young rams appeared a few hundred yards above her, feeding across the hillside. While she waited for them to feed on out of sight, another three rams appeared on the far side of the clearing. "Every sheep in Rock Creek, Montana, decided to feed between ten o'clock and one o'clock," she said. "I was surrounded by sheep!"

But no *big* sheep. Slowly, she worked her way up to the timber as the weather began to change around her. Clouds rolled in, and the sky rumbled gently. She waited out a brief rain shower in a grove of small firs, then continued on up toward the benches near the top. Another storm rolled in, a bigger one this time, and Lorenz decided she had better get back to her camp before it really started to come down.

Worried about the storm, she moved more quickly now, her rifle in one hand, her hat in the other, paying little attention to her surroundings as she pushed the pace up the mountain. And suddenly, three big rams jumped up in front of her and stood staring, 50 yards away. Just as startled as they were, Mavis Lorenz stopped dead. She had her hat in one hand, her rifle in the other. But she couldn't just drop the hat; the sudden movement might spook them. Very gently she raised her rifle, reaching for the fore-end with her hat still in her hand. The rams stared, unmoving; but they were not going to stay for long. They were all magnificent, she thought. But which one?

As the rifle reached her shoulder the middle ram turned away, offering his profile, and the hours of studying ram heads and photographs snapped into play. His horns dropped below his jaw line, the hole in the center of the curl was big, and the mass of the horns carried right into the third quarter. This, she thought, is a keeper. Not daring to drop to her knees, she held dead on his shoulder and pulled the trigger. The ram went down on the spot as his companions dashed away.

※

With shaking hands, Mavis Lorenz tried to concentrate on day and time, to make the requisite cuts on her permit. *Was this the sixth? Yes, the sixth...* Barely had she finished when the threatening storm finally cut loose, obscuring the mountain side in a welter of wind and rain, snow and sleet. Thunder rumbled and lightning flashed, darkening the sky like an early dusk. It was too dark to take pictures, and time was running short. Mavis Lorenz worked quickly to dress out the ram. A taxidermist had shown her how to skin it properly for a full-body mount, but even for an experienced skinner, doing that properly takes time.

Doing it for the first time, high on a mountain side, in a thunder storm, is another kind of problem. It took three hours, but she finally had her ram skinned and quartered, the head, horns, and hide safely up off the ground on a stump and the meat stowed away. It was six in the evening and darkness was falling around her when she started back down the mountain, alone, to get the help she needed to pack out her ram.

※

8

⁂

The Moose
of Fortymile

Prologue

At one time all the largest moose racks in Alaska came from the Kenai Peninsula. If you wanted a record-book moose, the Kenai was the place to go. There were big moose, and there were lots of them.

Why this was so is open to some speculation, but a huge forest fire that swept the peninsula before the turn of the century is generally given the credit. It replaced old forest with succulent new growth, returned vital antler-growing minerals to the soil, and the moose moved in in droves.

When Jack O'Connor published *Big Game Animals of North America* in 1961, he reported that in the Boone and Crockett Club's *Records of North American Big Game*, nine of the top ten Alaska-Yukon moose listed at that time came from Alaska (and one from the Yukon), with the top three all coming from the Kenai. But things change, and O'Connor saw the change coming.

"I believe time will prove that the moose heads run just as

⁂

large in arctic Alaska and the Wind River country of the Yukon," O'Connor insisted.

Fade to black. Cut to the headwaters of the Fortymile River, a hundred miles north of Tok, Alaska, and hard on the Yukon border.

❋

Klondike Gold, 1994

The Klondike Gold Rush was a century-old memory when John Crouse first set foot on the tundra around Fortymile, but evidence of the great gold strike lives on in the abandoned claims, the rotting sluices, and the piles of mine tailings. Here lived Jack London's *Men of Forty-Mile*—Big Jim Beldon, Scruff Mackenzie, and of course, the Malemute Kid.

From 1896, when George Carmack first discovered gold on Bonanza Creek on the Yukon side, until 1910, when the gold rush petered out, 100 million dollars in gold was extracted from the Yukon River drainage. Jack London left the territory with a fund of memories that he transformed into literature, and that in turn sent several generations of prospectors north to roam the rivers and pan for gold. Some of these men even managed to leave with more than they brought, while a few stayed on, discovering to their surprise that the real treasure was not the gold of the land, but the land of the gold.

John Crouse had no illusions of gold when he came north to the Fortymile River from his home in Cordova, on Prince William Sound. Crouse and his friends, Doug and Dennis Chester, came to hunt caribou and, with any luck, take a moose. Being an Alaska resident, Crouse was not unduly concerned with antler size. While non-residents hunting the Fortymile area are restricted to a 50-inch-minimum rack, Alaskans, who depend on the moose for meat, can take any bull, any size. And anyway, Crouse does not consider himself a trophy hunter. "What I like is hunting different species, seeing new places, exploring new areas," he says.

Although Crouse had hunted moose on a few occasions down near Cordova, he had never shot one, so the trip to Fortymile qualified on every count.

The three drove up the highway from Glennallen through the high mountains of the Alaska Range, reaching the town of Tok, on the Alaska Highway, on August 28, and prepared for the hundred-mile flight north by Super Cub. They arranged for the planes to come back on September 4, allowing them six full days of hunting, but there was a slight logistics problem: A pre-booked sheep hunter made it four hunters to go in, but there were only three Super Cubs to take them. Crouse found himself stranded at the staging area overnight. For lack of anything better to do, he spent his time studying the maps and regulations that were plastered all over the walls. And he received an unwelcome surprise.

"The game-management unit we were hunting was broken up into several smaller sub-units, and each had its own set of hunting regulations," he says. "There were also some special management units, and others that were closed completely because of a national park designation. I was reading over all the regulations, comparing them with where we were going to hunt, and I found that the drainage where I was hoping to hunt moose did not open until September 5, the day after we were due to leave!"

Crouse drew the pilots' attention to the problem. After thinking it over, they offered to fly in on the evening of August 31 and ferry the three hunters to a different area—one where they could start hunting moose September 1.

※

John Crouse arrived in camp a day later to find Dennis and Doug Chester already hunting. The country was "beautiful, but not really rugged," Crouse says. "There was spruce in the bottoms, which gave way to scrub birch and willows, and finally tundra as you got higher."

There were low mountains on the horizon, obscured in the morning by a constant light rain and fog. The three hunters would leave camp each morning and make their way up onto the ridges as the sun rose and burned off the cloud cover. Since the weather was warm and the main caribou herds remained far to the northwest, they saw only a scattering of cows and calves. Still, on the second day, Doug Chester collected a young bull. Everything was going, more or less, according to plan. "We hoped to get three caribou and one moose," Crouse says. "There's a lot of meat on a bull moose, more than enough to divide three ways."

Although he had lived in Alaska for five years, Crouse had never shot a moose. In his native Wyoming, he grew up hunting pronghorn antelope, mule deer, and elk. After graduating from the University of Wyoming in 1988 and qualifying as a wildlife technician, he migrated north to take a job with the Alaska forestry department in Cordova, a small town on the coast amid the rain forest of Prince William Sound. Once in Alaska he hunted different species, including Dall sheep, and although he has yet to get one, he says sheep hunting is already in his blood.

As a wildlife technician in Cordova, part of Crouse's duties include studying moose habitat and tracking them with radio collars. Cordova is in excellent moose country, and there are many with big antlers, but permits are mostly available on a draw system. When the Chester brothers suggested a hunting trip in 1994, he was eager to see something new—country where you do not have to don hip waders as soon as you get out of bed. Hunting moose around Cordova would, after all, be a little too much like the work he does every day.

❋

After two days of hard hunting, the trio had one caribou to show for their efforts, and the planes arrived right on time. A 5,000-foot spine of mountains separated them from the adjacent management unit with its early moose season. Flying east through the pass in the Super Cub, John Crouse studied the terrain below. Here the tundra was limited to the very tops of ridges, while the valleys and river bottoms were clogged with willows. He spotted a bull moose feeding on a hillside among the spruce and noted the habitat that seemed to attract them. The plane circled to get a better look at the big bull and the pilot noted that the velvet was almost off the antlers, which would "probably go a good 60 inches." Crouse made a careful note of the animal's location as they flew on down the drainage.

The Super Cub dropped the three hunters on a ridge a thousand feet up. They awoke the next morning to find their camp engulfed in cloud and the usual light rain falling. Crouse figured the moose he had seen was at least three miles back up the drainage, and they discussed strategy. Being a thousand feet above the nearest water source, the first priority was to fill water bottles. After that, they would work their way up toward a knoll, close to where the moose had been last seen, hoping for a break in the weather. If it cleared, they figured, they could sit on the knoll and glass the mountainsides.

It was noon by the time they worked their way down to the nearest stream. The rain continued stubbornly, although it was brightening a little, and it began to look like the weather might break up. They made the knoll and found themselves looking out over a deep saddle that divided them from the high, barren mountains to the west. Finally, the rain stopped and the sun began to peek through.

John Crouse moved slowly down the side of the knoll, looking for a vantage point to set up and start glassing. As he did so, he caught a sudden reflection sparkling from the bushes far below. Thinking it might be an antler tip, he dropped to one knee behind a slight rise, then squirmed to the edge and put his binocular to his eyes. A few hundred yards down the hill he saw one broad, newly-out-of-velvet and rainwashed palm of an antler, protruding from the bushes, glaring white in the sunshine. Moose. *Big* moose.

❊

Crouse sank back down out of sight and signalled to Doug and Dennis Chester, who were further up the hill and could not see the big bull. Together, the three worked their way down the hill behind a screen of spruce. When he estimated they were about 150 yards from where the moose was bedded, Crouse called a halt. They shed their packs, and in a low whisper he explained what he had seen.

"They wanted to know if it was a really big bull," Crouse says, "but I didn't know and I really didn't care. I could take any size bull, and we were there for the meat."

They all agreed they would shoot the first bull they saw, regardless of the size of the rack. Since Crouse was the one who had spotted the moose, it was his to shoot. Taking his rifle he crawled another 25 yards through the brush until he came to a low ledge. Prone, he pushed his rifle forward and squinted through the scope. All he could see was the bull's head and a bit of its neck—not enough to chance it.

"I whispered to Dennis that I couldn't see enough of it, that I wanted to wait for a better shot," he says. "At that moment, the bull stood up and looked our way..."

He could not have scented them, for the wind was in their faces. It was unlikely that he heard the whispering, either, but something had definitely alerted him. The bull stood broadside with his head turned directly toward them, searching the hillside above him. The huge antlers shone in the sun; shards of velvet dangled from the brow tines, and "pieces the size of gunny sacks" hung from each deep palm.

"I got back down over my scope," Crouse recalls, "while the bull stared straight at me. I tried to put the cross hairs behind the shoulder, but there was a branch blocking the shot. I had to try to move."

Gingerly, feeling the bull's gaze, Crouse inched to his right. The cross hairs found the spot, and the bullet hit with a resounding *whump!*

"The bull leapt into the air and whirled 180 degrees. I chambered another round and waited. He stood his ground for several seconds, just standing motionless. He didn't seem to be going anywhere, but I didn't want him getting any farther from our camp. The second bullet rocked him. He tried to leap forward but his hind legs collapsed. He toppled over backwards, and his antlers plowed into the soft earth."

Most hunters classify moose antlers by spread, but there is more to it than that. At one time, spread was the only official criterion for judging a moose rack, but now it is just one of several measurements that comprise its score for the record book—the others being the length and width of the palms, the total number of tines, and the overall symmetry of the head. This, said Jack O'Connor, "is as it should be, because some moose heads with very wide spreads and a high standing in the old records were actually quite narrow of palm, and spindly. The impressiveness of a moose head," he insisted, "is in its great mass."

When he stood by the huge bull, lying head down on the hillside, John Crouse says he was impressed by the size of the brow palms, and the overall width of each palm. He was more immediately impressed, however, by the mass of the animal itself. It took the three hunters more than an hour just to maneuver the carcass into a position where they could dress and butcher it. They then spent the rest of that day, all of the next day, and half of a third day getting the meat and antlers back down to their camp.

When the two pilots, Charlie and Ron, arrived with the Super Cubs to take them out, Charlie's first reaction was that it was the biggest set of antlers he'd ever seen. Ron wondered aloud if they would even be able to transport them out with the small planes. The antlers would have to be lashed to the struts under the wing, and he was afraid their sheer mass would cause too much air drag. Crouse suggested splitting the skull and transporting the antlers separately, but Charlie said no. "He wanted them to be measured for Boone and Crockett," Crouse says, "so the skull had to stay intact."

In the end they strapped them to Charlie's plane, and he managed to get them out as far as an abandoned mine, which had an airstrip to land a larger plane. As it turned out, the great antlers were too big even to fit into a Cessna 185, and they were forced to bring in a Cessna 206, with double cargo doors, to retrieve them. They completed the trip courtesy of a friendly truck driver on his way to Anchorage, who took the antlers to Doug Chester's place. There they stayed for the mandatory 60-day drying period, until they could be officially measured.

"The funny thing was, I didn't think they were all that big," Crouse recalls. "They were big, sure, but they did not seem all that wide. The spread was 65 inches, but I knew of a couple of racks that were wider than that."

But there is more to a moose rack than mere width. When the Boone and Crockett measurer was finished, he awarded John Crouse's Alaska-Yukon moose a total score of 261⅝—more than enough for a new world's record. A hundred years after the gold rush, the Klondike is still sending men home with riches, one way or the other.

Epilogue

There is an interesting side light to the tale of John Crouse's Fortymile moose. Two other Alaska-Yukon moose received awards at the 22nd Boone and Crockett Big Game Awards in 1995. The number-two moose was wider (almost 68 inches) than Crouse's, and weighed more (62 pounds compared to 55), but scored just a little over 246. Its palms were narrower and shorter, and it had fewer qualifying points. The number-three moose was wider overall and heavier still (70-plus inches and 77 pounds), but scored a little over 240 for the same reason.

As a wildlife technician who works with moose every day, John Crouse was particularly interested in the biological aspects of the animal he had taken. "I intended to bring the jaw out with me, but I just forgot it in the work of getting the moose butchered and back to camp," he says. "I did give it a good look at the time, though. That was really not a very old bull. His teeth were not worn down very much, and they weren't covered with tartar, which is what happens with older animals. I would say he was six or seven years old—no more than that."

That being the case, the new world's record moose might have had one or two years of improvement left in him before his annual antler growth levelled off and began to decline. Of course, we will never know for sure. On the other hand, where there was one bull like that there are bound to be more, and where there might be more, there will definitely be more people seeking them. That, too, is the history of the Klondike, as George Carmack would be the first to tell you.

9

❊

DAY ONE, TEN A.M.

There are two rules for seriously hunting trophy caribou: One, never shoot a caribou the first day, no matter how good he looks. Two, if he looks spectacular enough, know when to ignore Rule Number One.

Donald Hotter, fortunately, was an experienced hunter when he went to the Northwest Territories in 1994. Not only did he have 30 years of trophy hunting behind him, he had also hunted caribou several times before and shot four of them in Alaska, including one that placed high in the record book. So he knew caribou. He also knew the rules, and when to break them.

Humpy Lake is a small body of water 165 miles north of Yellowknife—just one lake among thousands, appearing on only the most detailed of maps. It is tucked into the endless tundra right on the edge of the tree line, where the scrubby black spruce peter out and give way to lichen-covered hills that roll on and on until they reach the Arctic Ocean. This is caribou country, classic and unforgiving. In summer—all eight weeks of it—the weather is fine and warm, and life would be very pleasant but for the incessant biting

❊

insects that make any breeze a welcome relief. By the end of August, however, the onset of winter becomes apparent, like a curtain about to rise when the theatre goes silent. The breeze has an edge to it, and the caribou are moving again. Their antlers have reached their spectacular best, the velvet is coming off as they savage any bush they can find, and the big bulls' thoughts turn to love.

Don Hotter and Wes Vining arrived at Humpy Lake in the second week of September, the ideal time to hunt trophy caribou. Vining, a booking agent from Cody, Wyoming, was interested in looking over a new camp he had taken on, and convinced his old friend Hotter to come along. As the bush plane flew in low, they noticed caribou moving on the shore across the lake from the camp, and made a mental note to check out that area the next morning.

Central Canada barren ground caribou range across the northern part of Canada from the Yukon to Hudson Bay. Like all northern caribou—and for that matter, almost every other northern species—they have enjoyed a remarkable comeback the last few years.

In the 1960s and '70s, the newspapers were full of stories about precipitous population declines among the caribou. Books like Farley Mowat's *People of the Deer* spoke of the decline in the great caribou migrations and the demise of the people (in that particular case, the Ihalmiut of the eastern Northwest Territories) whose livelihood, way of life, and even life itself were being wiped out as a result.

The barren ground caribou of the far north are loosely divided into three populations: Alaska (including the Yukon, lying to the west of the Mackenzie River), central Canada (from the Mackenzie to Hudson Bay) and Ungava (northern Quebec). In an article in *Gray's Sporting Journal* in 1976, Tom Brakefield gave an account of the decline of caribou numbers in Alaska. Most alarming was the Western Arctic herd, which had a minimum of 242,000 animals in 1970, but only 100,000 by April, 1976, and as few as 50,000 just six months later! Brakefield was pessimistic about the future of the caribou in a world of oil exploration and pipelines, snowmobiles and repeating rifles, and burgeoning wilderness roads.

To the east, in Canada's immense Northwest Territories (an area of 1.3 million square miles, more than twice the size of Alaska), the caribou were doing little better. There are seven major herds of barren ground caribou in the NWT, of which six are found on the mainland. The Beverley herd was the one Mowat wrote about in *People of the Deer*; between 1967 and 1974, its numbers declined from 159,000 to 124,000.

There were no easy answers as to why the caribou numbers were declining. It was not wolves, at least not in every case. It was not over-hunting, although there were documented cases of natives killing many more caribou than they could ever eat. It was not loss of habitat, although the land was certainly being altered by construction and exploitation. The inevitable conclusion was that a combination of all of the above, along with a generous dose of the modern world in general, was driving the anachronistic caribou to extinction.

Then, when it seemed that all was lost, the populations began to bounce back. In the case of Alaska's Western Arctic herd, a combination of wolf control, limits on hunting permits, and, perhaps, greater native awareness of the fragility of caribou numbers, led to a strong increase. The most spectacular single recovery was the George River caribou herd in Quebec, which increased from about 5,000 animals in 1955 to more than half a million by the mid-1980s. In that particular case, the most likely explanation is simply the cycles of nature. Caribou increase, and they decline; they decline, and they increase. There's not much we can do about it, and even less that we should try to do about it.

In the central NWT, in a huge area bounded by Great Slave Lake to the south, Great Bear Lake to the west, the Arctic Ocean to the north, and Bathurst Inlet and the Beverley herd to the east, lives the Bathurst herd of barren ground caribou. Inexplicably, during the years that saw the Beverley herd decline (1967-74), the Bathurst herd actually increased, from 144,000 to 174,000.

By the time Don Hotter and Wes Vining arrived at Humpy Lake in September, 1994, the resident caribou (members of the Bathurst herd) were in fine fettle in terms of numbers and, Vining was confident, ripe to yield some trophy heads that would raise a few eyebrows down south. He had studied the area closely and was confident that both the genetics and the habitat were ideal to produce a monster.

⁂

Early the next morning Hotter and Vining set out by boat with their guide, Leon Wellin. They cruised Humpy Lake, scanning the shore for any sign of caribou, and almost immediately spotted a small herd on the far shore. There were about 15 bulls in the group, so they beached the boat and stalked to within a few hundred yards. They then settled in to glass the antlers.

For a newcomer to the game, there is no harder head to judge than a good bull caribou. To anyone accustomed to whitetails and the occasional bull elk, even a mediocre caribou looks tremendous. That is the major reason so many are shot on the first day. It is also the reason so many should not be—hence Rule Number One. Caribou guides have great difficulty restraining first-time caribou hunters from pulling the trigger on the first set of antlers they see. With experience, however, comes judgement and the ability to calmly look over a caribou, even one that is putting distance between you and him, and not take the shot because the head does not measure up.

Experienced caribou hunters break down the antlers into their component parts and rate them accordingly, rather than seeing the head as a whole. You look for overall impression first (and briefly), then study the specifics. Does he have a really good top? If not, forget it; no bull with a poor upper is a decent trophy. If the tops are there, you then look for good bez tines, the palm-like protrusions that extend forward above the eyes. If the bez tines are good, you check the shovel—either a very large single, or a good double shovel, which is the ideal. After that, you check for the back tines that extend to the rear from the main beam where it begins to curve upward. If the bull checks out in every respect, you go back to looking at the whole to see if he has the mass and the aesthetic balance you are after.

Every mature caribou will be decent in at least one respect. Many will qualify in two of the three, but only the best trophies are good in all three areas, and it takes one in ten thousand to have it all, and have it in spades. Fortunately, Don Hotter was a widely experienced hunter who had pursued trophies over most of North America. He had been to Alaska eight times and taken every animal available except musk ox. He had been to British Columbia and Saskatchewan, to Ontario, to Wyoming, and his home state of Montana. He describes himself as both a meat hunter and a trophy hunter—a man who eats everything he kills, but "spends a lot of time thinking about horns, too."

A few years earlier he had taken a caribou in Alaska that scored just over 410 points B&C, so he and Wes Vining were well aware of what a good trophy was. One by one they studied the dozen bulls in the herd, and one by one they discarded them.

"Some had great tops but little on the bottom," Hotter says. "Some had great bottoms but no tops. Some had great tops and bottoms, but small spreads and no back tines. And then there were some that were pretty good, but had only one shovel. But wow! What excitement! We had fun looking at all these bulls and taking the time to be critical. What a great sport it is, to have a friend who also likes to hunt trophies and is willing to pass on hundreds of caribou, even if it means going home empty-handed because you don't find one that measures up."

In the end, although they were sure a couple of bulls would make the record book, the three hunters quietly crawled away without disturbing them. It was, after all, not even nine o'clock the first morning. There was lots of time and obviously no shortage of caribou.

❋

Abandoning a book head, even on the first morning, is a calculated risk. Being migratory animals, caribou come and go. Even in areas like northern Quebec, with its half-million caribou criss-crossing the land, it is possible to sit by a river ford for a solid week and see nothing. Just because the caribou are here today does not mean they will be here tomorrow. On the other hand, as someone once said, the secret to shooting big trophies is not to shoot little ones. Hotter, Vining, and Wellin returned to scanning the rolling hills and ridges of the endless tundra.

Within a few minutes, Hotter spotted several bulls a couple of miles away. Through their binoculars they could see a forest of antlers. After half an hour of careful glassing, they decided that at least two of the bulls rated a closer look. One in particular had "fantastic bottoms, good tops, and outstanding main beam length." The question was, how to get closer to them? Wellin suggested they go back to the boat and circle a hill that lay between them and the small herd, then climb a ridge, pinpoint the animals again, and intercept them.

When you say it fast, it sounds easy. But intercepting a moving caribou is an almost impossible task unless he is pausing frequently to browse. When a caribou is on the move, doing what he does best—migrating—he covers ground at an astonishing rate. A strolling caribou moves as fast as a man can trot on level firm ground, never mind slogging it over and through the tangled brush that covers the tundra. To intercept a moving caribou, you have to guess exactly where he will head and know the ground like the back of your hand to get there before he does.

Fortunately, Wellin knew the territory down to the smallest rock. A half hour later the hunters were in position, catching sight of the caribou as they moved up the valley at a fast walk, feeding as they came. One by one the bulls hove into view, with Wes Vining judging and mentally discarding each one in turn. "Not that one; the one we saw had better palms. Not that one; he's too narrow."

One bull. Two bulls. Three bulls. Four. Vining dismissed them one after the other. And then the fifth bull stepped out from around a hill, and Vining hissed: "That's him—that's the bull! Look at those palms. And that bez!"

Unaware, still feeding and walking, the big bull moved on behind a ridge. Carefully marking the spot where he disappeared, Don Hotter moved up the ridge trying to catch sight of him again. As he did so, a couple of the other caribou caught the movement and stared.

"I heard Wes say the big bull was no more than a hundred yards in front of me, but I still couldn't see him," Hotter says. "I inched further forward until, suddenly, there he was. I looked over my shoulder to ask Wes if this was the one."

The question required no answer. The look in Vining's eyes was enough.

"It was an easy one-shot kill, slightly downhill at 100 yards," Hotter said. "Ten o'clock in the morning the first day of the hunt, and I had the new world's record caribou."

❈

They had it, but at the time they did not really know it. They knew they had a great caribou, a phenomenal caribou, but just how good was he?

A preliminary measurement gave a score of 423 B&C points. If that was accurate—and they could hardly believe it was—and if it held up as the head dried, it would eclipse the old record by 11 points. Refusing to believe their good fortune, Hotter and Vining hunted on, trying to fill their other caribou tags. They took two other bulls, both of Boone and Crockett quality, but nowhere near the size of the first.

Back home, Bob Hanson, an official B&C scorer, scored the rack at 428⅛ points, proving once again that a truly great head gets bigger the longer you look at it, while a mediocre head always shrinks. The Humpy Lake caribou now seemed a sure bet to claim a new world record at the Boone and Crockett Club's 22nd big game awards in 1995.

But if the taking of the bull himself was quick and efficient, the claiming of the record more than made up for it in nail-biting suspense. In preparation for shipping the rack to Dallas for the awards meeting, Hotter had it mounted, then constructed a solid crate to ship it in. He loaded it into the back of his open pickup and left his wife, Judy, to drive it into town to the taxidermist, who would transport it to Dallas.

It was a blustery, rainy day, and to protect the precious trophy Judy Hotter wrapped a tarp around the crate. As she drove down the highway, a sudden gust of wind caught the tarp and billowed it out, lifting tarp, crate, and the about-to-be new number-one central Canada barren ground caribou out of the back and crashing down onto the tarmac. With help, Judy managed to drag the crate to the side of the road. Inside, the head looked all right, but the antlers...? There was something wrong! The impact on the pavement had cracked the skull just enough to allow the antlers to move!

The Boone and Crockett Club has strict rules of eligibility. In the case of antlered heads where spread is a measurement that makes up part of the overall score, both antlers and skull must be left intact to qualify. The crack in the skull, even though it did not break completely, was enough to disqualify the great bull—if the panel of judges so chose. Judy Hotter got the head into town to the taxidermist and called Bob Hanson, who immediately got in touch with the Boone and Crockett Club. He explained what had happened and asked for a ruling. Boone and Crockett said they'd get back to him.

"It took six weeks for them to make the decision to allow it into the competition in spite of the crack," Hotter says. "When I got to Dallas I could understand why they are so careful; there is so much that goes on, jigging around with heads to improve the scores. I could see their point. But it sure was a nerve-wracking six weeks. A lot of sleepless nights."

In the end, the B&C official scoring committee awarded the Humpy Lake caribou a score of 433⅜, smashing the old record by 21 points.

The story is unlikely to end here. In the same month of the same year, a hunter named Al Kuntz took another bull at Humpy Lake that scored 426⅛ points. Were it not for Don Hotter's monster, it would have been the new world's record. Hotter himself is confident that there are bigger bulls in the area and that one could well come along and eclipse his.

"In the group I took that bull from, there were at least two others that would have easily made the book," he says. "Wes Vining told me afterward that he should have shot one of those, except he was so preoccupied with me and the big one.

"I hate the thought of it, but we saw too many good bulls to believe that there is not another one, a better one, somewhere up there. For that matter, I may go back there myself and take Judy and my two boys. They are both hunters, and if someone has to break my record, I'd love it to be one of my boys."

10

❋

ONE WHALE OF A BEAR

To most Americans, the Aleutian Islands are as unreal as the dark side of the moon. They are a distant ethereal "somewhere," dimly recollected from geography books in long-ago classrooms—unless, that is, you were a pilot stopping to refuel on the Tokyo run during the Korean War, or one of the unlucky few who found themselves stationed there, living in Quonset huts in the icy rain 12 months a year. Then you would have memories of the Aleutians—memories of North Pacific tides, of mist and fog, of constant blowing rain. Your memories of sunny days would be very, very few, for they see barely a handful of those even in summer.

The Aleutians begin where the Alaska Peninsula ends, stretching out into the North Pacific like the tail of a cat. The islands are, in fact, a chain of volcanoes more than a thousand miles long, mostly uninhabited, left by man (with considerable relief) to the seals and whales and circling sea birds.

Unimak Island is the first of the Aleutians and one of the largest. It is 800 miles from Anchorage and farther still from every-

❋

where else—a piece of damp and windswept tundra. Unimak is home to two volcanoes, Pogromni and Shishaldin, and, at 9,300 feet, the latter is the highest peak in the Aleutian chain. Like most of the islands, it has no trees to speak of; its vegetation consists of short grass and low flowering plants. On Unimak, visibility is limited only by the shifting fog.

The landscape of Unimak has been sculpted by eons of volcanic eruptions and earthquakes. There are rocky spines and cliffs overlooking stony beaches awash in flotsam and jetsam. The Pacific tides carry everything imaginable before them, from the glass balls Japanese fishermen use to float their nets, to driftwood and empty oil cans, to ancient bottles with corks that should, but rarely do, contain letters from castaways. The tides also bring in carcasses of sea-going beasts of every kind, frequently hurling a whale up on shore and leaving it there, half buried in the sand, for the scavengers and the sea birds. And a good thing it is, too, for Unimak is also home to the most fearsome scavenger on earth—the Alaska brown bear.

❉

When we think of brown bears, the names that usually spring to mind are Kodiak and Afognak, Admiralty Island and Baranoff. But the Alaska Peninsula and the closer Aleutians also have substantial brown bear populations, and while they do not benefit from the abundant salmon runs that cause their down-coast brethren to grow so huge, they do have the carrion that washes up on shore.

In many ways bears are supremely adaptable, and the Alaska brown bear is no exception. The bears that inhabit Unimak—and their numbers are substantial—manage to emulate their various cousins in more ways than one. Their habitat itself is more reminiscent of the tundra roamed by the barren ground grizzly of the Northwest Territories than it is the coastal rain forest of Alaska, while their diet is closer to that of a polar bear on the ice floes than to an Admiralty Island brown bear.

Hunting on Unimak is a limited-entry affair, and prospective bear hunters enter a draw for the available tags. With a good bear population, ample food in the form of whale carcasses and the like, and limited hunting, Unimak would seem to be the ideal setup for someone looking for a big bear. However, its remoteness, isolation, and the high cost of even getting there, combined with its generally abysmal weather, discourages many prospective hunters. Only a quarter of those fortunate enough to draw tags actually manage to get to Unimak to hunt the bears!

John Frost (a.k.a. Jack, naturally) is an Anchorage surgeon who got his first glimpse of Unimak Island in 1980. Having drawn one of the coveted brown bear tags, he headed off completely on his own, armed with both a rifle and a bow, to attempt to take a big bear.

"I was fascinated by the prospect of taking a bear with a bow," he says, "although there are a lot of problems associated with it. It is foolhardy to tackle a bear with a bow, without a competent back-up gunner armed with a rifle. You can't stop a charging bear with an arrow.

"That first year on Unimak, I couldn't find anyone to go with me, so I went by myself. My plan was that I'd carry both rifle and bow all the time. If I was offered the perfect shot at a bear with a bow, I would take it; if I saw a really big one, though, a ten- or 11-footer, I'd play it safe and use the rifle."

In some ways, Unimak Island is perfect bowhunting terrain. There are lots of bears and the wide-open visibility makes spotting one relatively easy. On the other hand, lack of brush means that traditional, ambush-style bowhunting is almost impossible. You generally have to spot the bear and then stalk it, the most difficult method of all. For Jack Frost that posed no particular problem, for he was an accomplished hunter.

A native of Pennsylvania, Frost first saw Alaska in 1973, when he was serving in the air force. He fell in love with the country, decided to make it his home, and eventually set up his civilian practice in Anchorage. Although he killed his first game with a bow early in life ("a starling, at the age of seven") he was not a life-long bowhunter. During his first couple of years in Alaska he hunted with a rifle and took a wide range of trophies—moose, caribou, mountain goat, black bear, Dall sheep, and brown bear. He also found time to get his pilot's license and buy his own plane, the ubiquitous Piper Cub. And he studied and learned as much as he could about Alaska and the animals he hunted at every opportunity.

Gradually, Frost found himself growing away from rifle hunting. As his proficiency grew, he found it did not present as much of a challenge as it had before. More than that, however, he found that the most precious part of hunting—what he calls "being with the game"—was over much too soon when he hunted with a rifle.

"The best time in all of hunting is the interval between spotting the game and either killing it or spooking it. That's what I call being *with* the animal. You're making your stalk and the animal is close by and you can feel it. With a rifle, that period of time is frequently—too frequently—very short. With a bow, on the other hand, it is often a very long time, and usually ends with the animal spooked and gone, not dead."

So Frost returned to bowhunting. He found that archery equipment had undergone great technological changes since he had last hunted whitetails with a bow as a teenager in Pennsylvania. "The new compound bows that were coming out then (in the late 1970s), with sights, not only made it possible for me to become proficient much more quickly, but also to shoot a more powerful bow," he says.

His first year as a bowhunter, Frost found himself "on the receiving end of a false charge by a small grizzly." There being no place to run, Frost stood his ground and the bear stopped about 20 feet away. It was not the end of the bear, but it was the beginning of Frost's real fascination with the idea of taking a big bear the hard way.

Frost recognized the risks of hunting alone.

"The problem is, it's easy to find inexperienced guys who want to go along on a bear hunt and maybe even shoot one themselves," he says. "But it is very hard to find a capable, experienced person who has been in on many bear kills, who is steady enough not to shoot too quickly or unnecessarily and ruin a legitimate bow kill, but is capable of shooting quickly and accurately if the situation demands it. Most of all, you have to find such a person who is willing to take the time to go on such a crazy quest."

Jack Frost could find no such person for his first trip to Unimak, so he went alone.

"What you have to do then is consider shooting a brownie only under a very clearly defined set of circumstances," he explained. "The hunter should be above the bear in a safe, secure location, such as a tree, or a cliff, or a very steep bank. Second, the bear must be close and undisturbed for the shot. Finally, the surrounding terrain should be open so you can keep the bear in sight at all times after the shot. That minimizes the risk and uncertainty of following a wounded bear into the brush or alders."

Which is, of course, the most dangerous aspect of bear hunting.

Now to Unimak Island in the year 1980. Unable to find a competent back-up gunner, Frost went on his own. What he found at Unimak was a paradise of bears enveloped in a shroud of horrible weather. In a week alone on the island, he watched more than two dozen different brown bears, but the right situation never seemed to present itself. He could have used the rifle just about any time, he says, but never saw a bear big enough for him to justify it to himself.

As for the bow, "I did have one opportunity when an eight-foot bear came walking along a narrow stretch of beach, directly below a 12-foot bank I was on," he says. "I got out as close to the edge as I could, with my rifle cocked, safety off, by my feet. I waited until the bear was directly below me, then rose up to shoot. The bear was about 20 feet away when I released the arrow, and hard as it may be to believe, at 20 feet I missed! The arrow went high, and the bear took one startled look at me, and ran off—much to my relief! When I took a good look at that bank afterwards, I realized the bear could have climbed it and been on top of me before I even had a chance to move toward my rifle, much less pick it up and shoot."

Jack Frost killed no bear on Unimak Island that trip, but his education as a bear hunter made great strides.

※

Over the next several years Frost branched out, periodically taking time off from his practice as an arthroscopic surgeon to work as an assistant guide for an outfitter who hunts grizzlies in the Brooks Range. There he had the opportunity to be in on numerous bear kills with rifles. Still, what he really wanted was to take a big bear with a bow, and memories of Unimak remained fresh.

Six years later Frost got his wish. His name came up in the draw and he prepared once more to tackle the brown bears of Unimak Island. This time, however, it would be different—very different— in many ways.

"First of all, I had a back-up gunner," he said. "That was very important. My friend Tony Oney, who's a dentist in Anchorage, had some free time and he wanted to see if an arrow could kill a brown bear. So he agreed to go with me.

"Aside from being a dentist, he'd also been guiding in Alaska since the mid-1960s; he used to guide polar bear hunters before the Marine Mammal Protection Act in 1972, and since then he'd been taking out grizzly hunters. Tony is one of the few men in whom I would have the confidence to back me up in an attempt to kill a big bear with a bow."

Like many Alaskan hunters, Oney was also a pilot; they decided to take both planes down to Unimak, partly because it was safer, but also because it would give them the opportunity to thoroughly scout the island from the air. Since Unimak is 70 miles long and ten miles wide, an air reconnaissance was obviously the best way to pick a hunting area in the limited time they had available.

The 1986 spring bear season on Unimak ran from May 10 to May 25, but Frost and Oney had commitments in Anchorage until May 17. Then, just as they were preparing to head out, the weather turned nasty, heavy rains riding a 60-knot head wind, combined with turbulence and low ceilings all the way to Cold Bay, the last settlement on the tip of the Alaska Peninsula. Wisely, they stayed put. Two days later the weather cleared enough for them to take off for the nine-hour, 800-mile flight through the Alaska Range at Lake Clark Pass, then down to King Salmon to refuel, and on down the Bristol Bay side of the Alaska Peninsula, beachcombing from the air all the way to Cold Bay.

"There are all kinds of interesting things to see on those beaches," Frost says. "Wrecked boats, whale carcasses, walrus carcasses. There are always lots of eagles, and a few caribou and foxes. And bears, of course. You always see bears."

Frost and Oney landed in Cold Bay late on the 19th. Cold Bay, Alaska, is the last outpost on the mainland, if you can call the rat's tail of the Alaska Peninsula "mainland." It's the jumping off point for the Aleutians, the last major fuel stop, the last glimpse of civilization as we know it. It has gasoline, a bar, a restaurant, and a motel. By the time the two fliers set down, however, the restaurant was closed. They dined sumptuously on peanuts and a sandwich, leaning on the bar. Then they walked through the rain to the motel to get a room for the night. Cold Bay, Alaska, may be the gateway to the Aleutians, with all the grandeur that implies, but it is still a fishing village, not a tourist town. Amenities are, shall we say, sparse?

"When we woke up the next morning, though, it was hard to believe we were in Cold Bay," Frost recalls. "The sun was shining, there was no wind, and it was warm. Warm! According to the weather service, they only get three days a year like that, and we got one of them!"

Things were looking good. It was an ideal day for aerial reconnaissance. "So," he said, "after a hearty breakfast of aspirin and eggs, we saddled up our Super Cubs and headed for Unimak Island."

With perfect weather and full gas tanks, they decided to fly the entire circumference of the island, looking for beached whales or anything else that might attract a concentration of bears. As soon as they reached Unimak they began to see bears down near the beach, and within a few minutes Oney spotted a whale that had been washed up on shore, probably by the big storm a few days earlier.

The whale carcass looked to be about 30 feet long, and it had been partly buried in the sand. All around it were bear tracks, clearly visible from the air, and spread-eagled lazily right on the carcass, enjoying the sunshine, was a respectable-sized brown bear. Another one, equally large, was standing on a small bluff just back from the beach. It looked made to order for a bowhunter.

Staying close together, Frost and Oney continued on, flying low, beachcombing as they circumnavigated the island. They saw a few caribou, one "lovely white wolf," and a total of 18 bears in the two and a half hours it took them to cover the entire shore and end up back near the big whale carcass. They then found a stretch of beach about two miles away where they could land (by law, small planes with balloon tires are allowed to land only on the beach at Unimak), pulled the two planes up onto the grass above the high-tide mark, and began the laborious task of dragging driftwood logs up to tie the planes down. The glorious summer-like weather was not going to last forever. This being the Aleutians, it would probably not even last until sundown.

"It wasn't very comforting to think that every one of those big logs had been deposited there by the tide and the high winds," Frost said. "Many of them had clearly been washed up just a day or two before, in the big storm. We hoped if we lashed the planes down really well, a big wind would not come along and blow them away—and that is not a joke."

After making camp, they beachcombed away the afternoon, picking up one of the large, old, glass balls that the Japanese fishermen used before plastic ones took over the market. The old balls are worth money in an antique store. An even better omen was finding a can of beer, intact, that had probably fallen off a fishing boat. Good weather *and* a cold beer—who could ask for more? "All the signs were good," Frost said. "It wasn't even raining yet."

After Cold Bay, camp on the shore of Unimak seemed positively luxurious, and dinner was certainly better. In the last light of that one lovely day, they watched a nice brown bear foraging on the tundra a half-mile away from camp, and dropped off to sleep with visions of big bears dancing in their heads.

※

Sure enough, the fine weather was just too good to last. As darkness fell the wind sprang up and brought with it heavy rain, and it rained throughout the night. They awoke to find themselves in more typical Aleutian conditions: wet, and more wet. Shortly after dawn, the rain tapered off, and they set off down the shore, heading for the whale carcass but staying well back from the beach. The fresh breeze was not the best, quartering from behind them and blowing out to sea. Inland, they spotted a single bear, brown against the tundra, and a few minutes later a second one.

Finally, when they judged themselves to be about half a mile from the whale, they crawled up to the edge of the bluff overlooking the beach and began to glass. There, right where they expected it to be, was the whale. But no bears. They glassed some more, scanning the beach up and down, and studying the bluff behind it. "Then Tony spotted a bear lying at the foot of the bluff," said Frost. "If he would just stay there, it would be a perfect setup.

"We pulled back from the bluff and retreated inland a couple of hundred yards. We wanted to come back up to the bluff above and a little beyond the bear, so the wind wouldn't carry our scent to him. The tundra, although it had no trees whatever, nor even any bushes, was very irregular. There were lots of little humps 10 or 15 feet high, and hills, and valleys, and ridges. It was actually great for stalking."

In some ways, it was *too* good. "Then we came over a hump, creeping along, and almost walked onto a sow bear and two big cubs, curled up sleeping right in our path."

That presented a problem. The only way to get past the trio of sleeping bears without risking the wind carrying their scent straight to them was to cut between them and the beach; that, in turn, presented the risk of the wind carrying their scent to the bear they were stalking, but it was the lesser of two evils. Frost and Oney edged past and left them sleeping there. They now had a brown bear in front of them, a mother and cubs at their back, and two more out on the tundra to the side, working their way toward the beach.

Once past the sleeping family of bears, Frost and Oney crept up to the edge of the bluff. They found they had overshot the whale by about 75 yards, but that was good since the wind had shifted and was now blowing toward them. By this time the bear had roused himself and wandered back out, onto the carcass of the whale. Standing there outlined against the sea, Frost says, he looked huge. He also looked like he was carrying something in his mouth, but through his binocular Frost could see that it was in fact one of his lower teeth, jutting out at a crazy angle like the tusk of a wild boar.

"We backed away from the edge of the cliff, checked the sow and cubs, which were still sleeping a hundred yards behind us, then looped around to come out on the bluff as close to the whale as we could get," Frost said. "As we were making this maneuver, I saw another bear coming down the bluff toward us. That made the seventh bear we had seen that morning, and we were now nearly surrounded— five bears on three sides, and none more than 150 yards away. I can tell you, I was certainly happy to have Tony there with all that fire power."

Frost and Oney crawled back up the lip of the bluff. They found themselves right where they wanted to be. There was a 50-foot sheer drop down to the beach, and then about 50 yards of beach between the foot of the bluff and the dead whale.

"It was an almost perfect setup," Frost recalls, "except I really wished the bear was a little bit closer. I didn't want to have to shoot at 60 yards, especially with that stiff breeze blowing."

By that time, however, the second bear had dropped down off the bluff onto the beach and was walking toward the whale. Both bears looked big and were about the same size, but Frost assumed the snaggle-toothed bear was the meaner of the two, since he seemed to own the whale. As bear number two approached, "Snaggle-tooth" came down off the whale and moved to meet him. Tony Oney nudged Frost.

"You'd better shoot now," he said. "Looks like he's leaving."

"And suddenly, that seemed to make sense," Frost says. "Rather than wait to see if either one of them would come closer, I drew up, put the 60-yard pin on the bear, and let the arrow go."

Sixty yards in a stiff breeze is one very long shot, even for an accomplished archer shooting a 73-pound bow. The arrow hit the bear a little high and behind the shoulder. He lurched, then turned and ran down the beach. The second bear, nonchalant to a fault, watched this performance for a moment, then sauntered up onto the whale and claimed it. Meanwhile his erstwhile rival raced several hundred yards down the beach, found a place to climb up through the bluff, and reappeared on top, making his way out onto the open tundra with Jack Frost watching him every step of the way. Then began a game of cat and mouse—with two very worried cats and one extremely large mouse.

Being able to keep him in sight all the time, Frost and Oney carefully stalked the wounded bear, staying about 200 yards back. The big bear stopped and stood quietly for a long time, turning this way and that, then walked on another 50 yards and lay down.

"I studied him with the binocular all that time," says Frost, "looking for blood around his nose or mouth—you know, some evidence to show it was a lung shot, or to give some indication where the arrow had gone. But there was no blood—at least none that I could see."

The bear lay still for a moment, then got back to his feet and looked around, then lay down once again. A few minutes later he got up, walked several yards, and lay down again. And a few minutes after that repeated the whole performance as Frost and Oney stood in the distance, watching his every move.

"This behavior went on for a good half hour," Frost says. "He made seven or eight different beds, all within 50 yards of the first spot he went to, but none of them in a straight line. If he'd been doing this in some thick alders, I would have said he was purposely setting up an ambush on his back trail. But he obviously wasn't hit really hard—at least, he wasn't acting as if he was hit hard.

"He was really restless and agitated at first, but then he seemed to calm down and started lying longer without moving. But every time we thought he might be down for good, up came his head, swiveling around, and then he'd get up and move again."

Frost and Oney watched the wounded bear for a solid hour. With the bear still very much alive, it became obvious that there was only one course of action if Frost wanted that bear as a bow kill: He would have to stalk in over the open tundra, close enough to put one more arrow into the big brown bear—close enough, almost, to feel his breath.

Slowly, Frost and Oney circled around until they had the fresh breeze full in their faces. There was a small hillock between them and the bear, which allowed them to keep him in view as they approached, but to duck back out of sight if he looked up. Arrow at the ready, cartridge in chamber, they crept toward the motionless bear.

"Frankly, under those circumstances, I felt we had a real advantage," Frost recalls. "Being able to see him all the way, having Tony right behind me with his .338—I had a lot of confidence. Too much confidence, maybe, because I moved in close. Really close."

The bear was curled up like a big dog, facing away from them. Oney, with his rifle, let Frost continue in alone while he edged out to the side to keep a clear shot. When only 20 yards separated them, and Frost had paused to shoot, the bear raised his head and looked back over his shoulder right into the doctor's eyes.

"He knew we were there," Frost says. "But then he looked away again. I drew the bow and the arrow buried itself right to the fletching, just behind his shoulder."

Like a flash, the bear was on his feet and whirling to charge. He raised himself up, immense, fur standing on end, ears laid back, fangs bared, dead on his feet although he didn't know it. With his surgeon's detachment, Frost knew the bear was dead. The only problem was, he might be dead too!

"All I wanted to do was keep away from him until the second arrow did its work," he says. "But how? Run? Dodge him? He was standing up there, looking bigger and bigger, and I was afraid Tony was going to shoot and disqualify my bow kill. Crazy thing to think about at the time, but there it is.

"At the same time, I was just as afraid he *wouldn't* shoot. Or that he might miss. And all the time the bear was standing there with his ears laid back and that crazy tooth sticking out, just looking bigger all the time. And then…he closed his mouth, and his eyes glazed over, and he just settled back down into his bed—dead!"

There's an old joke the African professional hunters tell: A client wounds a lion and it runs into some thick cover. The professional is describing what a wounded lion can do.

"Cover 20 yards in a wink, old chap. Chance for one shot at the most, once they come out of the long grass. Incredibly fast they are."

"That fast, huh?" The client is sweating now. "Can you outrun a wounded lion?" he asks.

The PH looks him up and down, standing there, sweating, overweight, more than a little worried. "Outrun a lion, old chap? But I don't have to. I just have to outrun *you*..."

But back to Unimak Island.

"The bear was going to charge," Frost says. "The bear knew it. I knew it. Tony knew it. And he never fired a shot. 'Why didn't you shoot?' I asked him.

"I wasn't worried," Tony replied. "He was going to get you first."

※

The second arrow took the bear squarely in the heart and did its job quickly. It only *seemed* to take forever. The first arrow was not a bad shot, either—just a little high. It struck the spine but failed to break it and never got into the chest cavity. Although it caused a lot of bleeding, the brown bear had plenty left if the second arrow had been a little bit off. Fortunately...

※

Frost and Oney skinned the bear and got the hide and skull back to camp, packed up hurriedly, and escaped from Unimak just ahead of the inevitable break in the weather. They were into Cold Bay in time for supper.

And the bear? A Pope and Young Club official measurer scored the skull at 28³⁄₁₆—³⁄₁₆ bigger than the bowhunting record taken by the grandfather of it all, Fred Bear, in 1960. Potentially a new Number One—if the measurement held up, if it did not shrink a quarter inch in the 18 months before the next convention, if someone did not come along and shoot a bigger one in the meantime. If...if...if.

But when the skull was measured again a year and a half later, by the official panel of measurers at the Pope and Young awards convention in 1987, Jack Frost's Unimak Island brown bear scored 28 4/16—a new Number One in the Pope and Young record book.

"By that time, to be honest with you, I didn't really care," Frost said. "The size of the skull had nothing to do with the thrill of that hunt—seeing him standing there like that. No one can ever take that away from me."

11

❄

Bears on Ice

The small party of hunters had been stormbound in an igloo, out on the pack ice, for one entire day, and one entire night, and most of a second day as well. The wind was so constant and so solid that they no longer heard its high keening howl as anything more than background noise. The outside of the igloo, where the snow blocks had been carefully fitted together, was ground smooth and round and hard as an egg, and the low entrance was packed solid with the wind-driven snow.

Outside, the Eskimo dogs burrowed deep into the drifts and curled up with their noses under their tails as the wind pounded the snow down around them. Inside, the men huddled in the weird half-light, wrapped in caribou skins, living through the Arctic storm in the only way possible: Sunk in their own thoughts, both conversation and the will to converse long since exhausted, they now simply waited for the storm to end.

It was well into the second day when one of the Inuit sensed a change in the wind, not a lessening or even anything as tangible as

❄

a momentary hesitation, but *something*. An old man, the oldest hunter, crawled to the tunnel and hacked an opening large enough to let himself out into the maelstrom of howling snow and driving ice particles. He struggled a few yards from the igloo and stood upright, braced against the wind with his arms dangling at his sides and his eyes closed. For long minutes he stood there; five minutes stretched to ten, and ten minutes to half an hour.

And then, the spell broken, he hurried back to the igloo and spoke quickly. The other Inuit, and the white polar bear hunter they were guiding, began to stir, packing what few things were scattered about and hauling the dogs from their snowy dens. The half-wolf Eskimo dogs snapped and snarled as they were gathered into harness, the lead dogs quelling all insubordination with long teeth and longer memories.

Within minutes the sleds were righted and the loads lashed on, one man straining to hold the sled while another packed and tied. Last in was their client, Don McVittie. He took his place, out of harm's way and out of the way of the professionals who worked the dogs, and the party began a long and wild journey across the ice, running for the distant mainland through the Arctic night, with the wind pursuing them every staggering step of the way.

"To this day, I don't know exactly what happened," McVittie told me, some years later. "Did he feel the ice starting to go? Was there a worse storm coming? Was it better to chance the storm than stay out on the ice? All I know is, he heard something or felt something that told him what we had to do, and we did it. It was one of the strangest experiences of my life."

And, he said, one of the greatest. To be out on the pack ice, dressed in caribou skins and pursuing the great Arctic bear, is a defining fact in Inuit life; for a white man to share it is to gain a glimpse of the essence of existence in the most hostile and unforgiving country on Earth.

For the Inuit, the polar bear is an almost supernatural

creature that stalks their legends and their mystic beliefs. In some regions polar bears are believed to change form, to cohabit with maidens, to do any number of man-like or god-like things that give it powers far beyond that of a mere animal. For this reason, to kill a polar bear is a great achievement—a required achievement—for a young Inuit hunter.

Ben East, an outdoorsman and conservationist who wrote for *Outdoor Life* for many years,was a respected authority on bears among the outdoor writers of his time. Of the polar bear, he wrote: "The Eskimos have always called him *Nahnook*. Of all his names, I like best the one by which the Crees of James Bay know him, *Wahb'esco*. They accent the first syllable hard, and I have never heard them say it but that excitement came into their voices. They understand the kind of bear he is."

Jerome Knap, a Canadian outfitter who has been working the

Arctic for 20 years, says that an old Inuit once talked to him about his son. The son was full-grown, married, and had several children of his own, but in the eyes of his father, he was not yet a man "for he has not killed a bear."

The 1960s and '70s rank as the all-time low point in the history of the far north, in Canada and elsewhere. Caribou herds were at a low ebb and predicted to be on a one-way trip to oblivion. While white men spoke of oil pipelines and economic development, government officials herded and harried Inuit bands from their traditional way of life into southern-style schools, pre-fabricated houses, welfare, alcohol, and incest. Dog teams were traded for snowmobiles, rifles for bottles, and fewer young men ventured onto the ice in search of the bear.

In Alaska, white sport hunters who came north did so clad in quilted goose down and nylon, and flew low over the ice in airplanes, looking for paw prints in the snow that would lead them to a white bear. Magazines were full of grinning hunters, crouched behind a dead bear with the airplane in the background. Always, the sun was shining and the hunters wore dark glasses to shade their eyes from the glare.

In his 1961 classic *Big Game Animals of North America*, Jack O'Connor talked about polar bear hunting as it was then. Although he never hunted polar bear himself, O'Connor narrowly missed an adventure that might have cost him his life. He was scheduled to go with a friend but had to cancel at the last minute. The friend went anyway, the plane crashed, the pilot was killed, the friend survived for three days on the ice, was rescued, and spent several weeks in hospital. Under the circumstances, O'Connor can be forgiven for not playing down the dangerous aspects of hunting from a small plane.

In theory, at least, hunting polar bears with aircraft was ethically defensible. Usually, for safety's sake, two planes were used. When tracks were spotted, the hunter's aircraft would set down far ahead of the animal and the hunter would stalk it, while the second plane remained at a discreet distance. One could argue this was fair chase, although it could hardly be considered a great hunting experience. In practice, what happened all too often was that the second plane was used to drive the distraught bear toward the waiting rifle, eliminating the need for much stalking, or even a measure of healthy exercise.

O'Connor had a strong sense of ethics and was more than willing to call a spade a spade. If he found hunting from aircraft morally indefensible, he would have said so; instead, he gulped hard and tried to give a dispassionate, objective view of that side of polar bear hunting. And, in fact, he presents a pretty good case. For one thing, he quotes an academic paper "given to the 24th North American Wildlife Conference," which stated that such methods were unlikely to result in the great bears being shot out. It estimated that out of a world population of about 19,000 polar bears, the total global kill was between 900 and 1,350 bears annually, with 100 to 200 being killed in Alaska, 400 to 500 in the Canadian Arctic, 150 to 200 in Greenland, 150 to 300 by Norwegians, and 100 to 150 by Russians. While hunting from aircraft might be aesthetically displeasing, the paper's author concluded, there was evidence that it actually was beneficial since the people doing it were trophy hunters out after the biggest bear they could find. As a result, they killed far more males than females. O'Connor was also told that hunting from a plane is less damaging to brood stock because shore hunters—Eskimos and clients hunting by dog sled—generally saw and killed more females and their young.

Regardless, polar bear hunting as it was then done in Alaska became a scandal. The sight of planes skimming over the ice, shooting at wolves and bears from the air, became an anti-hunting icon driven by the certain knowledge that polar bear populations were declining, not just in North America but around the world. The concern was shared by serious hunters as well as their ideological foes. In 1966, the Boone and Crockett Club stopped accepting polar bears for scoring or for entry into its record book of big game animals. The scandalous hunting practices then common in Alaska violated the club's rules of fair chase; what's more, there was growing evidence polar bear numbers were at an all-time low and dropping quickly. Under the circumstances, it was simply wrong to hunt them, by ethical means or otherwise.

Alaska imposed an annual quota on permits, limiting the legal kill to around 300, but officials freely admitted they had lost control of polar bear hunting. Dishonest guides and unethical hunters continued to thumb their noses at the law, and the game department had neither the staff nor the resources to do much about it. A thriving black-market trade in legal permits (which were officially non-transferable) grew up in Anchorage, and many without a permit killed a bear anyway.

According to Ben East, by the early 1970s, Alaska had already prohibited the use of aircraft in polar bear hunting and was taking measures to eliminate other abuses. But its actions came too late: In 1972, Congress passed the Marine Mammal Protection Act, took authority over polar bears away from the state of Alaska, and ushered in a new era of polar bear management.

❄

There are five nations in the world with jurisdiction over polar bear populations, and all five have a hunting heritage both native and non-native. Truth to tell, while Alaska may have had the most high-profile abuses, several of the other countries were far from guiltless.

Norway, in particular, allowed what it called "safari hunting" for polar bears, mostly by non-residents who hunted from cruise ships nosing along the edge of the ice floes. When a bear was spotted out on the ice, the crew would mount a drive to crowd the bear in close to the ship and the hunter's rifle.

In one famous case, a wealthy American hunter, Dr. Richard Sutton, chartered a Norwegian ship and set out with his family to hunt polar bears, among other things, along the edge of the pack ice between Iceland and Greenland. Sutton was a well-travelled hunter who wrote many articles for *Outdoor Life* in the 1930s. He wrote a book called *An Arctic Safari* in which he describes their voyage. Altogether they killed about a dozen polar bears, usually shooting from the deck of the ship or after a short stalk on the ice. The bears were then hauled on board and skinned. While on the ship, the Sutton family lived a very luxurious existence, and this is probably where the misnomer *safari-style* originated when applied to Norwegian polar bear hunting.

Sutton's story reads like one of the old-time African hunters—Roualeyn Gordon Cumming, for example, who killed everything in sight and revelled in the fact. Ethically repugnant as Sutton's approach might have been, it was, after all, the 1930s, and even ethical hunters had very different ideas back then.

Probably of more consequence to polar bear numbers would have been the commercial hunting Norway allowed on the Svalbard Islands, in which up to 400 bears a year (Ben East's figures) were killed using traps and baited set-guns.

The USSR, as it was then, has an uneven history of polar bear management. During the Stalinist nightmare of the 1930s, when the commissars were busy providing the model for the black pigs of Orwell's *Animal Farm*, they hunted what they liked, where they liked, and took as many animals as gluttony demanded. There are documented cases of Party officials killing six, eight, ten Siberian tigers in a day, and polar bear kills were probably comparable given the opportunity. By 1956, however, Stalin was dead, there were new rulers in the Kremlin, and polar bear numbers were perilously low. In an effort to show the world they could lead the way in northern development (a fiction swallowed whole by Canada's leading writer on Arctic life, Farley Mowat), the USSR banned all polar bear hunting, and it has stayed banned—officially, at least—to this day.

Denmark, the fourth polar bear nation, rules over a small population of bears along the east and west coasts of Greenland, but the annual kill was, and is, no more than 150 bears, and then only by resident Inuit hunters.

Which brings us to Canada, and the Northwest Territories. When Ben East investigated the state of polar bear hunting in 1976, he found that hunting was continuing all along Canada's Arctic coast, just as it had for decades.

The Northwest Territories is a vast area of the Arctic more than twice the size of Alaska. There is a mainland territory, divided into the Districts of Mackenzie and Keewatin, and a huge archipelago of Arctic islands called the District of Franklin. The NWT is home to about 12,000 Inuit, two-thirds of the total Inuit population of Canada.

At the time of the Marine Mammal Protection Act, polar bear hunting in the Northwest Territories had, for many years, been limited strictly to native people for whom hunting the white bear was a tradition. There was an annual quota, under which about 600 bears were killed. This quota was very carefully divided up and allotted among individual bands and settlements. These communities then assigned bear permits to individual hunters.

Within this quota system, hunting was also open to non-resident—that is, trophy or sport hunters—but only under very strict rules. The use of planes and snowmobiles was outlawed, and you went out on the pack ice by dog team, with Inuit guides. In other words, you hunted the traditional way or not at all. Any bear taken by a non-resident came out of the quota allotted to the guide's village. It was hard hunting, expensive hunting, and there was no guarantee the hunter would even see a bear, much less take one. In 1976, the going rate for such a hunt was about $4,000—roughly the price of a relatively luxurious sojourn in Africa.

Ben East talked to Ian Stirling, the ranking expert on polar bears for the Canadian wildlife service, who told him, "The hunter is buying not a bear trophy, but the experience of living and travelling for a short time with the Eskimos, sleeping in an igloo and hunting as they hunt." The prospect of such a hunt held limited appeal, however. "Not surprisingly, very few hunters are interested," East wrote. "In 1975, for example, hunters numbered only four, one from the U.S., one from Canada, and two from Europe."

❄

The reticence of American trophy hunters is surprising, but there is an explanation. With more trophy hunters in the United States than anywhere else in the world, and with Alaska closed down, the U.S. should have been the greatest source of clients. Unfortunately, The Marine Mammal Protection Act of 1972 was intended to put an end even to this very limited and, by anyone's standards, very ethical and professionally regulated polar bear hunt—at least for American citizens, at least in theory. Under the Act, Americans were not only prohibited from hunting polar bears in Alaska, they were prohibited from hunting polar bears anywhere in the world, even where it was legal (that is, Canada's Northwest Territories). The importation of polar bear skins was outlawed. About the best one can say about the Marine Mammal Protection Act is that its authors were well-intentioned.

Having said that, you can also say this: The MMPA was one of the most arrogant and ill-conceived pieces of legislation ever passed by Congress, presuming as it did to dictate to other countries how they should manage their polar bear populations—countries that were just as concerned about preserving the great bears and which, in many cases, had much better histories of game management than the United States.

It was an extraordinarily political document as well, from the time it was conceived, until it was implemented, and for the next 25 years as Washington tried to enforce it. And, as a piece of game management legislation, it was of very questionable value. For many years, it was a detriment to proper polar bear management in northern Canada, where natives were unable to make best use of, and hence have a vested financial interest in protecting, the available resources—a principle which is widely accepted today from Zimbabwe to the Yukon, yet which seems foreign to the lofty thinkers in Washington. This is especially true when it comes to managing another country's affairs. Like similar legislation designed to protect the leopard by prohibiting importation, but which only served to make the leopard of no commercial value and rendered it vermin in several countries where it had once been a valuable sport-hunting trophy, the MMPA may well have hurt the polar bear more than it ever helped.

On the other hand, since its inception, polar bear numbers worldwide have bounced back strongly. Where some experts estimated the total population as low as 12,000 in 1972, by 1996 it was reckoned at around 30,000. The Marine Mammal Protection Act may have had a small hand in this resurgence, but that is the best one can say about it, and even that faint praise may be indulging optimism too far.

Anti-hunting groups, naturally, hailed it as a triumph for good and right, and vigorously opposed any changes to its provisions—however small, however well supported by the facts. One of the lawyers who helped write the original bill told Jerome Knap that polar bears were not even included in the first draft of the legislation, yet that ended up as the most high-profile provision because the bill was "hijacked" by animal-rights activists. Even the definition of a marine mammal was rewritten, specifically to allow the inclusion of the polar bear.

⁂

American trophy hunters may not be lily-white when it comes to certain hunting practices, and unquestionably some, on occasion, behave unethically. All too often, the trophy itself is given more importance than the way in which it was taken. But even allowing for that and pleading guilty on all counts, the American trophy hunter is still the greatest friend any game animal can have. Through organizations such as Boone and Crockett and Safari Club International, American trophy hunters are a driving force in conservation around the world. Aside from the direct contributions they make to conservation projects, the money that trophy hunters bring into and leave in a country allows the people there to live with their wildlife, protect their wildlife, and at the same time, make a living from the land. This is especially true in regions where there is little alternative to subsistence hunting. And it is not just the people who benefit: The animals do as well, because they gain economic value, and valuable properties are protected.

After 1972, the only jurisdiction in the world in which trophy hunters could still pursue the polar bear was the Canadian North—specifically, the Northwest Territories. The Marine Mammal Act struck directly at the native population of the NWT. Depriving the Inuit of the NWT of the substantial cash flow they might have enjoyed from selling some of their polar bear quotas to hunters from "outside" was a blow to the Inuit way of life, and deprived of the cash to be had from hunting, it would not have been surprising to see many Inuit turn away from their traditions. Yet their culture survived, and in some ways was even strengthened during that time. In spite of the best efforts of the hand-wringing liberals to bring the Inuit into the 20th century, in much of the Arctic, life proceeded as it always had. Polar bear quotas were allotted, and young men and old struck out over the pack ice in search of bearskins and official manhood.

As well, that great symbol of the frozen North, the dog team, was brought back from the brink. In the early 1970s, dog teams were, individually and collectively, in serious danger in Canada. Snowmobiles were faster, more efficient, and did not continue to eat ravenously throughout the idle summer months. Slowly but surely, snowmobiles began to displace dog teams across the Arctic and the liberal press shed oceans of crocodile tears about the "inevitable" demise of this romantic emblem of life in the north.

Two things saved the dog team, aside from the devoted efforts of a small number of enthusiasts who loved them for their own sake. First, Canadian government regulations prohibited snow-mobiles for polar bear hunting by sport hunters. The Inuit could use whatever means they chose for their own hunting, and given the choice they almost always used a snow machine. As long as they guided sport hunters, however, they had to have a dog team, and that ensured that at least a few would survive. Second, fearing that neglect and disease would kill off the dogs, the government financed an operation in the territorial capital of Yellowknife, run by a dog breeder named Bill Carpenter. Carpenter's goal was to preserve the Eskimo dog through a breeding program, and today many of the dog teams found across the Arctic are descended from Carpenter's original stock.

Jerome Knap, who first went north to form a hunting part-nership with the Inuit in 1980 (an enterprise which became Canada North Outfitters), says that in the early days his operations were seriously hampered by a shortage of dog teams. They had more pro-spective hunters, and more permits than they could possibly sell, sim-ply because they did not have the teams to pull the sleds. The law of supply and demand being what it is, the situation eventually righted itself, with the help of Bill Carpenter and government funding. For once in history, a tax-supported program actually did some good. For the record, after about ten years, funding was ended because the program had accomplished its purpose, and Bill Carpenter went on to other things.

The 1980s brought great changes in the Canadian North. It was the decade of land claims and native rights, and one outcome of this was recognition at all levels that the Inuit's traditions and culture were important and worth saving. Gradually, Inuit communities in the Northwest Territories were given more control over their own lives and destinies, and ultimately a plan was developed to turn political control of most of the huge territory over to its original inhabitants. One immediate and noticeable effect of this policy was the changing of certain place names, such as Frobisher Bay and Fort Chimo, to the names given them in the local Inuit dialects (Iqaluit and Kuujjuaq, respectively). To outsiders, most of these names are as unpronounceable as the Inuit way of life is, itself, inscrutable.

For the polar bear, so important to Inuit culture, this transition to native self-government, which began in the mid-1990s and will take place over a period of years, is most likely a positive step. Inuit communities have shown they can manage their polar bear quotas very effectively, balancing the needs of their culture, the demands of their young hunters, and their desire for the cash that selling a bear tag brings in. There is no reason at all why they cannot manage the polar bear on a territorial scale, and anything that takes decision-making away from Ottawa and hands it to the people in the territory has to be a step in the right direction.

Meanwhile, throughout the 1980s, in spite of Washington and its animal-rights activists and in defiance of the Marine Mammal Protection Act, American trophy hunters continued to go north to hunt the great white bear. They were technically in violation of the law, although it was an aspect of the legislation that was really unenforceable. They were not allowed to bring the bear skin back into the United States, but that did not seem to matter. Some successful hunters put them in storage in Canada and waited for the MMPA to be repealed or amended; others simply sent them to the big fur auctions in North Bay, Ontario, and tried to recoup some of their expenditure; still others went to great lengths to get the hides into the United States by hook or by crook, and not a few found themselves on the wrong end of the law. If nothing else, the Marine Mammal Protection Act provided jobs for quite a few enforcement officers who attacked their work with a zeal that would be commendable if the targets had been real criminals.

The motivation for going to all this trouble to shoot a bear you could not bring back varied from hunter to hunter. Undoubtedly, some wanted a bear because it was one of the so-called "North American 27" big game animals, and they needed a polar bear on their hunting resume, for whatever reason. Others may have been determined to get the hides back somehow. But many—probably the majority—went north looking for an experience that was like no other.

Jack O'Connor: "A few adventurous Americans have gone right out on the ice with Eskimo guides and their dog teams to hunt polar bear. This, I am sure, is a tough and often uncomfortable way to hunt, but it is a sporting way and one which should be a never-to-be-forgotten experience for anyone who attempts it."

That was in 1961. By 1981, it was the *only* way an American was going to hunt polar bear, and O'Connor's brief description barely scratches the surface of the experience that awaited them.

Hunting polar bears this way is an expensive proposition, and it always has been. In 1976, according to Ben East, such a hunt cost about $4,000. By the mid-1980s, the price was up to $10,000, and in the late 1990s the average polar bear hunter spends $12,000 to $14,000. That is money left in the Inuit community; it does not include air fare. For that kind of cash, you can hunt in Africa for two weeks, take a dozen species, and live in the lap of luxury. In the Arctic, you get (with luck) one animal, and life is anything but luxurious.

So where does the money go? First of all, maintaining a dog team is not cheap, and dogs eat for 12 months a year, not just during hunting season. As well, food and supplies of all kinds are dreadfully expensive in the Arctic because of sheer distance and the cost of air freight. Then, of course, there is the matter of clothing.

Most Inuit hunters will not go out on the pack ice, with its inherent dangers and the possibility of blizzards, with a hunter who is not properly dressed by Inuit standards. That means the full Inuit kit—mukluks, mittens, parka, and pants, all made to measure from caribou skins. When it comes to Arctic survival, there is no such thing as "close enough;" unless the clothing fits perfectly, it does not work the way it is supposed to, so the hunter's measurements are sent on ahead to give the women in the village time to make the garments. What you are paying for, incidentally, is not the clothing itself, only the *making* of the clothing and temporary use of it. At the end of the trip, the hunter has the option of buying his Arctic outfit; if he declines (and it does not come cheap) it is sold elsewhere—for use in situations where perfect fit is not critical, presumably.

This is also the reason why taking a non-hunting observer costs about $5,000 on top of the price of the hunt. Other than the trophy fee, a non-hunter costs about as much as a hunter—clothing, extra food, extra dog team, and so on.

At any rate, that is the kind of expense involved. A big chunk of the $14,000 is a trophy fee for the bear permit, paid to the Inuit community out of whose quota it comes. Given that there is usually considerable demand for permits from Inuit hunters themselves, and that the permits represent a large proportion of the disposable income the Inuit see, who can blame them for charging what the market will bear? None of the wealthy businessmen who go up there to hunt became wealthy by doing any less, after all. And it is no different than the Apache on the Fort Apache Reservation selling elk tags.

Even the most tradition-minded Inuit need currency to maintain their way of life, since they live in houses, operate snow-mobiles, carry rifles, and shoot ammunition. Polar bear permits are a major source of income, and the need for money is weighed against demand from the young men for the permits. If trophy fees were not considerably higher than the price that could be gained by shooting a bear and selling its hide, then very, very few would ever become available to outsiders. The law of supply and demand does not play favorites.

Incidentally, the price for a polar bear skin on the commercial market today is not high. A large, prime skin might go for $2500, according to Jerome Knap, but he says he has seen them sell for as little as $500, and suggests that $1500 is probably the average. If the total kill is 600 bears a year, and 100 of those are taken by sport hunters, the economics snap into clear focus: Sport hunters leave well over a million dollars in the local communities of the Northwest Territories, while the sale of polar bear skins, if those 100 were shot by natives instead, would bring about one-tenth that amount.

In the quarter century since the Marine Mammal Protection Act was implemented, a great deal has been learned about polar bears. In 1972, biologists *assumed* far more about polar bears than they actually *knew*, and the intervening years have seen a bull market in polar bear research. The most important fact to come out of all this scientific activity concerns migration patterns and the understanding of what makes up the world population of polar bears. The total is not made up of five or ten individual populations; in fact, it seems to be more or less one fluid world population, and any return to polar bear hunting, with the inevitable quotas, must take that into account.

Jack O'Connor suspected this in 1960, writing "The American polar bears are found off the coast of northern and northwestern Alaska along the edges of the Arctic pack. The ice moves and drifts with the currents of the ocean, and it may well be that an Alaska bear is a Siberian bear one year, a Greenland bear the next." As is so often the case with people like O'Connor, who was a keen observer of wildlife, he was absolutely right.

In May, 1992, American scientists darted a female bear at Prudhoe Bay, Alaska, and fitted her with a special satellite radio beacon. For the next four years, biologists from the U.S. National Biological Service tracked her movements—all the way from Prudhoe Bay, across the Arctic to northeastern Greenland, where she spent one winter, then even farther north to Ellesmere Island, and back to Greenland. Altogether, Bear #20365, as she is known, wandered more than 3,000 miles and ruined a large body of scientific assumptions in the process. Until that time the accepted theory was that adult polar bears develop seasonal migration patterns and denning habits, which were fairly predictable. This was the "fidelity rule," and it further stated that no bear would wander more than a few hundred miles at most.

The realization that this is not the case at all is of tremendous importance both to world polar bear management and to sport hunters hoping for a return to regulated hunting. It means that all management must be done on the basis of sound international agreements that recognize the fluid nature of polar bear movements. One renegade nation could make a shambles of even the best-laid plans by ignoring agreed-upon quotas or by losing control of the hunting within its jurisdiction.

Recent research places polar bear numbers at well above 25,000, more than double the estimates of 30 years ago, and biologists are optimistic about the bear's future—with some reservations, such as the impact of off-shore drilling. With most big game animals, the greatest threat is loss of habitat; in the case of the polar bear, its habitat is of little use to most of mankind, and so it is safe in that respect. That does not prevent mankind from polluting and degrading its habitat, however, and this the biologists see as the source of the greatest danger: pollutants accumulating in the Arctic food chain.

Technically, the polar bear (in spite of the MMPA) is not a "marine mammal" in the sense that the whale is, or even the walrus. It is a land-based mammal that spends a great deal of time in the water, but it has not grown fins or even developed a particularly appropriate fur coat for spending long hours in freezing water. Where sea otter fur traps a thin layer of air for insulation, polar bear fur merely gets soggy. What's more, there is not as much of it: Sea otters have about 645,000 hairs per square inch, polar bears only about 10,000. Since adult bears spend a lot of time in the water (they have been known to swim 40 miles without a rest), they need some way of keeping warm; they do so by maintaining a generous layer of fat between their hide and their vitals, and that fat comes, mainly, from eating fat-laden seals.

An active adult polar bear needs 12,000 to 16,000 calories a day, otherwise it loses weight, and severe weight loss is fatal in an Arctic winter. A yearling ring seal is worth 60,000 calories, of which 41,000 come from fat. The danger from pollutants lies in the fact that seals eat fish, fish accumulate toxins, toxins concentrate in the fat, and...well, you get the idea.

Logically enough, polar bears do not religiously den up for the winter as black bears, grizzlies, and brown bears do. Denning is most common among pregnant females. After mating in the spring, a pregnant polar bear will eat voraciously all summer, increasing her weight from 350 pounds to as much as 900; she then digs herself a den and crawls in. During the winter she gives birth to her cubs, and by spring they have grown their own fur coats and are mobile enough to follow her for what will be a two-year odyssey of adventure.

Obviously, a denning mother is at her most vulnerable in the spring, and some Inuit communities, especially those around the favored denning area of Pelly Bay, actually made a specialty of finding polar bear dens and killing both the mother and her young. About the time Canada established its quota system, it also outlawed the killing of females with cubs. That alone, given the large "resident" polar bear population of the Canadian North, probably contributed as much as anything to the resurgence in polar bear numbers.

❄

In April, 1994, the Marine Mammal Protection Act was amended to allow a very limited importation of polar bear skins to the United States. The only jurisdiction so favored, however, was the Northwest Territories. Even then, only bear skins from certain districts would be allowed in, depending on whether the American government considered the bear populations in those districts to be viable, and if they had management agreements in place with adjacent jurisdictions. For example, the eastern Arctic is divided into a half-dozen districts; those farthest east are ineligible until they have hammered out a deal with Greenland.

As with its entire history, these changes to the MMPA were

intensely political. The act was, not surprisingly, a source of ongoing irritation for the Canadian government and the Northwest Territories territorial council, who saw it as brazen, paternalistic, and unjustified interference with their own efforts to manage polar bears for the benefit of the Inuit, as well as the bears themselves. So there was international pressure on Washington.

Within the United States, Safari Club International had lobbied for years to have the act amended to allow sport hunters to bring home legally taken skins. This was opposed by animal-rights groups large and small, including one of the national humane societies. Inside the wildlife services themselves, there were those in favor of making changes and there were those against. Not surprisingly, then, changing the Marine Mammal Protection Act has been a long process of very small steps, hesitantly taken.

On the whole, however, the outlook for polar bear populations, and the prospect of legal polar bear hunting, seems to be improving.

Denmark, which administers Greenland, allows only resident natives to hunt bears, but has no closed seasons, no limits and no sex restrictions. The numbers taken each year are so small, however, they have little impact. Russia is an unknown quantity. On the surface, the Russian government is committed to wildlife conservation, but in practice the stories coming out of Siberia do not give cause for optimism. The polar bear may be relatively safe from helicopter-borne predation simply because of cost and inaccessibility. Either way, the chances of the United States lifting restrictions on Siberian bears are non-existent. Alaska could almost certainly support a harvest in the neighborhood of the old quota of 300 annually, but the prospects of such a hunt in the foreseeable future are very slim. Norway maintains its ban on polar bear hunting, where it is illegal to kill a bear even in self-defense.

Two other Canadian jurisdictions, the Inuit territory of northern Quebec and the Labrador coast, both have great potential as hunting areas. At the moment, both have a "hands-off" policy—that is, the provincial wildlife agencies of Quebec and Newfoundland do not interfere with Inuit polar bear hunting. If they go to a quota system, there is nothing to prevent them instituting sport hunting along the lines of the Northwest Territories.

For the Inuit of the Northwest Territories, the stronghold of polar bear hunting in the past, the future now looks reasonably secure. Self-government is being implemented in stages, polar bear numbers are high, the Marine Mammal Protection Act barriers are coming down, and there is growing interest in hunting polar bears. There are now several outfitters representing guides in the Territory, including Jerome Knap's Canada North Outfitters, and they are able to sell every bear permit with which the Inuit are willing to part.

Chances are, the quota will not go any higher than it now is (roughly 600 annually), and the number available to outside sport hunters will stay around 100. With the possibility of bringing the hide back into the United States, interest among hunters will naturally increase, and trophy fees will go up accordingly. Supply and demand.

❋

Jack O'Connor was a romantic who loved being in far places. For O'Connor, getting there was half the fun and most of the romance. The hunting may have given purpose to the journey, but the journey gave meaning to the hunt. Early in his career, in the late 1940s, he travelled to the Yukon by way of Skagway, sailing for four days in the mist and rain up the Inland Passage by steamer from Seattle, then by narrow-gauge railway through the mountains to Whitehorse.

> *When I arrived, I felt in my bones that I was really 2,500 miles from my Arizona home, that I was actually in the mysterious subArctic. I have been to the Yukon three other times by ship, and always I have the feeling of mystery, romance, and distance.*
>
> *I have also flown up from Seattle. The planes leave in midmorning and get to Whitehorse in time for lunch. When I fly up, my feeling when I arrive in Whitehorse is that I am just somewhere else and that Seattle, where I had breakfast, is just over the hill.*

❋

By 1960, air travel had made it possible for hunters to go to Africa, to hunt Alaska, or to enjoy three days of grouse shooting in Scotland and still make the Monday-morning board meeting. While the benefits are undeniable, O'Connor felt that being able to fly into Telegraph Creek in northern British Columbia to hunt Stone sheep, for example, robbed the experience of much of its worth, just as flying to Nairobi diminished the impact of being on safari. In 1946, when he first travelled to the Prophet and Muskwa region to go after Stone sheep, he rode and walked for two weeks just to get there. "It is the distance and the hardship that makes far-away game worth going after," O'Connor wrote, "and so it is with polar bears. In the days when the taking of a polar bear meant a hunt with Eskimos or a long voyage on a chartered steamer, the white bear was one of the world's great trophies. Nowadays, it is too cut and dried..."

Although he never hunted polar bears by plane, O'Connor knew many people who had, and he observed that, ethics and aesthetics aside, hunting by that method "would rob the experience of much of its sense of adventure and its atmosphere."

Sometimes, though not often, things come full circle. The quarter-century since the Marine Mammal Protection Act and all the other measures to regulate polar bear hunting took effect may well turn out to be the best possible thing, not just for polar bears, but for the hunters themselves. Today, you cannot hunt polar bears from aircraft or shoot at them from the deck of a ship while a steward brings you another drink. You have to want a polar bear badly enough to travel to a far distant place and live in an Inuit community for a few days, and ride a dog sled over the Arctic ice clad in caribou skins, and brave the wind and the snow and life in an igloo and the treacherous vagaries of the pack ice. And if that price is too high, well, no one forces you to pay it.

❄

EUROPE

12

✳

THE HILL STAG

The road, not wide to begin with, turned from narrow tarmac to narrower gravel and effectively ended at a rushing, foaming burn beside an abandoned stone cottage. A chain hung limply across the ancient right-of-way, which meandered on up the Valley of the Spey toward the mountain pass of Corrieyaireag, disappearing into the mist and blowing rain.

It was raining two days earlier when I stepped off the train from Inverness onto the empty railway platform at Kingussie; it was raining yesterday when I climbed the high hill behind the lodge to get a feel for the country and test my climbing legs. Both days, the rain had come and gone, the clouds clearing briefly, the sun eventually peeking out, rainbows appearing magically before the clouds rolled back. Typical mountain weather.

But today was different. Today, our first day of actual deer stalking, the rain was coming in sheets, the mountaintops were shrouded in fog, and the rugged heather of the hillsides was cut by thousands of tiny rivers, twisting this way and that, rushing to join

✳

the burns that boiled over the rocks and down to the Spey.

My stalker, Davie Fraser, sat in the Land Rover and peered at the hill through his binocular. As the mist eddied and swirled in the high winds, we would get glimpses of rock and heather before the fog rushed back to wrap the hillside once again. Straining to pierce the mist, we would periodically see deer along the ridges—hinds and small stags, mostly, but occasionally a larger one. The windows were heavily misted, but every time we rolled one down to get some air, we were soaked by the driving rain. By 11:30, Davie said enough was enough.

"There is nooo point in stayin' oot in this," he said. "It won't clear this mornin'. Maybe by th'afternoon…"

He got no argument from me, and we tortuously turned the Land Rover around with its trailer and eight-wheel-drive Argo, currently occupied by Colin, who in an earlier era would have been the "pony boy" but now was the designated Argo driver. Beside him sat my hunting partner, Jim Morey.

Jim raised his eyebrows as I hopped out and stood in the lee of the stone cottage, directing the Land Rover back and forth, twisting itself around to get back onto the road. The burn was a torrent by now, raging beneath a stone bridge built almost three centuries ago, but still as solid as the day the final rock was mortared into place. In the valley, the River Spey was spilling over its banks, and the burns were pouring more water into it all the time.

In 1798, a traveller was warned away from the Pass of Corrieyaireag by the governor of Fort Augustus, who described it as follows:

> Wild desolation beyond anything he could describe; and the whole of the road rough, dangerous and dreadful, even for a horse. The steep and black mountains, and the roaring torrents rendered every step his horse took, frightful; and when he obtained the summit of the zigzag up Corrieyaireag he thought the horse himself, man and all, would be carried away, he knew not whither; so strong was the blast, so hard the rain, and so very thick the mist. And as for cold, it stupefied him.

It was from the Pass of Corrieyaireag that we now retreated, racing before the wind and rain to the shooting lodge at Sherramore, to the warm coal fire glowing in the grate, to some steaming tea, and the enjoyment that comes only of being warm, dry, and inside, while a blowing rain pries at the windows.

❈

In September, 1715, the Highland clans rose in revolt in support of the exiled Stuart king, James Edward. The Jacobite rebellions of 1708, 1715, 1719 and finally and tragically, 1745, led to the complete suppression of the Highland way of life by the English and the lowland Scots. After 1715, the government sent Major-General George Wade north with orders to build a network of roads through the wildest and most lawless parts of the Highlands. A primary target was the shire of Inverness, along the Great Glen that has Fort William at one end, Inverness at the other, and Loch Ness and Loch Lochy in between. This was the country of some of the most notorious Jacobite clans—the Frasers and the Macintoshes, MacDonalds and MacPhersons.

General Wade began by building Fort Augustus at the western end of Loch Ness, beneath the gloomy, glowering hills of Monadh Liath. He then joined Fort Augustus to the outside world by running a narrow road up over the Corrieyaireag Pass, down to the River Spey, and east to Newtonmore. The clans watched these civic improvements with sullen resentment. The chiefs ordered their followers not to accept Wade's offer of employment, for the roads, they well knew, boded them no good. So General Wade's road was hewn out by General Wade's redcoats, while the clansmen watched from the hills.

General Wade's Military Road, as it is still identified on the maps, runs from Fort Augustus to Laggan, past Cluny Castle, stronghold of the MacPhersons, to link with the main road near Kingussie. Kingussie is an ancient town, and the MacPhersons an ancient family. They trace their origins to an abbot who lived in Kingussie in 1153. When he inherited the chieftainship of his clan, he was granted special dispensation to marry by the Pope, and the name

❈

"MacPherson" means, literally, "son of the parson."

Their religious origins certainly had no pacifying effect on later generations, and in 1704 they were able to muster "700 claymores" to fight on behalf of King James. MacPherson of Cluny was one of the most recalcitrant and notorious of the Jacobite chieftains. History does not record the emotions he felt on seeing General Wade's road push past his stronghold, across the glens and crags that had been MacPherson land for 600 years, held against all comers with fire and sword.

⁂

I looked up from my book. Outside, the rain had finally stopped—or at least slowed to a drizzle—and the wind was sweeping the sky free of clouds. In the distance, the Cairngorms showed snow-topped white in the late afternoon sun, and Davie's Land Rover was turning up the lane toward Sherramore.

The warmth of the sun brought the red deer out of their glades and glens to browse through the late afternoon. A rainbow was our constant companion as we gently cruised along General Wade's road, scanning the hills to the north of the River Spey. Safely deployed a mile and more away, the stags and hinds kept a watchful eye on us, but never stopped chewing. Every half mile or so, Davie would halt the Land Rover and put a telescope out the window, checking each stag he saw.

We drove all the way to the end of the tarmac, to the chain that blocked further progress up toward the pass, and once again turned around by the abandoned stone house. It was, I now knew, *Meall Garbh Ath*, the Hill of the Rough Ford. The house was an old stalker's dwelling, long since abandoned. So solid was the structure, however, that the roof line was straight as a die a century and more after it was built.

The bridge across the burn beside the house was one of General Wade's "improvements." We rested our scopes on the stone wall of the bridge and scanned the hills up toward Corrieyaireag. The greenish-brown heather was dotted with shaggy grey-brown deer—

the red stags of Scotland—Sir Edwin Landseer's *Monarch of the Glen*.
Our host, Mike McCrave, had been emphatic.

"You have to understand, you are not going to take a stag
like that," he told us, not that we had really expected to. I don't go to
Alaska expecting a 44-inch Dall sheep, either. I'd like one, but I don't
expect it. "These are hill stags, not park stags. There's a difference."

The difference is that the hill stags of Scotland are a truly
wild race, inhabiting the high peaks of the rough country. They roam
vast estates—in the case of Sherramore, 35,000 acres—as unhindered
by the occasional sheep fence as Montana's pronghorns are by three
strands of barbed wire. They live high, and they live hard. The hillsides (they never call them mountains in Scotland, though many of
them are) offer little but heather and coarse grass. Under those conditions, antlers do not attain the mind-boggling size and weight of
the red stags found in more hospitable climes.

"We have park stags in Scotland," Mike said. "In fact, I've
got an Italian client coming in tomorrow to shoot a 22-pointer on
an estate a couple of hours drive from here." He shrugged. "That's
what he wants. But you said you wanted to hunt, not shoot a park
stag."

So we did, Mike. So we did.

Back in the 1930s, Captain Paul Curtis, who was gun editor
of *Field & Stream* and an early lover of shooting both birds and stag
in Scotland, described how stag antlers are judged:

> The stags of Scotland are divided into five classes. There is a bonnie
> stag, a "royal" or better, though it might include a very exceptional ten
> pointer (the royal being a twelve pointer). Next comes a stag, that is a
> normal beast of ten points, weighing sixteen stone or so. Then comes
> the staggie, eight point beast but shootable; lower down the scale is a
> wee staggie, a little six pointer, but still shootable; and lastly there is
> a sma wee staggie, and heaven help the fellow who shoots one by
> accident, for it will surely draw down the wrath of the keeper in most
> emphatic terms.

Today, antlers are judged by point count, the same way we judge the North American elk, which the red stag closely resembles in configuration and body, if not in size. A classic "royal," or 12-pointer, has a crown of three tines at the end of each antler, with two single tines lower down along each shaft, and two brow tines. That is the ideal. Look at a reproduction of *Monarch of the Glen*, and that is what you will see. Such stags are few and far between.

One thing about hunting in Scotland that has not changed since Curtis's day is the role of the stalker. The stalker is a gamekeeper, his responsibility the well-being of the deer herd, and that means culling the old, the inferior, and the weak. He chooses the animal you will stalk and, with luck, shoot. It will not necessarily be the largest stag in a given herd, however, and that can cause problems for Americans who are accustomed to looking for the biggest and best trophy to be had.

"A stalker will never let you shoot a great stag that is in its prime," Mike told us. "They want to save them to father more of their kind; what they shoot are young stags that will never be great—you don't want their genes passed down—or stags that are over the hill. It's hard to explain to an American..."

But, the stalker's word is law. If you accept that, and accept the fact that your role in all this is to help manage the wildlife, then you are in for some of the finest and most interesting sport hunting to be had anywhere.

The key to it is numbers. In many parts of the Highlands today there are far too many deer and not enough people to hunt them, especially in the wildest and most rugged areas like Sherramore. They have difficulty attracting people who like to hunt hard and climb for hours in the cold and wet, in the hope of taking a hill stag that might have only six or eight points. And yet, for the price of a modest Colorado elk hunt, you can go to Scotland and take two hill stags, and see more animals in one day than the average elk hunter will see in a season. In the end, you have worked hard for your animal, and a trophy that carries those memories is a more worthy addition to your trophy room than the finest park stag that ever walked.

We were on our way back in now, with the sun casting long

shadows. By the Garva Bridge across the Spey, another one of General Wade's creations, we glassed a distant ridge. It was dotted with red deer, and we studied each stag intently. As I slowly passed the telescope along the ridge, mentally discarding each stag in turn, I saw what looked to be a pair of black branches sticking up from the ground. It was a stag's antler tips. He was lying down on the other side of the ridge, and only the top half of each antler was visible. Davie was looking at the same stag. He was more than a mile away, but through the Swarovski telescope his black antlers stood out clearly. Each one had a crown of three points on top. Each had a tine further down. That was all we could see. And the shafts were heavy. We could see that, too.

"What do you think?"

Davie studied him. "He's a fine beast. A fine beast, yesss."

"Shall we try a stalk?"

"There's no time tonight, no." He took his eye from the glass. "They'll settle down there for the night, yesss. I think they'll not go far. We'll come back in the morning, if you like..."

If I like! I drifted off that night to the sound of red stags roaring within a few yards of Sherramore Lodge. They come down in the darkness to nibble the lawn, and there was a lovely 12-pointer in the group. But that one was a pet, not a hill stag.

❊

In July, 1745, Prince Charles Edward Stuart landed on the coast of Scotland, planted his standard, and called the Jacobite clans to his cause. Their response was not overwhelming, until the Campbells took London's side. At that point, hatred of the Campbells tipped the scale and the Macleans, MacGregors, MacDonalds, the Camerons—all took the white cockade of Bonnie Prince Charlie and marched off into history.

Ironically, the first few miles of the bonnie prince's road to immortality were laid by General Wade. It began with a march over the Pass of Corrieyaireag down to the Spey, where an English army under General John Cope was waiting for him by the Garva Bridge.

General Cope decided that discretion was the better part of valor and retreated to Inverness. Prince Charles then made the fateful decision not to pursue him, but to invade England instead.

By the Garva Bridge today is a small fenced enclosure, full of sheep and pine trees, that is known as Johnnie Cope's About-Turn, and Cope's action inspired a song that Highland regiments sing to this day—*Hey, Johnnie Cope!* Bonnie Prince Charlie and his clansmen marched down from the pass and crossed the Garva Bridge unopposed.

It was bright sunshine when we crossed the bridge and turned the Land Rover hard right, following a dirt track up the hill along a deep burn. The rain of the night before had all the waterways in full flood. *Garvamore* is a corruption of the Gaelic meaning "big, rough ford," and it was living up to its name that day. The rushing water licked high up the stone arches that have supported the bridge for almost three centuries, and there was water in every pan, every crack, every tiny stream. We abandoned the Land Rover and took to the Argo, toiling up the slope to a plateau from where we could glass the surrounding hills.

Although you see frequent references to Scottish *deer forests*, they are forests without trees. A hill covered with nothing taller than two-foot high bracken is called a deer forest. Where trees do exist— and there are large plantations of pine and fir—they are referred to either as woods or as *forestry*. We now found ourselves on a naked hillside, glassing a distant line of hills across a wide expanse of forestry. As we scanned back and forth, the hill was as alive with deer as ants on an overturned anthill. You literally could not put the binocular anywhere without picking up 15 or 20 deer— stags, hinds, and calves. Some were lying down, some were browsing, and the sunlight glinted off their antlers.

One in particular was worth a second look, and a third. I still had visions of my black-antlered possible royal from the night before, but Davie had picked out what looked like a big ten-pointer, lying down facing us. He was about a mile away, but his antlers still looked high and wide. We studied him for long minutes. There was half a mile of open heather between us and him, then another half mile of forestry we might be able to approach through, and then he was on a slope a hundred yards beyond the last tree. If we could get to the forestry without spooking anything...

In a situation like that, your big problem is not so much stalking the animal as avoiding spooking anything else that will cause a mass departure of all the deer. With hundreds of pairs of eyes, many of them belonging to wise old hinds, this is far from easy.

"Colin will stay here with the Argo," Davie told us. "We will walk slowly—slowly, now!—and keep close together. Don't look at the deer at all. Keep your eyes down. Down, mind! And we will walk into the forestry."

Gently we traversed the heather, sloshing through puddles and running streams that lay hidden beneath the two-foot shrubbery. It was like crossing a minor delta, a spider's web of water, and all of us were soon soaked to the knees. Every few hundred yards we met a swollen burn that must be crossed, hopping from wet rock to wet rock, or simply wading through. But we made it to the forestry without sparking a stampede. So far, so good.

The forestry was about 50 acres of tree plantation, the evergreens in neat rows, with fire breaks cut at regular intervals. One such angled forward in the general direction we wanted to go. We were barely a hundred yards in, however, when the first small stag stepped out of the trees, looked us over, and bounded off.

"Slowly, now. Slowly, mind," Davie whispered. "Maybe they won't come out t'other side..."

Then came another staggie, and another. They criss-crossed the firebreak ahead of us as we walked. We paused at a Y-junction of two lanes, and Davie scanned what he could see of the hillside ahead. The deer were starting to move. Not quickly, not panicking, but they were moving. Davie was not disturbed by this. I looked far down the second fire break, which ended against a grove of solid shrubbery. The sun was streaming in, broken up by the branches, and I was sure I could see something there. I put the binocular on it, and sure enough, it was a stag lying right at the end, watching his back trail. He had been quietly lying a few hundred yards away, studying us. As soon as I put the binocular on him, however, he rose and was gone.

By the time we made it to the edge of the forestry, the far hillside was bare. It was as trampled down and nibbled and marked with droppings as a barnyard, but not a deer remained. We had spooked several out of the forestry, and they had provoked a general exodus. I was downcast by this, but Davie was calm.

"We will climb this hill and have a look around," he said. "It is almost noon. The deer will lie up then, and we'll go looking for them."

Jim Morey and I had both gone to Scotland expecting to climb, and we got our wish. The hillsides look steep, but reasonably even, from a distance; up close, you find they have been cut to ribbons by centuries of rainfall feeding creeks and rivulets, and the ravines range from a few feet to a few yards wide, and up to several yards deep. Add to this the clinging, clutching heather, and the climbing becomes as difficult as coastal Alaska.

As we climbed, the weather began to turn. Clouds swept in and the wind picked up, and by the time we topped the ridge, it was dark and blowing. A brief rainstorm soaked us, a patch of hail welcomed us to the Highlands, and then the clouds swept on, leaving us soaked and shivering in the brisk wind and sunshine. Davie Fraser, in his traditional stalker's garb of tweeds, shirt and tie, and deerstalker cap, was unperturbed. He calmly ate a sandwich in the lee of a large rock, waiting for the weather to pass. Davie has been a stalker on the estate for more than 30 years, and he adheres to all the traditions, from his tie and deerstalker cap to the iron rules of stalking and shooting. Some of the younger stalkers will go out without a tie these days, but not Davie Fraser.

There is no training school for stalkers; there are no examinations to pass. The only thing that counts is performance "on the hill," as the expression goes. To say a man is "tireless on the hill" means he will stalk all day in the roughest terrain. Having hunted these hills for so very long, Davie Fraser knows every nook, every cranny, every crag and burn and corrie. For all I know, he even knows the stags by name. At any rate, as we ate our lunch (our "piece," to use the correct stalking term) we watched the wind sweep away the rain. The sun lit up the snow-capped Cairngorms and turned the River Spey into a sparkle of diamonds, and Davie Fraser gave every indication that he knew exactly—exactly!—what the deer would do, and what he would do in response. Jim Morey and I were just along for the ride.

"The deer lie up in the afternoon, yesss," Davie said. "We will let them settle, yesss? Then we will take a wander along this hillside."

The hillside led north into the wildest parts of the Monadh Liath hills, up towards Corrieyaireag. Scanning the peaks, there was not a single sign of human life—no dwellings, no fences, no cattle, no sheep. There was just endless rolling heather, cut by hundreds and hundreds of glittering streams, fed by three days of rain, racing down the hillsides. During the night it had snowed on the higher peaks, and the dusting of white hung on even in the bright sunshine. It was lovely while the sun shone which, on past performance, would probably be about 20 minutes.

We packed up and began to sidehill, Alaska style, staying well below the skyline. The hillside undulated, and Davie was peering ahead with each step, trying to see around the corners, watching for the glint of an antler, the flash of a white rump. We were staying close behind and practically ran him down when he abruptly halted and dragged us down against the hillside.

"The beasts are there," he breathed. "Stay still. Still, now!"

Just beyond the hill there was a gap, then another hillside, and one by one the deer came into view. Once you picked out one, the others popped into sight like magic. There were two dozen stags scattered over the southern slope, basking in the warm sunshine. One, facing directly toward us, appeared to be the big old ten-pointer we had picked out early that morning. They were about 300 yards away. Too far for Scotland, where the stalk is the thing. Too far for Davie Fraser, who wanted us practically kissing their ear before pulling a trigger.

Davie was pulling his pack off and tucking it into the heather. The rifle, which he carried in its case, remained there and would do so until the stalk was complete and the shot was imminent. I took off my pack, keeping only my binocular, and we began to crawl along the hillside on our hands and knees, not daring even to glance up. The heather was soaking wet, and soon so were we. Finally, about 200 yards from the stags, we reached an impasse. The hillside folded into a deep ravine which we had no hope of crossing without being spotted. We would have to shoot from here, or not shoot at all. The stags, calm and unperturbed, lay quietly munching. One or two were on their feet, but mostly they gave the impression of a gentleman's club after a long luncheon, preparing to doze through the afternoon.

Hugged in tight against the hillside in a deep shadow, wrapped in the wet heather, it became very cold very quickly. But there we stayed, for one cannot shoot a stag that is lying down no matter how tempting a broadside target he may present. It is simply not done. Until they stood up, we could do nothing but watch, so watch we did. Our stag had either 11 or 12 points, we couldn't tell. There was a definite crown on one side, but the other had either a crown or two tines only. So well did the antlers blend in against the heather it was impossible to tell. When we grew tired of staring at him, we scanned up and down the hillside, comparing the others.

It was in the course of one of these window-shopping expeditions that another stag suddenly popped out at me, lying in shadow 'neath a black rock. His head was in profile, but his antlers were black and heavy—not as long as the other, but with this one there was no mistake: a "royal," a 12-pointer, a *bonnie stag*—and most probably the very one whose antler tips we had spotted the night before. Davie Fraser was already studying him, lips pursed together.

"He is the finer beast, sure enough," he intoned. "Yesss, indeed, yesss." A pause. "We will take that one, I think, yesss," and he slowly opened the case and pulled out the rifle. I sank back down into the heather and prepared to wait him out.

❋

Ewen MacPherson backed Bonnie Prince Charlie and, along with 600 of his clansmen, fought all through the Jacobite invasion of England. When the Prince withdrew to Inverness, the MacPhersons dispersed. When the Prince faced the English under the Duke of

Cumberland on the field of Culloden, the MacPhersons gathered again to go to his assistance, but were too late to join the battle. They met the remnants of the Prince's force fleeing westwards, and Ewen—called "Cluny" MacPherson, after his castle—helped the Prince to escape.

The Duke of Cumberland—known as "The Butcher Duke" to this day—laid waste to the land of the clans, concentrating his wrath on the shire of Inverness. Cluny Castle was burnt to the ground while Ewen watched from a distant hillside. He then went into hiding, and there he stayed, eluding the English for nine long years. For nine years, he lived in a cave on a high cliff overlooking the River Spey, or in a subterranean shelter dug for him by his clansmen. They kept him supplied with food, and in spite of their desperate poverty, not one succumbed to the temptation of a reward of 1,000 pounds Sterling that the Duke of Cumberland had placed on his head.

Nine years! Nine years without a bed, nine years without a fire, nine years wrapped in a plaid on a stone floor through the worst gales of winter. And I thought I had it bad, lying on this wet hillside in the heather...

"Get ready, lad. They're starting to move!"

Sure enough, our boy was still lying down but a couple of the others were on their feet and moving. The sun was near to setting, and the temperature was dropping. I was shivering in spurts, uncontrollable one minute, calm the next. Nerves or cold, it didn't matter which.

"Ready, now, ready... There! He's getting up! Wait until he turns, wait now..."

The stag was on his feet quartering away, then swung around broadside. As he did so, I pulled the trigger. The .270 cracked.

"You missed. Reload!"

Missed? All right. I settled the crosshairs just behind the shoulder and watched the recoil lift the reticle. The next few minutes were a confused tangle of shots, running stags, and contradictory whisperings. The borrowed .270 should have been dead on at 200 yards. I was shooting level, and there seemed to be little wind. Why, then, was every shot going in front of the beast?

By that time, the others were dashing off down the hillside, leaping from crag to crag. Our big stag was moving slowly down the hill, and Davie Fraser was considerably less than pleased. "Come on, then. We have to catch up to him."

I had no idea what was going on. The rifle had been steady enough, but I'd been missing; the other stags had run off already, but the big one was lingering behind. He was obviously hit, but where?

Davie had dropped everything but the rifle and was bounding along the hillside. As soon as we left the lee of the hill and stepped out into the ravine, a blast of wind like a waterfall practically knocked us off our feet. That explained the shots going wide, all right.

And then down we went at a dead run, keeping the distant, limping stag in sight as he picked his way down a deep burn. Davie ran far past him staying high on the hill with me hot behind him. We reached a deep, narrow ravine cut by a burn and jumped in, following it down the hill, trying to outflank the stag. Finally, just before the burn plunged over a 50-foot precipice, Davie climbed up and there was our stag, not 20 yards away, almost done in, picking his way down on three legs. At the sight of us, he lurched and collapsed, picked himself back up, and then went down with a final shot.

❄

After nine years, Ewen "Cluny" MacPherson dug up his remaining gold, distributed it among his loyal clansmen, and escaped to France. He died there, a year later, of a broken heart. His lands were forfeit to the Crown, and Cluny Castle remained a burnt out shell.

With the power of the clans broken and their way of life destroyed, the Highland landowners decided they could make better use of their property than by having tenant farmers who would provide fighting clansmen in time of strife. The time of strife was ended, so who needed them? The lairds began to evict the tenants in a sweeping movement that eventually came to be known as the Highland Clearances. With the people gone, the land could be leased to sheepherders from the Lowlands, and gradually MacPhersons, Frasers,

❄

Grants, and Macleans were replaced by new tenants: the Great Cheviot and the Scottish Blackface. Sheep were more profitable than farmers.

Many of the large Scottish estates were bought by Lowlanders, or by English industrialists. Sherramore Lodge, for example, was built around 1850 by an Englishman named Bibby, a shipping magnate from Liverpool. The grassy glens were populated by sheep, while the high crags were left to the red stag and the ptarmigan, and their safekeeping to men like Davie Fraser.

❄

The next day, we set out to find a stag for Jim Morey. Once again we travelled the familiar road to the end—past Garvamore and the ancient barracks where General Wade's garrison had once guarded the pass; past Johnnie Cope's About-Turn, and the Garva Bridge; past an abandoned crofter's house, while Scottish Blackfaces observed our passing with the disdain of those who belong.

Predictably, it was once again spitting rain, and the hills up toward Corrieyaireag were black and menacing. We circled around through some forestry, then dropped down into a ravine beside a deep burn and began to follow it up the hillside. There were stags on the hill which is called Tom Mor, a hill that, according to legend, was lit with fires whenever a death was imminent among the MacPhersons of Garva. Now it was snow-topped and shrouded in fog, and the rain fell heavier with each step we took. Finally, with it pouring down and visibility measured in feet, Davie called a halt in the lee of a hill and we wrapped ourselves in waxed cotton, prepared to wait it out. The rain turned to sleet and then to snow, burning our faces as we stood in flowing water up to our ankles.

"It never rains in Scotland," Jim said bitterly, echoing Mike McCrave's daily rallying cry.

"And the cheque's in the mail," I responded.

The rain let up a little. Davie hoisted the rifle case to his shoulder and began to climb once more. The burn had become a tiny torrent. When it rains in the Highlands, it is like turning on a tap; the burns fill up in minutes and you can sit and watch the River Spey

❄

as it rises. Now, every little rivulet was in joyous flood.

"We'll stop and have our lunch here where it's dry, I think," Davie said.

It was still raining, the steep hill provided no shelter, and water was flowing all around our feet. Where does he mean, where it's dry? Jim and I shrugged at each other and pulled out our sandwiches.

Having now done it a few times, I see the pattern of stag hunting in Scotland. First, you find the herd you want to stalk and pick out one or two worthwhile beasts. Then you climb up into their territory. As you do, some will scatter left, some right, and some will go over the hill. But by that time you are up amongst them. You then stop for lunch, giving the herds time to slow down, gather themselves together, get over their fright, browse a little, and then settle down for the afternoon. At which point you begin a careful stalk along the hillsides, looking for your beast. You take it near sundown, and by nightfall you are back on General Wade's Military Road and heading for home, a hot shower, a glass of something medicinal, and congratulations all around in front of a roaring fire.

Which is pretty much how it worked. Davie Fraser was leading us along the side of a steep, rocky hill, up near the snow line, stalking a stag that was just visible beyond a ridge. The stag moved, but we kept on with Jim Morey following closely behind Davie and me bringing up the rear with my camera.

We stopped to glass and take some pictures, and I was hanging on to a boulder, trying to get the right angle, when Davie hissed at me to freeze. Far below, three hinds had stuck their heads around a ridge and were studying the hillside up and down. We shrank into the slick grass and lay motionless, digging in with bootheels and fingernails to keep from sliding down. For long, long minutes the hinds watched; then a stag head appeared, and another, and one by one they spilled slowly up over the ridge until it was dotted with deer. They were down a good 150 yards at a steep angle, too close for us to dare to move, and we carefully looked them over. At first there was not much in the group, but as one stag after another appeared, the antlers got better. If we were lucky, a big stag or two might be bringing up the rear, and they were walking, in effect, right into range.

Finally, a big ten-pointer topped the ridge. Davie looked, and looked some more, and eventually he nodded. Jim stretched out slowly and poked the rifle down the hill, trying to find a steady position where he would not go skidding down the slope like a toboggan. Then the stag turned, Jim fired, the others streamed across the ridge and out of sight, and the big ten-pointer slowly tumbled down the slope to come to rest deep in the wet heather.

By the time we picked our way down, the hillside was empty of all but the lone stag. His legs were gathered under him, and his chin was resting on the heather as if he were sleeping. The sky was black, and snow was sweeping down from the Pass of Corrieyaireag, and the hill stag's shaggy coat was white with the heavy flakes.

13

✳

THE INNSBRUCK
SANCTION

Lunch ended, as I recall, shortly after two in the afternoon. We sat, my tour guide and myself, in an upstairs room of an ancient inn, sipping a dry red and watching the mountain-fed waters of the River Inn surge by under the bridge outside. The dry red was Austrian, and the innkeeper was proud that his cellar could offer local vintages that compared well with the French. My companion was one of Innsbruck's licensed tourist guides, professionals who know every nook and cranny of the lovely old town, and can tell you instantly who married whom among the Habsburgs in 1503 and the exact date in 1611 that the Black Plague hit each house along the narrow streets of the old town. She was discussing wines with the innkeeper as I gazed out at the river.

My mind, however, was not on red wine, but on red stag, for that morning, in a centuries-old palace of the Habsburgs, I had seen the most fantastic array of stag antlers imaginable. The finest trophies of the chase, going back centuries, taken by the most privileged of hunters in a hunting-mad society, lined those walls for all

✳

289

to marvel at. And, in an hour or two, I would be climbing a nearby Alp to crawl into a shooting blind overlooking a ravine in the hope that such a beast might happen by in the waning minutes of daylight. It gave the wine a special flavor.

But this story is not about red stag. As it turned out, no stag happened along that afternoon as whipping rain and unseasonable cold kept them tight under cover. The strange weather, though, did have a direct effect on the game we were really there to hunt, the high-peak-loving little chamois, and so this story rightly begins in that Habsburg palace with its stunning array of horns and antlers, and its portrait gallery of Habsburg princes through the ages.

Innsbruck, for those who missed the 1976 Olympics, is the capital of the Austrian province of Tirol. The Austrian Alps loom over the city in every direction, snow-capped even in summer. The name *Innsbruck* means *Bridge on the Inn*, and the city has been, since Roman times, a crossroads. This is where the north-south and east-west passes through the Alps converge, and its favored location has conveyed on Innsbruck a history that is more interesting than it is peaceful.

The first recorded settlement was a Roman encampment, and my guide could even show me the outermost limits of the Roman walls. The sandaled feet of barbarians trod the passes through the Dark Ages, before giving way to the Holy Roman Empire and its Habsburg emperors. One of the Habsburgs had the temerity (in recent history—only two or three hundred years ago) to marry a commoner. She was prevented by law from living in the royal palace so he built for her, on a slope overlooking Innsbruck, a palatial residence of her own. This *schloss* is now a museum housing an art gallery, and it was here that we repaired to brush up my knowledge of the Austro-Hungarian Empire.

At first, wandering among the van Dycks and Dürers and the lone Velasquez was about as interesting as history could be. Gradually, however, I was overwhelmed by the minutiae of who married whom and when, and who they begat who in turn married whom, and began amusing myself by searching each succeeding portrait for the tell-tale effects of rampant inbreeding. The Habsburgs had a penchant for marrying cousins, and over the centuries it brought about the famous "Habsburg lip" for which the dynasty became notorious. This evolutionary progression was revealed in surprising detail by century after century of masterful portraits. Whether the Habsburgs' intellectual decline was also a result, or whether it was a legacy of an early Habsburg, the Spanish princess "Juana the Mad," I leave to the historians.

After paying my dues in the portrait gallery, I was conducted to the museum of arms and armor, one of the finest in Europe, which is housed in the great hall. And there, lining the ceiling, were the stag antlers. One after another they marched down the wall, each seemingly more spectacular than the last. In some cases, the beams were as big around as my arm; others were graced by spectacular basket crowns you could have used as fruit bowls. On one set I counted 36 points, including twin pairs of guard tines that were each eight or nine inches long. My guide was chattering merrily on about the relative merits of Italian Renaissance armor compared with that made in Germany, but I was not paying much attention. Those antlers, and the prospect of going into the mountains later that day on the admittedly long chance of seeing one in the flesh had brought me completely out of the Middle Ages into the present. All I wanted now was a good lunch and my mountain boots. The Habsburg age, for all concerned, was past.

It is a strange feeling donning green wool hunting pants and mountain boots in a five-star hotel in the center of town, walking through the lobby past a huge portrait of the Empress Maria Theresa (who was, even after a dozen children, gorgeous) and out to a taxi stand to take a cab…and go hunting. In Innsbruck, however, you turn no heads.

This is the single most hunting-mad town I have ever seen. The entire Tirol, with its mountains and estates, its red stag and roe deer and chamois, is hunting country—albeit hunting with a distinct and curious flavor imparted by 2,000 years of civilization. It is hunting ruled by tradition, with its own customs and obligations, but so closely woven into everyday life that you soon forget you are engaged in an enterprise that in most modern urban circles is highly suspect, not to say outright *verboten*.

Innsbruck owns many fine restaurants, and all, it seems, rejoice in the names of animals: the Black Stag, the Red Eagle, the White Horse. The buildings have been part of Innsbruck for four or five centuries; you enter through solid wooden doors that have withstood many a siege and climb narrow stone staircases to upper rooms rich with woodsmoke and roast venison. The walls are hung with horns and antlers and paintings of the chase.

Walk the streets in loden green, the traditional garb of the *jaeger*, and you draw approving nods. Other hunters search for a little sprig of pine in your lapel—the sign of a successful stalk that the hunter is allowed to wear the next day as a badge of accomplishment. If a fellow hunter sees the sprig, he offers his hand with a smile and *"Weidmann's Heil!"* The correct response is *"Weidmann's Danke."* It is a sign of recognition among enthusiasts.

My cab driver was not a hunter but, as a diner, he heartily approved of it because he knew where those delicious little brochettes of roe deer originated. We chatted happily about food all the way out to a little town where I was meeting Jim Morey, who heads Swarovski Optik in the United States, and the Swarovskis' chief game keeper, Walter Sailer, for a late-afternoon expedition into the mountains to get Jim a red stag. It was an impromptu hunt, an unexpected but highly flattering invitation to hunt an animal for which the trophy fee normally runs into many thousands of dollars. In Austria, there is virtually no hunting on public land, and the fees for hunting large trophy animals on private land are beyond the reach of all but the wealthy. It is not unusual to spend four or five thousand dollars for a year's fishing rights on a hundred yards of mountain stream.

Game animals are graded and licenses issued based on the number of animals of a particular size in a herd and which ones the game keepers want culled for the good of that herd. Trophy fees, like-wise, are determined by the size of the animal. So, if you are issued a license to take a red stag, you might pay $1,000 for an over-the-hill eight-pointer, or $10,000 for a gold-medal-level 12-pointer, or $20,000 for a spectacular 16-pointer that would feel at home in the palace of the Habsburgs. What level Jim was authorized to shoot, should we see one, I did not ask. I don't think he knew him-self, and Walter was being rather circumspect. If he said shoot, Jim would shoot; if not...not. European-style hunting takes some getting used to.

I was studying the Pension Clara's mini-museum of hunting when Jim and Walter arrived from the latest round of celebrations for Swarovski's 100th anniversary. It had been an outdoor affair; while I was touring the palace and wolfing venison brochettes, Jim had been standing in the whipping rain listening to sermons. He arrived thor-oughly wet and miserable, but the prospect of climbing a mountain in that same whipping rain cheered him up considerably. There is a message there.

At any rate, we piled into Walter's four-by-four and began the winding climb up the mountain, passing first through gently treed slopes and chalets, on to high country pasture, then into a terrain of rock faces, evergreens, and sudden country inns that appeared around hairpin corners. After about an hour, we reached a roadblock at the entrance to an Austrian army shooting range. Walter keyed in the code, the barrier lifted, and we continued on up the mountain. The trees began to thin, as did the fog, and I realized we had been climbing through clouds. Looking down, the valley was a long green vessel filled with shifting fog. We arrived at a mountain herdsmen's camp, boarded up tight for the winter, pulled the car in under the lee of a building, and disembarked. The trees were black-green and dripping, the nar-row winding trail that led up to the shooting blind was a mile of slippery mud, and it was a long, long way to the bottom. All we could do now was shiver and wait for a red stag or darkness, whichever came first. Darkness won.

❈

That evening we were joined at the Hotel Maria Theresa by a Texan named Shawn Ferris. The next morning hunting was to begin in earnest, and now the quarry was not red stag but chamois. This is a completely different type of hunting, as different as hunting Dall sheep in the Brooks Range is from stalking Rocky Mountain elk in the forests of Colorado.

The chamois is a delightful fellow about the size of a pronghorn, with little fish-hook horns. An eight-inch head is extremely good, and a 13-incher would be a new world's record. While a chamois's horns may not impress a sheep hunter, the country they inhabit certainly will. They are critters of the high peaks—above timber-line, above the alpine grass, higher even than the gravel slides. When a chamois wants to, he can dance along the mountaintops like any mountain goat—which, of course, is what he is. And if the chamois are up high, the only way to get one is to climb up there yourself and shoot one on his own turf.

The chamois are not always up that high, of course. They descend to the sheltered valleys for the winter, driven down by the bad weather of autumn, and the bad weather of autumn was exactly what we had been having for several days—rain and wind and cold. We arose, however, to a spectacularly sunny day, a crisp October day that was beautiful for climbing or simply sitting on a mountainside, gazing across distant peaks into distant valleys. Because of the previous bad weather, however, the chamois might be down low—at least, to start with. As the day wore on, they would almost certainly begin to climb, and climb, and climb.

Like red stag, licenses are issued for chamois by sex and grade. We had tags for a Class-Two buck, a Class-Two doe, and a Class-Three doe. This was all a mystery to me. Jim explained that a Class-Two buck was roughly equivalent, in chamois terms, to getting a tag allowing you a 36-inch Dall as opposed to a 40-inch Dall. The does, well—an old Class-Two doe might be as big or bigger than a Class-Two buck, while a Class-Three would be a young, dry doe which would be expected to pay for her virtue by making way for more productive females. They were expecting a hard winter in the Tirolian Alps, there were too many chamois for the range, and our job was to cull the above-mentioned. Again, European-style hunting takes some getting used to. It was the job of Walter Sailer and our other game-keeper, Herr Mims, to point out which animal to shoot.

We began seeing chamois before we ever left the cars, brown and white critters glued to cliffs that soared up to our right and left. Walter and Herr Mims studied them all closely, murmuring to each other in German. We rounded a bend and surprised a pair on the road, one of which was exactly what Shawn, with his Class-Two buck license, was looking for. Walter and Shawn bailed out as the bucks disappeared around a corner and spent a few minutes trying for a shot, but thankfully did not get one. Road hunting for chamois is not much of a story, even though you shoot when the game keeper tells you to. We split up, with Jim, Herr Mims, and myself continu-ing up the mountain on foot while Walter and Shawn began a long stalk up a high valley into a mountainous cul-de-sac that ended with steep walls on three sides. Glassing the peaks a few thousand feet above, we spotted some chamois, so we were climbing into an area where we knew there was game. This gives spirit to any set of lungs.

It was shortly after nine when we heard a distant shot and looked back down to where we had started. Walter's four-by-four looked like an olive green toy tucked in among the distant evergreens. We glassed carefully for a few minutes, but seeing nothing, we con-tinued up the mountain.

I should tell you, I am not a ropes-and-pitons man. If I have to hang on with both hands, I don't want to go. The particular Alp we were on was steep and rocky, with some (to me) impassable preci-pices and some difficult, scary parts, but overall the trail was a hard climb but not terrifying. The groomed state of the trail should have told me something, but it was still a shock when, climbing with our packs and rifles, we looked back and saw a pair of hikers climbing after us, brightly clad, sunglassed, backpacked, and striding purpose-fully upwards with walking poles swinging.

"*Volks marchers,*" Jim said.

"Folks what?"

"Hikers," he said. "It's very big here, hiking in the moun-tains. There are trails all over."

Scarcely had he said it when another hiker came down the trail toward us. Then another appeared. And another and another. Altogether I counted 28 hikers in that group, and they descended smack through the area we wanted to hunt. Hunting in a crowd—another unfamiliar aspect of the chase in Europe.

"So much for the chamois," I said, bitterly.

"Don't worry," Jim smiled, "they aren't going anywhere. They're used to people up here. It may even be an advantage."

As the busload of *volks marchers* marched past, they looked at our rifles.

"*Grüss Gott,*" they offered—the standard greeting in the devoutly Roman Catholic Tirol.

"*Grüss Gott,*" we replied. They studied our rifles and smiled and chatted with Herr Mims before volksmarching on by, wishing us luck. There are actually three religions in the Tirol—Christianity, hunting, and in the winter, skiing. Those who don't hunt wish they could. That seems to be the only difference between hunters and non-hunters in the Tirol. Being accustomed to non-hunters eyeing my rifle with disapproval, it took a while before I could smile and say "*Grüss Gott*" without expecting an anti-hunting lecture. In the next few hours, though, I got a lot of practice. That sunny October day the mountains were crawling with *volks marchers*. If we saw one, we saw a hundred. We also saw chamois, but not many and not shootable, and we descended in the late afternoon with a serious thirst.

❉

We found Shawn at the four-by-four, proudly cradling the finest chamois Jim had seen in a half-dozen years hunting the Alps. Shawn had had to walk all of a quarter-mile to get it and was back at the hunting car, tag filled, before the sun even crested the mountains.

Sometimes in hunting the planets converge and you are presented with a windfall. The spate of bitter weather on the weekend had kept the *volks marchers* at home and driven the chamois down into the valley for shelter, and Shawn and Walter had walked from the car right into a browsing flock. A short stalk, a 400-yard dash up the scree, and Shawn had his chamois—and a real beauty, at that. Now, the opposite was about to occur for Jim and me. The weather had turned fair once again, the hikers were on the trails, and a combination of sunshine and humanity was urging the chamois back up toward the peaks.

When Jim and Walter and I returned the next morning for a second assault, the chamois were just brown-and-white dots on the rock faces near the skyline, thousands of feet up. Thousands of feet. Up. Knowing my own limitations when it comes to mountaineering, I asked Walter if he did any rock climbing. "*Ach, nein,*" he smiled. "I do not like the cliffs. I had a bad fall when I was very young." I was reassured. I should not have been. My definition of cliff, and Walter's, turned out to be two very different things.

We set out up the valley, following the trail Walter and Shawn had taken the day before. After a quarter mile of brushy undergrowth, it broke out onto the scree—a gravel-covered mountainside of oversized rocks stretching all the way to the head of the valley. We climbed until we hit a trail that angled up the mountainside.

There was no sign of yesterday's chamois, which had included several suitable does. As we climbed, we passed the blood trail where Shawn's buck had been dragged down the slope. Then we were in snow, inching higher up the mountain with each step. Walter led, using a pair of ski poles for balance. With his rucksack, breeches, and high wool socks, and the rugged peak that towered overhead, he reminded me of *The Eiger Sanction*— a reassuring thought.

We took only one rifle, Shawn's new .257 Weatherby with a Swarovski 2.5-10 x 56mm scope. This is considerably more rifle than a chamois demands, except for one small but significant consideration: When wounded, a chamois will use its last breath to get as high as possible before expiring and plunging onto the rocks below, shattering its graceful horns. A rifle that puts one down and keeps it there is worth the extra weight. With its 26-inch barrel, the new "Made in America" stainless Weatherby was a true all-weather, ultra-long-range unit, but it had the one thing that counted: punch. Still, as I climbed higher, it did get heavier.

The sun finally topped the Alps at our backs and penetrated into the furthest recesses of the high valley. The last vestige of frost disappeared, although the heavy, wet, permanent snow on the mountains took little notice except to become heavier and wetter, and the temperature began to climb right along with us. We reached the point where the mountain valley narrowed to nothing and lunged upwards, then crossed to the other side and continued our ascent. We could now look back down at where we had been. The trail across the opposing scree was a narrow line, falling further below us with each step.

The slope we were on was steep, with sharp rocks and clefts that ranged from mere cracks to deep ravines. As we got higher the terrain became more difficult, and it was a blessing whenever we found ourselves on a narrow stretch of *volks marchers'* trail. When we came to a stream babbling out of the mountainside, Walter called a brief halt. I wedged my pack in behind a rock to keep it from sliding down; when I went to put it back on I lost my grip on the rifle and, in saving it, let go of the pack. It tumbled and bounced 20 yards down the mountainside before a protruding rock saved it from going all the way to the valley floor, hundreds of feet below. Until that moment, I had not realized just how steep it was.

We were following a trail with a rock face to our left and a rugged drop to the right when we rounded a corner and found…nothing. The mountainside fell away to infinity, and the gap was negotiable only by clinging to a steel cable bolted into the rock face and skipping across the chasm. By the time I reached the other side, the sweat soaking my back was from neither heat nor exertion.

After that, the slope topped out a bit. The scrubby evergreens that covered the lower levels gave way to grass, which became shorter and thinner as we climbed. Finally, it too gave up and now there was only gravel and rock, ice and snow. We were into the hanging glaciers and rocky peaks, the part that looked so pristine and picture-post-card-like from below. Now, as I perched on it, it was just one more treacherous old mountain waiting its chance.

Keeping close to the vertical wall, we began to traverse this high ridge, stalking each valley that cut into the wall, studying it carefully before continuing on to the next. It was like walking down a hotel hallway past a series of open doors, behind any one of which might lurk a flock of chamois. But one by one, the high mountain valleys came up empty. Then we came to the largest valley of them all.

From far below we had seen one stark pinnacle that reached up to the sky, a miniature Matterhorn towering above all the others, flanked by a fold in the rocks. Now, standing at its base, what had looked like a fold was, in fact, a deep valley. The thin grass petered out among the rock slides, and in the center of this valley was a rocky knoll. Between us and the knoll was a small glacier, and from the base of the glacier bubbled a clear mountain stream. It was, in every sense, a high-country idyll—complete with chamois! For there, beyond the knoll on three sides of the valley, appeared brown-and-white dots, nibbling, wandering, or lying in the cool snow—one, two, four, a dozen!—chewing and gazing down at us with interest, but no panic. Now, all that separated us from our goal was a 500-yard stretch of wide-open gravel that a ferret could not have crossed undetected. Not disturbed in the least, Walter calmly removed his pack and braced his telescope in the "X" of his ski poles. Jim and I then set about looking like *volks marchers* and pretending we had not the slightest interest in any chamois that ever lived.

Sometimes, faced with an unalterable obstacle, the best course is to make the obstacle the cornerstone of your plan of attack. It worked for Hannibal, it worked for General Wolfe; maybe it would work for us. For the next half hour we sat and moved about, making no attempt at all to hide and doing everything possible to convey the idea that we were not concerned about being seen. Gradually, the chamois lost interest in us and began to move about again, nibbling. When he was sure they were accustomed to our presence, Walter casually shouldered his pack, motioned us to keep close, and began a slow, meandering progress up and over the glacier toward the rocky knoll that would shield us from the chamois and, eventually, provide a platform within shooting range (we hoped) of two Class-two does.

We crawled up onto the knoll and peeked over a boulder. On the scree in front of us, and out to the left and right, were scattered two-dozen chamois. One old doe was lying in the snow about 300 yards away, and she had a nice set of horns; in another group, on the scree about 150 yards out, were several does that might qualify for the tags we held. Again Walter settled down to study them and decide which we should shoot. Jim and I, meanwhile, began figuring out how we could take two does from the same group, in rapid succession, with only one rifle between us.

Finally Walter pulled back and told us which he wanted us to shoot. There were seven in a group; we were to take two young does that were standing together off to the right side; mine was the uppermost of the two. I laid the rifle over a pack on top of the boulder and went over the plan once more to make sure I was shooting the right one. She was facing away from me, and Walter kept whispering to wait until she turned. This, naturally, she stubbornly refused to do. But, finally, she turned her head and her body followed, and I touched the trigger. As she coughed blood, I rolled out of the way. Jim grabbed the rifle and settled in. His first hurried shot missed and set the flock in motion.

"Jim!" Walter hissed. "You missed!"

Jim's doe crossed the scree at a dead run, and his second shot dropped her in a skidding heap on a patch of glacier snow.

"Not that time, I didn't!"

Walter then seized the rifle and turned his attention to my doe, which was still on her feet and trying to move toward the sheer rock face. At the shot she collapsed where she stood, then slowly slid down the scree to come to rest against a rock. The whole episode took less than a minute. The remaining chamois dashed off, some left, some right, some straight up. Very quickly, however, the echoes of the shot died away. The chamois calmed down and began to browse once again. It was not quite noon.

Walter and Jim and I gathered up our two does, dragged them across the glacier onto the grass where we could look out over the valley, and settled down to have lunch ourselves, munching Austrian sausage and dry smoked ham, and scooping cupfuls of water from the icy alpine spring. As we sat, we glassed the far side of the valley and the mountains beyond, and the valley beyond that. A mile up the valley and high above us, on the very peak of a jagged line of mountains, a human figure appeared, and then a second. Then came a helicopter, hovering briefly above the two climbers before slowly descending, close to the rock face, until it was far below us. From where we were, we had a clear view. The helicopter stopped moving and hovered in close to the rock beside the very trail we had climbed that morning. Walter was watching the affair intently.

"What is it?"

Walter murmured in German, peering through his binocular.

"Search and rescue," Jim said. "A *volks marcher* was killed there on the weekend. They found his body yesterday. I guess the two on top are trying to find where he fell from, and the helicopter is looking at where they found him."

❄

Having climbed a mountain and killed a chamois, I thought most of the work was done. I was wrong. Walter cut the heads and hooves from our two animals and stuffed the carcasses into his backpack. I wrapped the heads in paper and put them into my pack, and we started down, Walter going on ahead on his alpine legs, knowing that with the weight he was carrying he would have to stop often. Rather than retrace our steps, which was the long way to the bottom, we stayed on the trail and continued our ascent, climbing higher and higher toward the main trail that would take us back down.

With Walter out of sight, Jim and I picked our way ever upwards as the mountainside became rockier, steeper, and more jagged and cut with ravines, and the trail clung to rock faces that fell away to nothingness. At times the track was little more than a gesture a few inches wide, and we encountered the helpful steel cables more and more often.

As happens in mountaineering—my brand of mountaineering, at least—I began to anticipate bad spots before they occurred. The sight of a cable bolted into the rock made me sweat before I even saw the precipice it was put there to help me cross. Jim Morey, ever helpful, burst into song. *"I love to go a-wandering..."*

It didn't help. With my pack weighing 60 pounds or so, and carrying the rifle as well, my legs were already shaky.

"Keep moving. Don't look down," I repeated, under my breath like a mantra. "Keep moving. Don't look down. Keep moving. Keep moving. *Keep moving..."*

We were now into the most alpine of Alps, sheer cliffs and rock faces and hanging glaciers. As well as cables, we started to find steel pitons driven into the rock, to be climbed like a ladder. One set descended into a chasm until the two walls were only a few feet apart; we then stepped over to the other side and climbed back up to the trail. Keep moving. Don't look down. Keep moving. Keep MOVING!

We rounded a bend to find Walter waiting for us.

"There is a more direct route down, right here, but it is riskier than the trail," he said. "I am going to take it because it is shorter. Do you want to try?"

Uh, no, Walter, thanks very much. Riskier than this? Riskier than cables and pitons? Uh, no, uh, Walter. You go ahead. See you at the bottom. Maybe.

Walter then plunged over the edge and into some junipers that clung to the mountainside by sheer force of will. Jim grinned cheerfully, I grimaced a reply, and we pressed on, across a hanging glacier turned greasy slick in the warm sunshine, with the trail growing narrower and rockier before it suddenly all ended at the main trail. The sight of that thoroughfare, to-ing and fro-ing down the mountainside, as broad as a sidewalk and flanked with shoulder-high junipers, was as welcome a sight as I can remember. Jim and I were stretched out on the grass beside the four-by-four when Walter staggered in a half-hour later, scratched and bitten, sweating and bleeding. He never did find the shortcut, and ended up just bulling his way down. Some shortcut.

"Think it's time for a beer, Walter?" we asked. He grinned.

We were sitting outside the *gasthaus* working on our second glass of frothy lager, the mountains that loomed behind us once again the stuff of postcards rather than of terror, when an acquaintance happened by. He looked at our lapels. We had forgotten the sprig of evergreen, but the bloodstains told the tale. He smiled shyly and offered his hand. "*Weidmann's heil!*" he said.

ASIA

14

❋

TIGER, TIGER, FADING FAST

AN OPENING POLEMIC

An old *Punch* cartoon went something like this: Two big game hunters are standing before a wall of trophies, looking at a rhino head.
"Alas, the rhino's almost extinct," says one. "Yes, it's really too bad,"
replies the other, "too bad, indeed. I'm going out next month to get
mine, before they're all gone."

Fade now to a recent Safari Club convention, where I ran
into an acquaintance I had not seen in some time. "Where have
you been?" I ask. "Siberia," he smirks. "Tiger hunting." And seeing
the look on my face, he adds: "There aren't many left. I wanted to
get one."

Once again, life imitates art.

This chapter was originally intended to be a progress report on the state of the tiger worldwide. There was to be a brief look at India, where Project Tiger supposedly saved the Bengal species from extinction, and where numbers were inching high enough that, once again, for control purposes, it was dreamt that they might be hunted by sportsmen. It was to look at Siberia, where the giant tiger of the north was being hunted—and managed—with an eye to preserving both hunted and hunter. And it was to be an update on the status of the lesser- known subspecies in Manchuria and Indochina.

Alas, reality intruded on these starry-eyed premises to the point where it seemed irresponsible to even mention the word "hunting" in the same breath with tigers because, while the reports do tend to be contradictory and there are disagreements among tiger experts as to actual numbers, there does seem to be consensus on one major point: The road of the wild tiger may pass here, or it may pass over there, it may be quite short or it may be a little longer, but in the end it leads to only one place: Extinction.

But how can that be? How can the most-heralded conservation campaign of the century—India's Project Tiger—which brought the Bengal race back from the brink 20 years ago, now be once again looking over the edge?

The short answer is, we were fools to think, as one Indian official rashly put it in 1980, that the tiger was "saved from extinction forever." It was not. It is not. The longer answer is, forces that are many centuries old, forces most of us had no idea we were dealing with, are what threatens the tiger today.

At the turn of the century, it is estimated there were 100,000 wild tigers of all species roaming the forests and jungles of Asia. Today there are maybe 7,000 wild tigers in the world. That is the optimistic estimate; others range as low as 5,000. Of those, approximately 4,000 are known to be in India's tiger preserves. That leaves anywhere from 1,000 to 3,000 divided among the other subspecies—Siberian (Amur), Manchurian (Amoy), Indochinese (Corbett's), and Sumatran. Three other subspecies (Bali, Caspian, and Javan) are either known or assumed to be extinct—all three having disappeared since 1972, when all tigers were placed on the endangered species list.

In 1900, there were about 40,000 Bengal tigers in the Indian subcontinent. By the time the British pulled out in 1947, hunting and an exploding population had combined to reduce the number to a fraction of that, and by the time legal hunting was stopped in 1970, there were only about 1,800 tigers left. Project Tiger established preserves for them with strict controls and close supervision. The tiger bounced back. Meanwhile, of course, the Indian population continued to grow and land became scarcer and more precious; human settlements crowded up against the boundaries of the preserves and some farmers even crossed the line to graze their cattle and steal timber. With more and more tigers, less and less room, and fewer and fewer natural prey animals, but with both cattle and humans readily available, no one was really surprised to see a sudden resurgence in man-eating and cattle-lifting, and the whole situation was a ready-made political hot potato in India.

There were a few suggestions that regulated sport hunting—with trophy fees for the government and jobs and money for the locals—might alleviate the situation and put the tiger on a firmer economic footing, but opposition from the usual quarters caused those suggestions to come to nought. And there, as of 1990, it stood.

The situation in Siberia was less clear, but no less volatile. Hunting the Siberian tiger has never been a major sporting proposition. A few intrepid hunters braved the tundra under the Czar, and in Stalin's heyday (an era of unbridled excess worthy of Orwell's *Animal Farm*), Communist Party bosses would hold tiger-hunting fests and take five or ten animals at a time, and all done in a manner that would put the elephant-back hunts of the Victorian maharajahs to shame. Part of the backlash against Stalinism that occurred in the Soviet Union in the 1950s was an internationally trumpeted effort to save the tiger, similar to what happened with the polar bear. Officially, all tiger hunting in Siberia came to an end. Then the Soviet Union also came to an end, as did the communist system and any semblance of game regulations in Russia's far east.

For reasons best known to the revolutionaries themselves, fundamental changes in government always seem to bring with them a complete breakdown of game laws. It happened in India in 1947;

it happened all over Africa in the 1960s (and is still happening), and it has happened (less flagrantly or with less publicity) in Siberia. Or perhaps we should say that, in Siberia, it has happened with the complicity of many in the hunting community and behind a facade of respectability. Over the past several years, after the initial flurry of optimism and excitement about Russia's conversion to an open-market system and the opening up of a new hunting and fishing frontier, reports have filtered out of Siberia about unchecked corruption, rival hunting camps hijacking each other, and shooting bears, mountain sheep, and Siberian elk from helicopters.

Although Siberia is a big place—at almost five million square miles it is larger than the entire United States, including Alaska—the haunt of the Siberian tiger is relatively small. They now inhabit a narrow strip of territory about 800 miles long in the Sikhote-Alin mountain range in the Ussuriland region. This is near—well, it's not really near anything. Tigers are territorial, and each adult male requires 500 to 600 square miles of land to call his own. To support a population of 100 adult male tigers, then, you would need 50-60,000 square miles of uninhabited wilderness. Altogether, there are *at the absolute most* a few hundred Siberian tigers roaming the *taiga*. Most estimates now put the numbers at 200 or fewer. Considering that it is generally accepted that the point of no return for a subspecies is 120 animals, that puts the Siberian tiger in dire straits.

As for the Manchurian tiger, the high estimate is 40 animals, the low estimate around 20. May they rest in peace.

Of the remaining subspecies, the Bali tiger became extinct first, followed by the Caspian tiger in the 1970s, and the Javan tiger around 1980. The Indochinese (Corbett's) tiger is, at this point, an unknown quantity. It inhabits the jungles of Burma, Thailand, Malaysia, Kampuchea, Laos and Viet Nam. A grand total, at a guess, might be 2,000, but most experts consider that a wildly inflated number. The Sumatran tiger, the only one of the island subspecies still extant, numbers in the hundreds. Some are on preserves, some are in zoos.

If one wanted now to sum up those things that threaten both the Siberian and Bengal tigers, probably the word "greed" would do nicely. Another way to put it would be "prosperity." The 1990s brought unprecedented wealth to Southeast Asia and the Pacific Rim. Money. Big money. Oriental peoples, notably the Chinese, place great faith in what are known as "traditional" medicines. Politically incorrect Eurocentrics, such as your obedient correspondent, may consider the use of tiger whiskers in aphrodysiacs to be criminal, but good liberals insist such sentiments are "judgemental" and we must not say such things anymore—especially since China is a huge market for jeans and compact disks and personal computers and all the other disposable crap of the consumer age.

So demand for tiger parts has risen point for point with Far Eastern prosperity, and poaching of tigers for their skins, teeth, testicles, penises, paws, claws, whiskers, gall bladders, body fat, and eyeballs has become a serious business. Efforts to persuade (or pressure, or blackmail, or force) the Chinese to halt the trade have run up against a stone wall, partly because the tiger counts as little but a bargaining chip in a series of endless trade negotiations. Given a choice between saving the tiger and protecting the copyrights of a pack of crack-dealing rap stars, guess who the trade negotiators pick every time?

The problem is compounded by the fact that it is not just the Chinese. People of Chinese origin are prominent in Singapore, Malaysia, Indonesia, and throughout the Far East, and their so-called "traditional" medicines are in widespread use among people who hold considerable political power. As well, other eastern races (notably the Koreans who, you may have noticed, are not exactly penniless) also want animal parts for various purposes. What it boils down to is, the tiger's best friend at this point is the U.S. trade department. If that does not make them vulnerable, I don't know what would.

And speaking of trade, there is the matter of American investment in Siberia. Great thing for everybody, so they say. Get those Siberians involved in the free market. Jobs. Money. Prosperity.

Self-professed altruism aside, the two great attractions of Siberia are the vastness of its forests and the scantiness of its environmental regulations. It does a clear-cutter's heart good to look at those rolling expanses of evergreens with nary a Greenpeace in sight.

Recent news reports have North American pulp and paper companies moving into Siberia in a big way, and guess what they have their eye on? That's right—the last haunts of the Siberian tiger, which just happen to be in some of the few remaining stands of virgin timber in all of Asia. The tiger is a dweller of the deep forest glades, and the surest way to wipe him out is to cut down the trees, as those who deforested the Indian *terai* proved so well.

With Siberians willing to sell out the tiger for U.S. dollars and Chinese *yuan*, with American companies lusting for the timber, with Indian peasants demanding to know "What's more important—people or tigers?" and with the Indian government pondering the fact that tigers don't vote and listening to shrill cries of "land, land, land"—well, altogether, the outlook for the tiger is anything but burning bright.

✳

Tiger Trade

The foregoing should be sufficient to arouse the rage of ethnic Chinese, American timber barons, peasant-worshipping humanists, global free-traders, poverty-stricken Siberians, and American trade negotiators—an unlikely cabal to accuse of conspiracy but that is, in fact, what it amounts to. This is the front arrayed against the tiger, whether through circumstance, greed, or political expediency.

Over the past decade, a remarkable variety of publications has discovered the plight of the tiger and laid it before the public. The list includes *The Economist*, Britain's highly respected business-affairs weekly; the *Congressional Quarterly Weekly Report*; *Science News*, repeatedly; *Wildlife Conservation*, repeatedly; *Newsweek*, and, in a superb cover piece in March of 1994, *Time*. On some points, they agree; on others, there is disparity. Tiger numbers, for example, are estimates at best, guesswork at worst. In India, where a tiger census is carried out every year, numbers are pretty well known, although it was disconcerting for wildlife officials to discover that individual reports had been padded to make the guardians look good, and that some of those cats roamed only in the imaginations of the census takers.

Usually, these magazine articles have coincided with a newsworthy event, such as a Congressional move to invoke trade sanctions or a meeting of the Convention on International Trade in Endangered Species (CITES). From all of this research, however, a frightening picture emerges. The forces threatening the tiger today are the same that have always threatened it, only more so, and the hiatus period of the early 1980s, when the success of Project Tiger was being trumpeted, was nothing more than a breathing space brought about by the near-annihilation, deliberately and with Chinese government encouragement, of the Manchurian tiger.

To an ethnic Chinese, a live tiger is a walking pharmacopaeia. There is no part of its body that is not used in some form of medicine, stimulant, or aphrodysiac. The spectacular striped pelt of a prime tiger may sell for as much as $15,000, usually ending up in the den of some Arabian princeling (another race not noted for its devotion to conservation). By comparison, however, that money is just a sideline. The real money in tigers is in the bones and the organs, with tiger bone selling for up to $600 a *pound*.

Tiger bones are prized by the Chinese, ground up into a fine powder for use in pharmaceuticals to cure rheumatism and lengthen life, and even made into a type of wine that is noted for its restorative powers. The whiskers supposedly can either poison or strengthen, depending on the use, but are prized for both purposes. Tiger eyes, made into pills, are thought to calm convulsions. According to *Time*, in 1994, tiger penis soup in Taiwan cost about $320 a bowl. Why would you want it? Why, to make love like a tiger, of course; tigers can copulate *several hundred times* in a weekend, when the female is in heat. Then there are gallbladders, testicles, body fat, the meat itself; all have their folk uses—and their value.

China has its own subspecies, the Manchurian or Amoy tiger. While the rest of the world was trying to save the tiger in the 1970s, China was deliberately trying to eradicate it as a pest, a threat to humans, an impediment to progress. Through the '50s and '60s, thousands of Manchurian tigers were killed; being thrifty folk, the Chinese carefully stockpiled the bones, the penises, and everything else of value, stripping the bodies like an abandoned Cadillac in the South Bronx. The body parts went to the state-sponsored pharmaceuticals industry, which for a while enjoyed an over-supply. With a temporary glut on the market, prices for poached parts dropped—and so, for a while, did poaching. Then, in the late 1980s, the Chinese stockpile began to run low.

By the early part of that decade, Project Tiger had been declared an unqualified success, and one Indian official even boasted to the *New York Times* that the tiger could be considered "saved forever from extinction." Little did he know that Project Tiger had, in effect, done little more than build up a reserve of tigers that would become fodder for a Chinese black market that was about to boom.

Around 1985, Indian officials began discovering a pattern which, by the end of the decade, had become an epidemic. Tigers were being poached increasingly in the Indian preserves, and even tigers that had died of natural causes and been buried years before were found to have had their graves plundered and the valuable bones stolen. And in India, a mafia-like underworld of organized poaching and processing was in full swing.

Typically, after a tiger has been illegally killed in an Indian preserve, its body is smuggled into Delhi's Sadar Bazaar, the Indian end of the illicit tiger trade. There it is skinned and dismembered, with the pelt usually going to Arabia. The rest of the tiger's parts, now dried or otherwise preserved, are carried over the Himalayas by trains of porters, crossing into China over the roof of the world, down across the Silk Road of Marco Polo, in an illicit traffic older than civilization.

TRAFFIC is an organization that monitors trade in endangered species for the World Wildlife Fund. In 1993, it mounted a large sting operation in India and uncovered an organized underworld of families running a poaching operation. Indian police seized a cache of 850 pounds of tiger bones, roughly equivalent to 42 adult tigers. Halfway around the world, French police in the city of Metz arrested two ethnic Chinese who had a cache of 24 tiger penises.

In China, impervious to the cries of conservationists and immune to world opinion, production of tiger-bone remedies, licensed by the government, was not officially halted until 1993! Two years earlier, in an effort to preserve this industry under a guise of respectability, China had tried to get international acceptance for a scheme that would allow tiger "farming," with cats bred in captivity purely for parts, and those parts eligible for export exempt from CITES regulations. The plan was dropped because conservationists believed (rightly) that any semblance of legal trade would provide a smokescreen to shield the illegal trade, and anyway, there was no possible way that animals raised in captivity could satisfy the burgeoning demand throughout the Far East.

Although China is the major culprit, Taiwan and South Korea are not far behind. South Korea allowed the legal importation of tiger bones right up until July, 1993, and only outlawed the trade under the threat of severe sanctions. Even now, it appears, the South Koreans have made little effort, if any, to enforce the law, and the trade has simply gone underground. Customs data from 1988 through 1992 show Korea imported 50 to 100 tigers a year. Meanwhile, in preserves throughout India, tiger numbers were beginning to decline, plunging by an average of 35 per cent over the five-year period between 1988 and 1993.

Being the most susceptible of the three to pressure from the West, Taiwan has done, on the surface, the most to curb the trade, but to quote *Time*, "All three (China, Taiwan and Korea) have a well documented history of paying lip service to agreements protecting endangered species while continuing to do business as usual." In Taiwan's case, the official conversion to hypocrisy occurred a little earlier, that's all, although Taiwanese police officials insist they do not receive credit for the "real progress" they claim to have made. Indications are, however, that this alleged progress consists of little more than driving the trade underground. In early 1994, an undercover investigation of pharmacies in four Taiwanese cities found that tiger-bone medicines were readily available in 13 of the 21 stores the investigators visited.

It is difficult for Westerners to appreciate the depths of devotion that Oriental people have to potions made from tigers, bears, and other wild animals. In 1988, I hunted brown bears in Alaska with a guide who had recently had a Japanese hunter as a client. The Japanese do not hunt, as a rule, and firearms ownership is almost unknown in Japan. Yet this man had flown to Anchorage and booked a full-scale brown bear hunt in the spring of that year. A few days into the hunt, he shot a big brownie with a rifle he had rented in Anchorage. Once the bear was dead he showed little interest in it, beyond insisting that the guide open it up and remove the gallbladder immediately. As soon as this was done, the client had him call in a light plane to take him, and the gallbladder, off the sand bar and back to town.

"What about the hide?" the guide asked, perplexed.

"You keep it," the Japanese businessman shouted as he climbed in. If the whole venture cost him a dime under $20,000 I would be surprised—and all for a bear's gallbladder. Such are the powerful forces driving the global black market in tigers and tiger parts.

Against these forces there is little defense except trade sanctions—and trade sanctions, as everyone knows, are a force that is used with great hesitation against any country that has actual economic power. Needless to say, Taiwan, South Korea, and China have considerable economic power. For every conservationist who values the tiger above any mere financial concern, there are a hundred businessmen who would deeply resent having their free access to these thriving markets limited or eliminated for anything as trivial as a few tigers. Trade sanctions are similar, in a way, to the atomic bomb. Having the use of it makes you very strong, yet very weak at the same time. You can use it, but do you dare to do so when you could hurt yourself just as badly as your opponent?

⁂

False Spring

One of the fundamental laws of commerce is that where there is a demand, a supply will inevitably grow to meet it. The demand for tiger parts is certainly there, and crocodile tears notwithstanding, China, Taiwan, and Korea are unlikely to do much to curb it. They might outlaw the trade for public relations purposes, but it is still highly doubtful whether any of those governments could put a stop to it even if they really wanted to.

At the other end is the supply, and the largest pool of remaining tigers, probably amounting to 80 per cent of the world's total, is in India. The most recent valid count of India's tiger population shows about 3,750 living on preserves scattered throughout the country. There is no doubt whatever about the sincerity of the Indian government in its original support for Project Tiger, nor about the devotion of thousands of Indian game wardens and guards who try to protect the tigers on the preserves. But the fact is, they are facing growing pressures from a number of directions. The first and most obvious is the increasing Indian population, projected to reach 1.6 billion shortly into the next century. The tiger preserves, never very large to begin with, are now mere islands of forest in a sea of humanity. Not surprisingly, the villagers press up against (and often into) the preserves, while the tigers spill out over the edges. Conflict is inevitable.

A system is in place to compensate villagers who lose cattle and families who lose members to the tigers' jaws; conversely, if a villager kills a tiger he faces fines and imprisonment. This is all well and good, although the villagers complain that the compensation paid for their losses, material and familial, is not nearly as high as the fines levied for a dead tiger.

A good analogy for this situation would be to imagine some Washington bureaucrat turning Central Park into a tiger preserve with no fences, and the tigers free to wander out onto 59th Street and chew on people leaving the Plaza Hotel. It might cause some problems with the Manhattanites, and you could reasonably expect the mayor of New York to become a bit testy about it. Well, that is basically the problem facing virtually every one of the tiger preserves in India. Local politicians tend to side with their constituents, and tigers vote only with their teeth.

Actually, that is rather a delicious image. It is hard to imagine anyone in the rest of the country siding with the New Yorkers—at least nobody who has met one. At the same time, can you imagine the personality of a Bengal tiger that was born and raised in Manhattan?

A finite territory can hold only so many tigers. When saturation point is reached, various natural means limit their numbers. For example, when they become crowded, adult tiger males kill cubs to prevent future competition for territory. Still, as the preserves reach the limit, the number of prey animals drops. Also, older animals that lose territorial battles are forced to look elsewhere for food; geriatric tigers are Jim Corbett's natural man-eaters, and that is often what happens. Imagine Central Park as outlined above, with 100 tigers in residence but only enough deer to feed 50.

In India there are no buffer zones between human habitation and cultivation, and the tigers' forests, because there is not enough land to allow such a luxury. In some places it is common, apparently, for villagers to plant sugar cane right up to the very boundary of the preserves, and sugar cane is thick cover, ideal for a tigress to have her cubs. Picture it.

Chances are, only the very poorest or most desperate would choose (!) to live close to the tigers' lair, so let's people the area surrounding Central Park with a few thousand denizens of some South Bronx hellhole. We'll give them an annual income of $300 and tell them one dead tiger can be sold on the black market for $50,000. Then we'll arm them with poison and a few primitive weapons. And, oh yes—we'll tell them not to kill the tigers; we'll tell them it's illegal, just like the drug trade. Say goodnight, tigers.

Probably I am libelling the Indian peasants mercilessly, but the end result is about the same. These are the pressures facing the

Indian government—no, the Indian people, who are really the ones who will have to make the choices that will either save the tiger for all time or merely lengthen the tortuous road to extinction.

For the average Indian peasant, with nothing to look forward to but a lifetime of scratching a bare living out of a patch of dirt, some Chinese businessman holding out a fistful of cash is an extraordinarily powerful inducement. Add to that the memory of tigers eating your younger sister, and—well, it's easy to criticize.

Through the late 1980s, tiger poaching began to pick up in India, and by the early 1990s all the hard-won gains of 20 years of Project Tiger appeared to be in jeopardy. One preserve lost 18 tigers to poachers in a three-year period, in spite of having 60 armed guards patrolling the forest to protect them. Another, bordering on a tribal area in Assam, lost an estimated 50 per cent of its 90 tigers in a four-month period: The Boro tribesmen, in revolt against the Indian government, were killing tigers and trading the parts for guns and ammunition.

While demand in China provides the immediate economic incentive for poachers, the other factor that imperils the tiger is sheer numbers of human beings. Since 1972, the beginning of Project Tiger, India's population has grown by another 300 million. The pressure of numbers and poverty is almost incomprehensible. And, as tiger numbers dwindle further, the prices offered for tiger parts will skyrocket, adding further incentive for poachers, and so on, and so on, and so on.

Taiga, Taiga

In Russia, the tiger story is similar to India, but on a far smaller scale.

Amur tiger numbers reached their all-time low in the 1930s, with only about 30 cats surviving. Fearful the tiger would be lost forever, the Soviet Union belatedly decided to protect them; since Moscow's control over every aspect of life in Siberia was almost absolute, it could offer much better protection than the Indians were able to later. The Second World War was a fortunate respite for the tigers as well, since the Russians were preoccupied with Guderian's divisions of Tiger tanks; this was immediately followed by a horrible famine in many parts of the Soviet Union. Altogether, the tiger got a decade of peace, followed by the death of Stalin and the end of Stalinism.

By the 1980s, there were about 400 Amur tigers living in the wilds of eastern Siberia, and another 50 or so were hanging on by their toenails in northeastern China, in addition to the surviving pockets of Amoy tigers in China, which totalled a few dozen at most.

The end of the Soviet Union in 1991, and an almost complete breakdown of authority in Siberia, coincided with the surge in prices for tiger bones in China, Taiwan, and Korea. With the ruble descending to joke value, Siberians naturally began to kill bears and tigers for the pharmaceutical trade, using whatever means they had available—helicopters, horses and dogs, snares, poison, machine guns. A steady supply of hard currency gave poachers the means to start paying off police and wildlife department officials, and the trade gathered steam.

In 1992 alone, *Newsweek* reported, between 15 and 25 per cent of the remaining population of Amur tigers was killed by poachers. In the following year, 1993, Russian officials estimated another 80 to 100 tigers were killed by poachers. A computerized model created by biologists working at the University of Minnesota has found that once tiger numbers in a limited population drop below 120, even a slight increase in poaching levels will doom the remaining population. Tigers simply do not reproduce fast enough to offset losses from guns, snares, poison, and natural deaths.

The Amur tiger's numbers in 1990 were estimated at 400 or so. In 1992 and 1993, poaching took 150 to 200 of those. It is just a matter of time, and not much time at that, before the Amur tiger crosses the point of no return. Offers of assistance to protect the tiger, mainly infusions of cash to finance patrols and offset the power of bribes (counter-bribes, in effect), came from various western conservation organizations, but most ended up sitting, often for months, in the "in" baskets of Russia's immense and glacial bureaucracy. Observers from groups such as Britain's Tiger Trust could do little but watch helplessly as the killing continued.

By mid-1994, however, a combination of money and public opinion was starting to have an effect. The Russian government launched Operation Amba, an anti-poaching campaign designed to protect all Siberian wildlife, but especially the hard-pressed tiger. Assistance came from both the Tiger Trust and the World Wildlife Fund in the form of vehicles, pay supplements for game rangers, and training. It was hoped that these measures could buy time for the tiger until international pressure finally put an end to the illegal trade.

As bad as the poaching is, it could probably be stopped or severely curbed if the Russian government were really serious about putting its still-formidable powers of observation and enforcement to work. But what about the other economic threats? The eastern *taiga* holds vast reserves of timber, and at least two Western pulp and paper companies are moving in to exploit the very forests in which the Amur tigers dwell. In 1993, the magazine *Wildlife Conservation* reported that the Weyerhaeuser company of the United States and Hyundai Corporation of South Korea had each signed contracts with the Russian government that would allow clear-cutting in the forest habitats of the Amur tiger.

Clear cutting the timber is bad enough, but to have it done by a South Korean company sends chills down the spine. Perhaps I am succumbing to terminal conspiracy paranoia, but I am reminded of what happened in northern Botswana a few years ago when a Korean company received a contract for a major road-building project. Construction lasted many months; during that time the Koreans, who love eating dog meat, scoured the villages around the Okavango Delta, buying up all the dogs they could for the pot. When I was there in late 1992, there was not a dog to be found in the northern part of the country, from Francistown to Maun.

Given the Korean penchant for tiger-based pharmaceuticals, imagine the possibilities with the company moving in with equipment to clear-cut forests. It would be the simplest—and most efficient— thing imaginable for them to kill tigers one way or the other and ship them back to Korea. With ample funds for bribes and the prospects of big money at home for the tiger carcasses, it would in fact be surprising if they did *not* poach the big cats. As I say, I may be succumbing to conspiracy-theory paranoia, and there is a big difference between buying domestic dogs for the stew pot and illegally poaching wild tigers. Yet the image persists.

Forests of the Night

In a December, 1995, report in *Science News*, a group of American researchers published the results of a study carried out at the University of Minnesota in St. Paul. Using data collected at Nepal's Royal Chitwan National Park over a period of 20 years, the researchers (from the Maine Department of Inland Fisheries and Wildlife and the University of Minnesota) created a computer model that projected the results that should be expected from different levels of poaching.

The model was based on a group of 120 tigers—a typical population for an Indian preserve, for example. Every year, five to 10 animals will be lost to poachers. That can be considered more or less normal. If that number is raised to 10 a year for three years, and then poaching stops, that group will have about an 80 per cent chance of not becoming extinct within the next 75 years.

Raise the poaching level to 15 animals a year for three years, and the probability of extinction becomes an even bet. Poach 15 animals a year for six years, however, and the tiger group is as good as wiped out. It has almost no chance of not becoming extinct; similarly, if you poach 10 animals a year for nine years. The poaching pressure becomes too great for the tigers to resist, since they still face the normal hazards of life such as bad weather, disease, and injury. What's more, reducing the number of tigers also diminishes the gene pool, which weakens the tigers' natural defenses and their ability to withstand unexpected disasters.

In light of these findings, it is obvious the poaching levels that prevailed in Russia in 1992 and 1993 would have wiped out the Siberian tiger in short order, and it must be assumed that many of the tiger populations on Indian preserves are now at risk. Poaching in Nepal, which has a population of a few hundred Bengal tigers, is reported to be dropping. But not in India, and it is in India where the battle to save the tiger will be won or lost.

Nagarahole National Park is in the southern part of India, a region of blazing sunshine and teeming human populations. It encompasses an area of 250 square miles supporting a tiger population of about four dozen cats which, in tiger terms, is dangerous overcrowding. They have 250 armed guards to protect them. Surrounding Nagarahole are 250 villages crammed with people, and 6,000 Indians live inside the boundaries of the park itself. There is no room to maneuver—for the cats, for the people, or for the Indian government. There is no margin of error. There are no buffer zones.

During the first 20 years of Project Tiger, the Indian government spent about $30 million to protect the species, and millions more poured in from the Tiger Trust, the World Wildlife Fund, and dozens of other organizations. Yet, according to some of the more pessimistic observers involved in the tiger tangle, all that has been accomplished with that money and effort is to create a reservoir of livestock destined for the Chinese pharmaceuticals industry. Virtually everywhere you look, tiger numbers are dropping.

And yet we have hunters—self-styled "sportsmen," "hunter-conservationists," "harvesters" of wildlife—who would pay big money to go to Siberia and shoot a tiger. And smirk about it.